The Individual and th
State in China

Studies on Contemporary China

The Contemporary China Institute at the School of Oriental and African Studies (University of London) has, since its establishment in 1968, been an international centre for research and publications on twentieth-century China. *Studies on Contemporary China*, which is sponsored by the Institute, seeks to maintain and extend that tradition by making available the best work of scholars and China specialists throughout the world. It embraces a wide variety of subjects relating to Nationalist and Communist China, including social, political, and economic change, intellectual and cultural developments, foreign relations, and national security.

Editorial Advisory Board

Volumes in the Series include

Chinese Foreign Policy, *edited by Thomas W. Robinson and David Shambaugh*
Deng Xiaoping: Portrait of a Chinese Statesman, *edited by David Shambaugh*
Greater China: The Next Superpower?, *edited by David Shambaugh*
The Chinese Economy under Deng Xiaoping, *edited by R. F. Ash and Y. Y. Kueh*
China and Japan: History, Trends, and Prospects, *edited by C. B. Howe*
China's Legal Reforms, *edited by Stanley Lubman*

The Individual and the State in China

Edited by

BRIAN HOOK

CLARENDON PRESS · OXFORD
1996

Oxford University Press, Walton Street, Oxford OX2 6DP

Oxford New York
Athens Auckland Bangkok Bombay
Calcutta Cape Town Dar es Salaam Delhi
Florence Hong Kong Istanbul Karachi
Kuala Lumpur Madras Madrid Melbourne
Mexico City Nairobi Paris Singapore
Taipei Tokyo Toronto
and associated companies in
Berlin Ibadan

Oxford is a trade mark of Oxford University Press

Published in the United States
by Oxford University Press Inc., New York

British Library Cataloguing in Publication Data
Data available

Library of Congress Cataloging-in-Publication Data
The individual and the state in China / edited by Brian Hook.
(Studies on contemporary China (Oxford, England))
Includes index.
1. Civil rights—China. 2. Civil rights and socialism—China. 3. Individualism—China.
4. Communism and individualism—China. 5. Civil society—China.
I. Hook, Brian. II. Series.
JC599.C6I53 1996
323'.0951—dc20 96-10752
ISBN 0-19-828931-6

Typeset by Best-set Typesetter Ltd., Hong Kong
Printed in Great Britain
on acid-free paper by
Biddles Ltd., Guildford & King's Lynn

Contents

List of Contributors

ROBERT F. ASH is Senior Lecturer in Economics with reference to China and, until recently, Head of the Contemporary China Institute at the School of Oriental and African Studies, University of London. He has published widely on various aspects of the Chinese economy, including *Land Tenure in Pre-Revolutionary China* (1976) and *Economic Trends in Chinese Agriculture* (1993).

MICHEL BONNIN is an Assistant Professor at the École des Hautes Études en Sciences Sociales (EHESS) in Paris and heads the French Centre d'Information et d'Études sur la Chine in Hong Kong. He specializes in the study of social and political trends in contemporary China, and his most recent publication (edited with J.-P. Béja and A. Peyraube) is *Le Tremblement de terre de Pékin* (1991).

YVES CHEVRIER was Head of the Centre de Recherche et de Documentation sur la Chine Contemporaine at the École des Hautes Études en Sciences Sociales (EHESS) in Paris. He is a research fellow at the Centre National de la Recherche Scientifique (CNRS) and specializes in the history of ideas and political culture at the turn of the century, and post-Mao reforms, especially in the urban sector. His latest publications include a contribution to *Chinese Society on the Eve of Tiananmen*, edited by D. Davis and E. Vogel (1990).

THOMAS B. GOLD is Associate Professor of Sociology at the University of California, Berkeley, where he has taught since 1981. From 1990 to 1994 he chaired the Center for Chinese Studies there. He was educated at Oberlin College and Harvard University and has studied at Fudan University in Shanghai. He studies Chinese societies on both sides of the Taiwan Straits. He has written *State and Society in the Taiwan Miracle* (1986) and numerous articles on Taiwan's political economy, democratization, and the consequences of this for the expansion of private life more generally as well as the emergence of a public sphere in the PRC. He has also written on Chinese youth, popular culture, and civil society on the mainland.

BRIAN HOOK is a senior member of the Department of East Asian Studies at the University of Leeds, and the former editor of *The China Quarterly*. From 1958 to 1963 he served in the Government of Hong Kong. He was Head of the Department of Chinese Studies at the University of Leeds from 1979 to 1982 and again from 1985 to 1988. His interests include the institutional development of the PRC. His current research is on the retrocession of Hong Kong. He is editor of the *Cambridge Encyclopedia of China* and series editor of the OUP (China) Regional Development Series.

LUCIAN W. PYE is Ford Professor of Political Science Emeritus at the Massachusetts Institute of Technology, and the author of numerous books in comparative politics and political culture, including most recently *The Spirit of Chinese Politics*, *Asian Power and Politics*, and *The Mandarin and the Cadre*.

DAVID SHAMBAUGH is Reader in Chinese Politics at the School of Oriental and African Studies, University of London, and editor of *The China Quarterly*. He has published widely on Chinese domestic politics, military affairs, and foreign relations, and the international politics of East Asia. He is author of *The Making of a Premier: Zhao Ziyang's Provincial Career* (1984) and *Beautiful Imperialist: China Perceives America, 1972–1990* (1991). He has edited *American Studies of Contemporary China* (1993), *Deng Xiaoping: Portrait of a Chinese Statesman* (1994), and *Greater China: The Next Superpower?* (1994), and co-edited *Chinese Foreign Policy: Theory and Practice* (1994). He is currently writing a book on the Chinese military.

ANDREW G. WALDER is Professor of Sociology at Harvard University. He is the author of *Communist Neo-Traditionalism: Work and Authority in Chinese Industry* (1986) and *Chang Ch'un-ch'iao and Shanghai's January Revolution* (1978). He has in recent years published a series of articles on the political and organizational dimensions of China's economic reforms, and is currently at work on a book about mass political movements in China during the Cultural Revolution of 1966–71.

GORDON WHITE is a Professorial Fellow at the Institute of Development Studies, University of Sussex. A political scientist, he works on the politics of economics and development with particular interest in China and East Asia. His most recent books are *Riding the Tiger: The Politics of Economic Reform in Post-Mao China* (1993) and (with Paul Bowles) *The Political Economy of Financial Reform in China: Finance in Late Development* (1993).

Introduction: Reshaping the Relationship between the Individual and the State in China: Issues in the Approach to a New Equilibrium

Brian Hook

From the adoption of the policies of reform and opening out at the beginning of the 1980s it was clear that their implementation would have significant implications for the relationship between the individual and the state in the People's Republic of China (PRC). At the time, there was, of course, no clear indication as to the scope, intensity, duration, or indeed, actual durability of the policies. Such had been the anarchy of the recent past it was difficult if not daunting at the time to look far ahead with confidence, however convincing were the arguments for the grand design. To a very great extent therefore, while the strategic and tactical packaging of the new policies for reform and opening out, with references to statistical targets for the millenium and beyond, contained clear implications for the key relationship between the individual and the state, there was little if any perception of the issues that would be raised in the way ahead.

At a point midway through the second decade of the implementation of the reform and opening-out policies, it is self-evident that the PRC has embarked on what would appear to be an unprecedented and indeed irreversible quest for comprehensive modernization. Thus any questions and doubts as to the scope, intensity, duration, and durability of the policies that existed at the beginning of the 1980s have been either answered or dispelled in the interim. It is clear, moreover, that in the halting progress towards this grand design of modernization, there are forces at work that have disequilibrated both the pre-existing and traditional notions of the proper relationship between the individual and the state. It remains unclear, however, as to the actual extent of the consequential disequilibrium and the degree to which it will induce and compel a reshaping of that relationship. The indications are the greater the pace of modernization, the greater the disequilibrating forces acting on the old structures and therefore, the more pressing the need for measures to promote and achieve a new equilibrium in the key areas of the relationship.

The Scope of the Book

As a book, *The Individual and the State in China* is intended to cast light on some of the main issues that have emerged and are emerging in this process.

It does so by focusing on key areas and specific relationships that are not only important for their role in the social, political, and economic development of the state but also in the shaping of individual identities. These foci include the relationship between workers, managers, and the state, the peasant farmer and the state, the soldier and the state, the intellectual and the state, and youth and the state. While each is intended to be a self-standing case study they are clearly linked by the common theme of the book. The studies are preceded by an overview and followed by a concluding chapter.

The overview sets out the cultural, historical, philosophical, and political assumptions the combined effect of which was to contribute to what until the advent of Marxism-Leninism became accepted as axiomatic in the relationship between the individual and the state. It is evident a more accurate reflection of reality, given the degree of authoritarianism implicit in the traditional relationship, would be to refer to relations between "the state and the individual". The overview refers also to the impact of the Maoist state and alludes to the emergence of disequilibrium in the relationship in the Dengist state. The concluding chapter addresses the question that to some extent is begged by the foregoing chapters, namely whether from the current disequilibria there could emerge a new overall equilibrium, a principal balancing force which would come from development in civil society.

Midway through the second decade of reform and opening out, the main issues that are affecting the axiomatic assumptions, the six focal relationships, and the conclusions about the prospects for civil society are relatively clear. On the side of reform, the developments in agriculture, industry, and business and in the legal system are among the more significant. On the side of opening out, the developments in international trade are clearly by far the most significant. At the same time moreover, as we have seen, these developments have been accompanied by the PRC's playing a major role in the management of world affairs, an interaction that cannot fail to have consequences for its own internal affairs.

Historical Considerations

While the implementation of these policies has for obvious reasons attracted much attention, it is important to note they were initially predicated on the four modernizations: agriculture, industry, science and technology, and national defence. Moreover, while it is conventional to view them and to measure their effect within the timespan of the 1980s to the present, it is necessary not to lose sight of the fundamental thrust of modern history. By taking a longer timespan, we are reminded that for one and a half centuries the search for wealth and power has motivated those who seek both to shape the Chinese state and, they would contend, in its interests, to manage the lives of its individuals. In such an historical context, Deng Xiaoping and his supporters should be seen as the representatives of and successors to the earlier generations of China's self-strengtheners. Their aim is the same; only their prescriptions are distinct.

In the mid-nineteenth century, the first generation of self-strengtheners, including Liu Zexu, Zeng Guofan, and Zuo Zongtang, prescribed strong warships and efficient guns; the second generation, including Li Hongzhang and Zhang Zhidong, added economic wealth to that basic prescription; by the turn of the century the third generation, including Kang Youwei and Liang Qichao, hoped to transform imperial autocracy into constitutional monarchy; the fourth generation, represented by Sun Yat-sen (Sun Yixian) and Chiang Kai-shek (Jiang Jieshi), experimented with the concept of a republic incorporating aspects of western democracy and the basic philosophy of the Confucian state. The fifth generation was represented by Mao Zedong, whose supporters succeeded in emancipating China internationally by creatively applying Marxism-Leninism to China at a time when the forces of patriotism and nationalism were at their strongest.

The outcome of the Maoist period, which had its conspicuous achievements but which manifestly failed to enrich China, was, as we have seen, the spur to the formulation of Dengist policies. Thus, the complementary policies of reform and opening out, predicated on the concept of creating socialism with Chinese characteristics and based on the prescription of developing a socialist market economy, with all the implications such formulations may have for the relationship between the individual and the state, are primarily designed to complete the task of joining wealth to the recently restored power of China.

In such an historical context, the equilibrium supposed to exist in the relationship between the individual and the state has clearly been in some flux for over a century. The difference between the late nineteenth century and the late twentieth century is, however, one of scale and effect and it is therefore very marked. In the late nineteenth century, the impact of disequilibrating forces was localized so that what was axiomatic in the assumptions about the relationship generally prevailed over the challenges that emerged, surviving, *mutatis mutandis*, into the early years of the twentieth century. This remained so until the May Fourth Movement, which appears as a clear punctuation point in any account.

Contemporary Issues

In the late twentieth century, despite the latent authoritarianism of the Dengist state, a quality that was never more in evidence than in Tiananmen Square on 4 June 1989, the impression is of the widespread application and generalized effect of the disequilibrating forces. This is accompanied by a belated recognition that modernization in the cause of achieving wealth and power will entail unavoidable consequences. Among them, it will inevitably empower the individual to the extent that the authority of the state will, of necessity, be moderated and the relationship between the individual and the state permanently modified. This appears to be a fundamental departure from the philosophical premises that generated the *ti-yong* dichotomy which so effectively hindered the progress towards modernization in the closing decades of the nineteenth century.

If this is so, the questions that remain to be answered are no longer whether the individual will enjoy greater liberty at the expense of the authority of the Chinese state, but rather to what extent greater liberty will be enjoyed and how fast it will come. Neither of these is open to a ready answer at the time of an impending succession in the leadership. There seems little reason to suppose, however, that the protégés of the late revolutionary, and economic theorist, Chen Yun (Liao Chenyun), who died probably aged 90 in April 1995, are in the wings simply biding their time: once Deng Xiaoping passes on, they would, as Chen Yun had hoped in his lifetime, be able to place clear limits around the ongoing reform process. The reimposition of a planned economy in which market forces would be neither crushed nor liberated but contained like a "bird in a cage" seems highly improbable. Nor does it seem at all possible that China could revert to the stage where the availability of consumer goods was subordinated to the creation of agricultural surpluses to pay for them and where the intrinsic value of such goods as an incentive to productivity would be questioned.

On the contrary, despite efforts by the centre to control the opportunistic exploitation of the reform and opening-out policies by provincial authorities, the so-called "traffic-light philosophy" which Chen Yun is said to have ascribed originally to the Guangdong authorities, and to which Lucian Pye refers in his overview, has actually been rather pervasively adopted. According to this view, the provincial authorities respond in three ways to the centre's attempts to impose controls: a red light means, rather than stop, they make a detour to circumvent any control; an amber light means they ignore the warning and keep going at constant speed; a green light means they open the throttle and go full speed ahead. Although the centre under Zhu Ronqji has clearly achieved some success in macro-economic management it is evident that provincial authorities, in the absence of the further development of political institutions, can no longer deliver the response that the centre might wish, even if they aspired to do so. Among the reasons why they can no longer so respond is the changing relationship between the individual and the state.

The migration from the land is evidence of such change. First, it shows the difficulty experienced in many areas in making a living from agriculture sufficient to support the primary group, and commensurate with current aspirations. Second, it suggests disillusionment with the outcome of the reforms. Third, it shows the lure of those urban areas, notably the coastal cities, where modern forms of industrialization are advanced.

The peasant household remains at the core of rural reform, having replaced the collective as the basic unit of production. Moreover, it remains central as a primary group-identity structure for the individual farmer. The shift, however, of upwards of 100 million employees from the agricultural sector with more to follow reflects a major change in the relationship between the peasant farmers and the state. This huge migration reflects both market forces to which the individuals are, perforce, responding in the absence of state planning, and the erosion of state authority. In the past, such authority would have been exerted through the *hukou* or household registration system to maintain agricultural output and restrict migration from the rural to the urban areas. Having abandoned the principle and practice of control, the state would find it exceedingly difficult if not impossible to reimpose it.

In industry, where profit is at stake, no matter which form of ownership (though the degree of motivation is linked to the rewards), workers are beginning to enjoy more power in relation to management than before. Save for the loss-making state-owned enterprises that in certain places in China still remain the sole source of employment, where the primary group-identity structure, the *danwei* system, must remain intact as a form of social insurance pending the completion of restructuring, and where clientelism and dependency in the workplace undoubtedly remain, the implications of consumer demand have brought great change in both management and employment practices. These have been reflected in the new labour law.

In business, the most striking changes in the relationship between the individual and the state following the reforms have been encouraged by the emerging dominance in the retail market-place of consumer demand and the expanding scope for individual initiative. To a large extent both reflect the purchasing power of individual urban households, not only in major cities but in urban areas throughout the country. According to advertising specialists Saatchi and Saatchi, among the characteristics of the Chinese consumer market are the relative youthfulness of consumers, reflecting national demographics, the high percentage of their incomes which is actually disposable, reflecting a working population not burdened by huge mortgages or crippling debt, a rapidly acquired brand consciousness, and a high level of media consumption. Allowing for self-advertising by the specialists, these characteristics cannot be ignored by those who do business and by those in the state bureaucracy who regulate it. The former aim to maximize profits and the latter are increasingly aware of the direct link between sales and tax revenues as the tax system is modernized. The relationship which has emerged, which involves the population as a whole, is in practice an inversion of that which existed under the planned economy.

In other sectors, including foreign trade, the stock markets, and securities trading, there are complaints about the prevalence of corrupt or unethical practices. To a large extent these may be attributed to an undeveloped legal system, opportunities for the abuse of state power that are unique to a bureaucracy-dominated, bureaucratically managed socialist market economy and the opportunity for certain individuals to make huge profits in circumstances of sustained rapid growth. In this context, the reform and opening-out policies, which in 15 years have not only enabled the PRC to re-enter the mainstream of world trade but also enabled it to be the beneficiary of some US$ 112 billion of direct foreign investment, are increasingly exposing the PRC to international legal norms, standardized accounting systems, and recognized auditing practices. While, in the short term, little can be done effectively to control rampant corruption and pervasive unethical practices that affect the relationship between the individual and the state, in the longer term, the exposure to international standards should have an effect throughout the country leading to a reduction in the abuse of state power, less corruption, and an improvement in business ethics.

The exposure to international standards resulting from the opening-out policy has had one other significant impact on the relationship between the individual and the state in the PRC. This has occurred in the field of human rights. It has involved not only international support for the rights of dissidents, such as those accused of counter-revolution in the crisis of 1989, and Tibetan nationalists, but also for certain individuals regarded as victims of the Chinese penal system. In such instances, the relationship between the individual and the state, despite developments in the legal system, has failed by Western standards to strike a fair balance between the rights of the individual and the authority of the state. They have become, therefore, the object of criticism. Whether such criticism ever directly induces reform is doubtful. It does, however, as in the case of Harry Wu, the US citizen detained in the PRC in the summer of 1995, occasionally work to the benefit of the individuals at risk in the system. Moreover, to the extent it is part of the international discourse on the subject, it will have an indirect effect on the formulation of policy and therefore on the evolution of the relationship between the individual and the state.

The international dimension of the current policies is also responsible for what is arguably the single most important issue potentially to affect the relationship between the individual and the state over the coming years. Whereas the economic issues, without exception, appear to have induced a marked withdrawal of the state, enabling the individual to enjoy greater freedom in economic activity, the same cannot be said of the political sphere. The political demise of Zhao Ziyang and his supporters against the background of the crisis in international communism, culminating in the violent suppression of the so-called democracy movement, signalled an end to the modest retreat of the state in the political sphere in the 1980s.

Coinciding with the terminal decline of the Soviet Union, the events of 1989 also signalled the determination of the Dengist regime to strengthen its Leninist structures and to ensure its political survival in an internal environment characterized by the need for economic liberalization. Accordingly, the ability of the state to defend its interests from internal and external threat appears to have strengthened considerably in the 1990s. This is true for both the internal security forces and the People's Liberation Army (PLA). Judged by the massive pre-emptive responses to perceived security threats posed by the presence of large numbers of foreigners on the occasions of the Asian Games and the UN Women's Conference, the internal security organs of the state have undergone both expansion and professionalization. Similarly, judged by the PRC's performance in the international arms market, in its enhanced force-projection capability as a maritime power in the South China Sea, and in its Taiwan-directed demonstration of military firepower, the capability of the armed forces is being continually upgraded. These measures appeal to patriotic and nationalist sentiment. Moreover, while the armed forces are presented primarily as defenders of the national interest in times of international conflict, very few individuals are not aware they are, as was evident in 1989, the ultimate guarantee of internal stability and order. Provided therefore they remain united in purpose, they are a factor in ensuring that the disequilibrium presently perceived in relations between the individual and the state does not threaten the party-state system.

The Content of the Book

These issues are reflected in the content of the chapters of the book, the organization of which was referred to earlier. In the overview interpretation, Lucian Pye indicates that while the Confucian tradition ascribed moral virtue to the state and to its officials, and depreciated the worth of the individual, who was expected to defer to the interests of the collective, represented by the family, kinship group, or government, there was some ambivalence about individualism itself. Although the individual was expected to conform within the group, he was also expected to excel at self-improvement. Pye concludes that on balance, the highest ideal in the Confucian tradition was learning to be selfless.

According to this tradition, Pye maintains, the ultimate sin was selfishness. Consequently, politically, the Chinese developed no legitimate channels for interest articulation; political participation was passive and associations tended to shield their members from the state rather than make demands on it. In short, instead of there being pressure groups there were protective groups which sought privately, often surreptitiously, to get special favours for their members. The justice system, rather than regarding the individual as being legally accountable, relied upon the concept of collective responsibility.

Regarding the system that developed after 1949, Pye notes that while on the one hand the old system of collective responsibility based on the authority of the family was attacked, on the other hand the communists introduced a new system of collective responsibility based on work units or *danwei*. At the same time, the tradition of conformity made it easy for the Communist Party to introduce the practice of giving everyone a class label. He notes that the Dengist reforms have indeed relaxed the collective controls and given the people more scope for individual autonomy, as illustrated by both the vast floating population swept into the urban areas on the tide of rural emigration and the scope for private enterprise. He concludes that while on the one hand more individual freedom may, in time, generate a stronger civil society in China, the subject which is taken up in detail by Gordon White in the concluding chapter, on the other hand many Chinese may actually feel rootless as their collective world erodes. He suggests that such a feeling of rootlessness, induced by the perception of the erosion of their collective world, could make people candidates for authoritarian movements. Thus, the evolution of the relationship between the individual and the state will be fundamental in determining the future of the country.

In the chapter "Workers, Managers, and the State: The Reform Era and the Political Crisis of 1989", Andrew Walder explores the significance for the urban work-force of the changes that occurred in the 1980s. Such changes culminated in the system of work-unit control failing to avert workers' dissatisfaction over wage issues and inflation from turning into popular protest in response to student political appeals. He seeks to explain the changes in urban industrial life that led to the active participation of workers in the political demonstrations of 1989. While many interpretations have placed emphasis on the distress caused by inflation and concern caused by economic corruption, Walder explains why corruption actually was an issue that so motivated workers and why workers were able so readily to mobilize in support of student hunger strikes.

Regarding the exercise of cadre privilege and the abuse of power in, to take an example, the key issue of the allocation of factory housing, Walder notes paradoxically this became more frustrating under the more transparent, reformed system than it had been under the opaque Maoist system. This was because it was perceived by the work-force to be a blatant subversion of the democratic process introduced in the reforms precisely to defuse the perennial conflict over housing allocations. Consequently, by 1989, cadre privilege seemed even more illegitimate and intolerable than it had been in the past. Such conflict over housing allocation, pay, benefits, and job tenure in the workplace, together with the interruption of the rapid rise in real incomes that was encountered in the late 1980s, were issues that engendered workers' protests. At the same time, the decline of the party organization within factories and the increased autonomy of enterprises from party and state agencies provided the unprecedented opportunity for workers to mobilize for protest. The author describes the response of the workers to the news of student demonstrations, the formation of protest brigades within factories that marched in street processions, and the emergence of self-proclaimed autonomous labour federations on the streets. Walder concludes that the political lessons of 1989 show that the process of urban economic reform is fraught with enormous political risk. This lesson appears to have been drawn by the party in its ultra-cautious approach to the question of the reform of loss-making state-owned enterprises.

The link between the relationship of the worker and manager to the state and that between the peasant and the state was illustrated in 1985. Then, against the background of euphoria surrounding the attempted liberalization of agricultural production and distribution, the maintenance of state control over farm surplus, to ensure adequate supplies at tolerable prices for the population as a whole, quickly re-emerged. A decade later, the Chinese state is preoccupied by the issue of food production for a rising population from a smaller agricultural base. The background to the current problem in the agricultural sector, epitomized by the shedding of upwards of 100 million agricultural workers, leaving agriculture to be managed in many instances by women and the aged, is set out clearly by Robert Ash in his chapter on the peasant and the state.

He shows that the changing roles of the peasant and the state, given shape by the institutional and economic reforms initiated after 1978, have had a significant impact on the structure of farming. The pre-eminent role of the state as arbiter of what should be produced gave way to peasants' own decision-making powers. Consequently, the peasants cultivated crops that offered the greatest monetary reward: the structure of land use favoured by the peasants in their quest for income maximization no longer reflected the state's priorities. The state's economic involvement in agriculture declined. Budgetary support fell. In the early 1980s farmers, whose incomes had risen appreciably, responded positively to the challenges but, by the late 1980s, because the momentum had not been maintained, agricultural stagnation, linked to a deteriorating infrastructure, had become a problem. The inability to resolve the issue of land tenure, the shibboleth represented by the privatization of land, became an intractable problem. Moreover, the shifting economic relationship between peasant and state did not result in its becoming embedded in a system of farming guided by demand and geared towards commodity production. The author concludes that unless such dilemmas are resolved an effective balance of economic power between the peasant and the state will remain elusive.

In his analysis of the key relationship between the soldier and the state in contemporary China, David Shambaugh considers "the soldier" in the collective rather than the individual sense. There are methodological and non-methodological reasons for his approach. First, unlike access to workers, cadres, peasants, youth, and intellectuals, access to individual soldiers is severely restricted for security reasons. Second, unlike the other individuals who are the subjects of this book, the military, because of its cohesiveness, has a corporate or collective identity and as such has a special relationship with the state as its ultimate guarantor.

The study focuses on the mechanisms established by the Communist Party to exert and maintain control over the People's Liberation Army (PLA). As the latter part of the title, "The Political Work System in the PLA", suggests, the scope of the study is the politicization of the military rather than the militarization of the political process in China. Drawing on unique Chinese materials and interviews with PLA personnel, Shambaugh explores in depth and brings to the surface new details about the structure and functions of the political work system in the PLA.

This unique system in the Chinese communist forces has evolved since the 1 August 1927 Nanchang Uprising, which gave birth to the latter-day PLA. As the author shows, it is the basis for the marked contrast between the Western model of a professionalized and apolitical military, as envisaged in Samuel P. Huntingdon's conceptualization of civil–military relations, and the current communist Chinese model. According to Huntingdon, the professional military existed to serve the state. Moreover, the relationship between the military and the state hinged on the existence of a socialized, professional officer corps. In China, by contrast, the military is an instrument of political power as is abundantly clear in the quotation from Mao Zedong that political power grows out of the barrel of a gun.

The author demonstrates it is the historical interconnection of the revolutionary military and the party, together with the organizational penetration of the military by the party, that have defined civil–military relations in the PRC. The revolutionary struggle in China produced a uniquely socialized officer corps, the peacetime role of whose members, who were categorically neither professional nor praetorian but "revolutionary soldiers", set the PRC apart from the developing states. The argument advanced by Shambaugh is that the politicization of the military is at the core of the relationship between the soldier and the state: in the 60 years and more of its existence, the PLA's identity has been, to quote the author, "inextricably intertwined in the party-state".

This, Shambaugh maintains, has led to the "soldier" being ready to come to the support of certain leaders or of certain factions within the party-state. He explains this phenomenon not as a praetorian intervention but as an outcome of the parallel symbiotic relationships between the party and the state and the party and the army. The PLA's role in maintaining the party-state was never more in evidence than during the 1989 crisis. Accordingly, although conventional professional values and ethics exist in the PLA, showing that, as in certain other countries, the professionalization and politicization of the military are not mutually exclusive, the strict conceptual dichotomy perceived in the Huntingdon schema cannot be applied to the PRC. The PLA is unique however in that in the party-state system, revolutionary soldiers as distinct from professional or praetorian soldiers can, as Shambaugh indicates, legitimately pursue multiple missions in the Chinese economy, polity, and society.

This chapter contains detailed documented accounts of the PLA as a political actor, the history of political work in the PLA, the organization and structure of political work in the PLA, the three systems—political commissar, party committee, and discipline inspection—and the five phases of political work in the PLA since Tiananmen. Shambaugh explains that the relationship between the soldier and the state has evolved through stages. In the first, the early shared identity of interests sustained a political-military symbiosis. In the second, after the purge of Peng Dehuai and the ascent of Lin Biao during the late Maoist period when politics impinged on the post-revolutionary professional mission of the PLA, the symbiotic relationship weakened. In the third, under Deng, nascent military autonomy emerging from the beginnings of corporate professionalism threatened the effectiveness of party rule, which depended on the party-army. Consequently, the party had to regain absolute control over the PLA.

This fact, which is of fundamental importance to the outcome of the succession in China, is reinforced in the postscript. Here, the author deals with the implications of two developments and one trend. The first development was the ouster of the "Yang family village" (the CMC secretary and GPD chief, Yang Baibing, and his half-brother, CMC vice-chairman and State President, Yang Shangkun) at the time of the 14th party congress in 1992 and the subsequent changes in personnel, command, and control structures. The second development was the emergence of the PLA as the arbiter in the succession to Deng, where its support has been sought by Jiang Zemin. The trend concerns the increasing involvement of the PLA in commerce. This Shambaugh sees as a further incentive to ensure the PLA's support for the existing party-state system: a post-communist China would bring renewed pressures for depoliticizing the military. In considering the approach to a new equilibrium in relations between the individual and the state this trend, which could retard the pace of generalized reform and impede progress towards political reform in particular, is clearly very significant.

The changing relationship between the intellectual and the state, the subject of Michel Bonnin's and Yves Chevrier's chapter, "The Intellectual and the State: Social Dynamics of Intellectual Autonomy during the Post-Mao Era", is closely linked to the development of the challenge to the party-state that was crushed by the Chinese security forces in 1989. In this chapter, the authors analyse the role of Chinese intellectuals and their relationship to the state in terms of how they joined the mainstream of post-

Mao social change and how their initiatives helped to shape it. Rather than analysing the role of the intellectuals and their relationship to the state in the context of intellectual or political history, the authors focus the analysis on how the intellectuals established themselves in small groups, and instituted publishing houses and other business or research ventures, in the new sphere of economic and social initiative allowed by the reforms. The particular contribution to knowledge made by the chapter is in its presentation of information mainly gathered from personal interviews with participants contacted outside China after the 1989 crisis.

The authors recall the basic patterns governing the relationship between the intellectuals and the Maoist state, first, in order to clarify the scope of the post-Mao evolution and secondly, because the new associative setting, notably the salons that characterized the changes in the 1980s, had roots in the social dynamics of the Maoist state in the 1970s. They note that the instrumentalization of the intellectuals which had, in practice, developed in the social dynamics of the Maoist regime, had been counterbalanced over time by the more traditional practice of patronage and advice in the context of ideological controversy and factionalism. They point to the fact that many of the new intellectual associations and ventures in the 1980s were built around salons and based on personal friendships established when the party-state system lacked the power needed to control society. It was particularly so in the period of factional disintegration and loss of legitimacy after the Cultural Revolution.

The authors differentiate three types of relatively autonomous organizations reflecting intellectual emancipation that emerged within the changing economic and social context. The first were non-official, non-governmental associations which, because of the non-state sector in the economy and the official recognition of social pluralism, were free from direct links to the state. The second were associations linked to administrative organs, research bodies, and state collective enterprises, but not supervised by political organs. The third were research groups or institutes under central party organs, which revived the traditional advisory function of Chinese intellectuals. The authors trace the evolution from such aspects of what was to become characteristic of the activities of intellectuals in the late 1980s to the development of a political dimension and thence, ultimately, to overt politicization and confrontation. They conclude that the Tiananmen crisis was but one step in the emergence of civil society based on social autonomy within the political framework, a step away from the "bleak landscape of totalitarianism". Although small, it was, however, a significant step, which they envisage will be followed by others (not always forward), in which an important factor is the transformation in the role of the intellectuals.

In his chapter on youth and the state, Thomas Gold employs the life-course approach of sociology to explore the relations between youth and the party-state in China. This provides a coherent way to link the progression of individuals and cohorts through the life-span with the socio-cultural context and the historical events through which the progression occurs. It delineates the social construction of transitions between the stages in life and the definitions of the activities characteristic of each stage.

After a discussion of youth as a stage in the life course generally, Gold reviews youth as a stage in the Chinese life course traditionally, and under communism prior to the Cultural Revolution (CR). He then examines the different effect of the CR, which he identifies as being of challenging significance similar to the Vietnam War and the Holocaust to their respective cohorts and societies, on three youth cohorts, before turning to the changing relationship between youth and the party-state during the reform period.

He notes that three birth cohorts have passed through the youth stage since 1949. They have had radically differing relations with the party-state, bringing serious consequences for the party-state and its relations with succeeding youth cohorts and for the integration of Chinese society. The revolutionary party attempted a thorough transformation and reconstruction of the life course of the Chinese people. This involved changes at all levels from nation to family, the environment in which people lived, the agents and content of socialization, people's definition of self and relation to society, the scope for autonomy in decision-making, and the ability to control one's own life.

The 1950s cohort received an education emphasizing ideological and moral education as well as standard academic subjects. It was disrupted by the CR in its youth stage but it learned, among many things, self-sufficiency. The 1960s cohort, by contrast, passed through the youth stage at a time of relative stability and predictability. The reforms have offered them opportunity. The author regards them as a "swing group". The 1970s cohort is, however, at the extreme of alienation: although it is the beneficiary of the reforms it expects quick success and gratification. Consequently, when its expectations are not met, frustrations are quick to emerge. This led to some of its members participating in the pro-liberalization demonstrations of 1986–87 and 1989.

The author concludes the party-state has tried to redefine and manage the youth stage but has done so inconsistently. This has resulted in wide gaps between cohorts and generations making it difficult both to integrate Chinese society and to control it. It appears that the 1950s cohort may have benefited most from the upheavals, being the most self-sufficient, realistic, and skilful in the use of power. It will be for that cohort to channel the talents and energies of its juniors, including its own offspring, the products of the single-child policy, the 1980s cohort.

It will be evident from this introduction that the concept of civil society has been referred to explicitly by most of the contributing authors. Even where the term does not appear, the significance of the development of civil society may be inferred from the text. It is appropriate therefore that the concluding chapter, written by Gordon White, should focus on the dynamics of civil society in post-Mao China. In it, the author separates the sociological from the political meaning of "civil society" and uses the former to investigate the emergence of an intermediate associational sphere in China during the era of market reform.

The emergence of civil society, the author maintains, reflects both a political and a market dynamic. The market dynamic embodies rapid and profound social changes accompanying the spread of a market economy. On this basis, in the process of the emergence of civil society, it is possible to detect a dual impetus towards organizational change, both from new groups and forces in society seeking greater influence and access, and from party-state institutions seeking to control and channel them. The resulting organizational constellation of civil society is multi-layered.

This organizational constellation includes a "caged" sector of official mass organizations such as the old-style mass organizations of the pre-reform era, e.g. the All-China Federation of Trade Unions, the Women's Federation, and the Young Communist League. It also includes an incorporated sector of semi-state, semi-popular social organizations alluded to by Bonnin and Chevrier, which emerged at national and local levels during the reform era. Among them are business and trade associations, professional associations, academic societies, and sports, recreational, and cultural clubs. These could be regarded as constituting "semi-civil society". In addition, there are the interstitial "limbo" world of semi-formal and informal organizations and a suppressed sector of underground political and criminal organizations.

Examples of semi-formal and informal organizations, whose numbers grew during the period leading up to the Tiananmen crisis and in the early to mid-1990s, when the pace of economic reform accelerated, are the urban associations which are not officially recognized or which gained such recognition through connections. They included the salons of intellectuals in 1988–89, which in the 1990s have been superseded by informal associations that are less explicitly political, uniting like-minded people in clubs, common-interest groups, karaoke parlours, dance-halls, and bars. Examples of the suppressed sector, "underground civil society", include a variety of political and social organizations, the latter reflecting an increase in religious sentiment, as well as secret societies and other criminal organizations.

The chapter ends by evaluating the methodological utility of the term "civil society". White concludes that while it is an intrinsically political rather than a scientific concept it is of considerable heuristic value in analysing the current socio-political dynamics of Chinese society. In view of the complex and contradictory political character of the social constellation, he considers that it may prove a problematic basis for a stable transition to democracy. He notes that since the Tiananmen crisis there has been a growing consensus that if liberalization and democratization are to occur, there should be a gradual, managed process.

This appears to represent the desire of political elites and to reflect the wishes of influential members of China's incipient civil society. The entrepreneurs are worried about political instability; the industrial working class fears the erosion of a privileged position in society, insecurity, and exploitation; the intellectuals fear chaos or rule by an "illiterate" majority. Such preoccupations suggest that civil society in its present limited form may be an obstacle rather than an impetus to democratization. Indeed, for a successful transition towards democracy to occur, the indications are it would have to be sponsored by reformist elements within the political elite. For the moment, they remain in a small minority. The paramount consideration, for which there appears to be majority support within the political elite, is to maintain a high rate of economic growth while not putting at risk the political equilibrium on which the survival of the party-state depends.

The State and the Individual: An Overview Interpretation*

Lucian W. Pye

It could be that no people have ever outdone the Chinese in ascribing moral virtues to the state or in deprecating the worth of the individual. First Confucianism and then the Chinese version of Leninism went all out in extolling the importance of rulers and society and in minimizing the rights of individuals. The gap between the moral worth and the recognized rights of state and citizen in China was and remains huge both because of the way the Chinese have consistently given paramountcy to the state and the ways in which they have subordinated the individual to the group. The extraordinary imbalance in the relations of the state and individuals provides both the structural and the cultural bases for the human rights practices which are now the most contentious issues between China and the west, especially the United States. What is outrageous to Americans can be for most Chinese normal expectations—although since Tiananmen a majority may feel that the state has gone too far.

In Confucian China the state stood alone, as does the state and its Siamese twin the Party in the People's Republic, as the sole nation-wide institution. At the other extreme, both Confucianism and Maoism denied the autonomy of the individual and made self-sacrifice for the state the highest ideal of citizenship. Yet today, as China goes through its crisis of ideological legitimacy, cracks are appearing both in the public's awe of state authority and in the general hostility toward individualism. But to appreciate the enormity of the challenge of any significant change it is necessary to recognize the massive weight of cultural inertia which favours the state and inhibits the growth of a vibrant civil society.

It is true that some societies have gone further than the Chinese in glorifying the state with pomp and circumstance. Others have turned worshipping the state more into a religion. What is distinctive and extreme in the case of China is that government and the world of officialdom have consistently monopolized power and authority on a national basis. There have been no other organized elites or institutions with recognized rights and adequate nation-wide authority to check, counter and discipline the state.

Indeed, in the case of China it makes little sense to speak of state–society

* I have benefited from the helpful criticism of Thomas Gold, Merle Goldman, Brian Hook and David Shambaugh.

relations, because the Chinese have never had a national civil society.[1] Apart from their government the Chinese had no established institutions with authoritative reach that could extend across the entire country. Thus state and society did not have a nation-wide relationship: it was always an imperial or a national government confronting local communities, fragmented interests, parochial private groupings, or semi-illegal secret societies.[2] Except possibly when Buddhism was first introduced after the Tang, China never had an organized religion that was institutionally capable of restraining state authorities such as existed in Christian, Muslim, Hindu or Buddhist societies. The non-development of feudalism and capitalism in China also meant that there were no alliances of merchants or traders, no coalitions of cities or estated noblemen to balance the state authorities. In modern times the diversification and differentiation generally associated with modernization was arrested in China, in part because of the practice of relying upon enclaves to contain the impact of the west. In some of the Treaty Ports there were elements which might in time have become the bases of political power, but they were never a serious challenge to the Chinese state.[3] The closest the Chinese have come to having a society-wide balancing force to the state has been the intellectuals, Confucian scholars in the past and in modern times the emergence of a westernized intelligentsia. But for reasons which will be explored, Chinese intellectuals have only been able to contribute to the eroding of state legitimacy; they have not been able to act as a sustained counter-force to the Chinese state.[4]

As for the vulnerabilities of the individual, the conventional wisdom, which in this case is not far off the mark, is that Chinese culture is group-orientated and essentially hostile to individualism. The individual has consistently been seen as merely a disciplined member of some larger group and the group's interests are always assumed to take precedence over those of the individual. At the core of Chinese ethics and morality there has always been the ideal of depressing self-interest and glorifying self-sacrifice for the collectivity. The cultural basis of self-identity was never given a quasi-sacred dimension, as in cultures in which it is believed that each person has a unique and precious soul and that therefore each individual

1. For a general analysis of state–society relations in China, see Thomas B. Gold, "Party-state versus society in China," in Joyce K. Kallgren (ed.), *Building a Nation-State: China after Forty Years* (Berkeley: Institute of East Asian Studies, University of California, 1990), ch. 5.

2. For a good description of informal groups in traditional China, see Mark Elvin, *The Pattern of the Chinese Past* (Stanford: Stanford University Press, 1973).

3. On the limitations to the political influence of the Treaty Port Chinese, see Rhoads Murphey, *The Treaty Ports and China's Modernization: What Went Wrong?* (Ann Arbor: University of Michigan Center for Chinese Studies, 1970).

4. For an excellent evaluation of the role of Chinese intellectuals, see Merle Goldman with Timothy Cheek and Carol Lee Hamrin (eds.), *China's Intellectuals and the State: In Search of a New Relationship* (Cambridge, Mass.: Harvard University Council on East Asian Studies, 1987), especially "Introduction: Uncertain change" by Goldman and Cheek.

deserves respect and has certain inalienable rights, based on the inherent worth of human life. Instead, in Chinese culture the individual's identity has been consistently derived from particularistic relationships with others. It is always some relationship, such as position within the family or other particularistic consideration, which determines self-identity for the Chinese. Therefore they are expected to make sacrifices without hesitation for the group which provides them with their identities.[5]

It is, of course, true that the Confucian state was expected to treat the individual with benevolence and compassion, and that today the government is the "people's" government. The individual's relationship to the state, however, has all along been one of dependency and not one based on the rights of individuals. Over time there have been ups and downs in the relationship between the state and the individual. When state authority has been strong the sub-groups that gave identity to the individual have usually also been firmly in control. Traditionally when the state became weakened the primary groups of family, clan, guild and secret society became increasingly important institutions, so there was still little increase in individual autonomy. Yet what is significant today is that the decline in the legitimacy of the Beijing regime is being accompanied by a loosening of institutional sub-groups and a marked increase in people seeking individual freedom.

This is the trend to be analysed in this article. It is necessary to start, however, by clarifying the issue of individualism in the Chinese cultural tradition. This will lead to an examination of the cultural practices that have inhibited the advancement of the interests of individuals, such as the techniques of state control, and then, finally, to questions about the current situation and what can be expected in state–individual relations in the post-Tiananmen environment. There are increasing signs of hope for the growth of respect for the individual but the weight of tradition cannot be easily set aside.

The Ambivalent Character of Individualism in Chinese Culture

The conventional wisdom that the Chinese are group-orientated is, paradoxically, matched by the equally conventional view that the Chinese are individualists. Chinese and foreigners alike nod their heads in agreement with Sun Yat-sen's complaint that the Chinese people were "like a plate of sand." Although Dean Acheson did not get universal support for his plea to allow the "dust to settle" (made in his 1949 White Paper about the "fall" of China), there was less criticism of his belief that the collectivism of communism was incompatible with the Chinese tradition of individualism, and

5. One of the best anthropological studies of Chinese identity-formation in the family context involving "worldly and other-worldly residences" is still Francis L. K. Hsu's *Under the Ancestors' Shadow* (New York: Columbia University Press, 1948).

hence communism could not last long in China. Thus there would seem to be a basic contradiction about individualism in Chinese culture which needs to be cleared up. Indeed, the answer to the contradiction can provide us with deeper insights into the distinctive Chinese pattern of state–individual relations.

The confusion about individualism has, in fact, been extensively debated among students in the study of Chinese philosophical thought and political rhetoric. Wm. Theodore de Bary has long argued that in Neo-Confucianism there was a powerful notion of individual perfectibility.[6] In analysing the concept of the self in Ming thought, de Bary has stressed the extent to which the Wang Yang-ming school in particular advanced ideas about the importance of individualism akin to what can be found in western thought. In addition to Wang Yang-ming's dictum that "Study must be for one's own sake," and not simply to please others, de Bary cites Wang Ken's "celebration of the self," and Li Chi's "the importance of being selfish."[7] Thomas Metzger also agrees that with Neo-Confucianism the Chinese mandarins did experience inner tensions about self-realization, for they had a ". . . moral-psychological sense of living along a perilous divide between moral success and moral failure."[8]

Yet what makes the Wang Yang-ming school stand out in the history of Confucianism is precisely the fact that it went against the grain of the more traditional Confucianism and its orthodox interpretations. Moreover, as Benjamin Schwartz has noted, while the goal of moral advancement in Confucianism might call for a striving for self-realization, there was no appreciation of liberty and individual rights.[9] Donald Munro has identified some Chinese philosophical ideas which are consistent with elements in the western concept of individualism, but he also sees limitations on true autonomy.[10]

Even after allowances are made for the important qualifications about self-realization and self-perfection, it still remains true that the dominant feature of Confucianism was a pervasive hostility to the notion of personal autonomy and individualism. The goal of self-improvement was moral perfection according to established standards, and hence it sought excellence in terms of conformity to cultural norms, not in terms of the uniqueness of

6. Wm. Theodore de Bary, *Self and Society in Ming Thought* (New York: Columbia University Press, 1970).

7. *Ibid*. pp. 145–225.

8. Thomas A. Metzger, *Escape from Predicament: Neo-Confucianism and China's Evolving Political Culture* (New York: Columbia University Press, 1977) p. 197.

9. Benjamin I. Schwartz, *The World of Thought in Ancient China* (Cambridge, Mass.: Harvard University Press, 1985).

10. Although Munro acknowledges some of de Bary's interpretations, he is in the main closer to the standard view, holding that in Chinese culture there is really no place for a "private self" because the self is defined by society and government. See Donald Munro, *The Concept of Man in Contemporary China* (Ann Arbor: The University of Michigan Press, 1977), pp. 45–55.

each individual. There was a hierarchy of moral achievement in which only the elite could strive for self-development while the mass of the people were ruled by example. Above all, however, there was no notion of individual rights.

The debate over what were the precise limits of individualism in traditional China will no doubt go on indefinitely. There will be those, such as Tu Wei-ming, who will argue that Confucianism found a happier balance between self and community than the western liberal balance between majority interests and human rights for the individual. Philosophical discourse aside, in practical political terms John Fairbank's observations on the limits of individualism in Chinese culture fairly accurately summed up the traditional situation when he noted that, "To say that liberalism rests on individualism under the supremacy of law is more sensible and gratifying than to say, as one does in Chinese, that the doctrine of spontaneous licence (*ziyou zhuyi*) rests on the doctrine of self-centredness (*geren zhuyi*) under the supremacy of administrative regulations (*falu*)."[11]

The Chinese instinct has indeed been to see individualism as nothing more than self-centredness. Lee Kuan Yew, in upholding authoritarian practices in Singapore, has emphasized the evils he ascribes to western individualism and the superiority of a virtuous form of communitarianism which in his view can be found in Confucianism. The campaigns against "bourgeois liberalism" of late 1986 to mid-1987 and again after the Tiananmen Massacre revealed the continuing hostility of the Chinese elite toward western individualism. In March 1987 Zhao Fusan, then vice-president of the Chinese Academy of Social Sciences, wrote an extended essay attacking individualism by extensively quoting American scholars who had criticized contemporary western culture for being too ego-centred and lacking in a sense of moral responsibility. Citing western views from Tocqueville to Daniel Bell and concentrating particularly on Robert Bellah *et al.*'s *Habits of the Heart*, Zhao argued that the "culture of individualism is morally vacuous and socially irresponsible" and "the ideologies of western capitalism are in a morbid state and had developed into a cancerous state." By contrast, in China's cultural tradition, "individuals have always been closely linked with society . . . [and] individuals have never been placed above society, and the values of individuals have always been unified with the responsibilities of society."[12]

Zhao, like Lee Kuan Yew, but not like Reinhold Niebuhr, sees the alternatives as Moral Society and Immoral Man. The issue however is falsely formed when it is posed as a stark choice between the individual and

11. *The China Quarterly*, 96 (1983), p. 739.

12. Zhao Fusan, "Some thoughts on certain aspects of modern western culture: reading notes," *People's Daily*, as quoted by Richard Madsen, "The spiritual crisis of China's intellectuals," in Deborah Davis and Ezra f. Vogel (eds.), *Chinese Society on the Eve of Tiananmen: The Impact of Reform* (Cambridge, Mass.: Harvard University Press, 1990), p. 247.

the community. The more basic question that should be asked concerns the sources of the communitarian values: are they an expression of the majority interests of society or are they the values of an authoritarian elite? Genuine communitarian values evolve out of the process of individuals interacting with each other and working to harmonize their separate interests. If the communitarian interests represent only the values of the state elite, no matter how intrinsically worthy they may be, the result is still an authoritarian state.

Learning to be Selfless

The contradictions about individualism in the formal philosophy of Confucianism also turn out to be a source of psychological tensions when we examine the experiences that the Chinese generally go through in arriving at their individual identities. Both in the past and today the dominant cultural practices in bringing up children have tended to instil conflicting and contradictory ideals about individualism. Children are taught to be selfless and to defer to collective norms, but they are also expected to gain recognition through achievement.[13]

The contradiction is intensified by what is explicitly taught and what is implicit in their experiences. Chinese children are generally told that their identity is totally derived from belonging to some larger group or community, and it is therefore from this "Other" that the individual receives his or her "greater self" or *da-wo*. What is generally left vague is where the boundary should be between the *da-wo* and the *xiao-wo* or the "lesser self." Worse still, there are few clearly-defined standards for identifying the conditions when it may be permissible to assert the interests of the lesser or private self. Self-sacrifice is glorified to such an extent that the safest rule for the individual is to pretend always to selflessness. The tension, however, is made more acute because the tendency is for parents to be very indulgent in the early years, so that the child learns the pleasures of wilfulness, but the adult world then imposes demanding controls which teach the child that reality requires yielding to the wishes of others.[14]

13. For a discussion of the conflicting tendencies in Chinese socialization practices, placed in historical context, see Jon L. Saari, *Legacies of Childhood: Growing up Chinese in a Time of Crisis, 1890–1920* (Cambridge, Mass.: Harvard University Press, 1990), especially ch. 4.

14. For a more detailed analysis of the psychological dimensions of the Self–Other problem in Chinese culture see "The psychological roots of China's opposing political cultures," in my *The Mandarin and the Cadre* (Ann Arbor: Center for Chinese Studies, University of Michigan, 1988). That analysis in turn was based on evidence found in such works as Michael Harris Bond (ed.), *The Psychology of the Chinese People* (New York: Oxford University Press, 1986); David Y. H. Yu (ed.), *Chinese Culture and Mental Health* (Orlando, Fl.: Academic Press, 1985); Kenneth A. Abbott, "Cultural change and the persistence of the Chinese personality," in George de Vos (ed.), *Response to Change: Society, Culture and Personality* (New York: Van Nostrand, 1976); Donald J. Munro (ed.), *Individualism and Holism: Studies in Confucian and*

The Chinese socialization process thus seems to produce an unresolvable tension between dependence upon an Other for identity while generating a craving for wilful assertiveness. Individuals are expected to be not only meek and conforming but appreciative of the group that provides their identities. Yet there is also the unforgotten pleasure of having once been the happy object of indulgence, which leaves, if not a hankering to be heroic, at least an instinctive appreciation for the posturing of others, and hence a love for the dramatic. Liu Binyan has described quite explicitly this tension in his own life and how it contributed to the appeal of communism for him:

As for myself, I joined the revolution mainly to liberate myself, to realize myself. I could not say precisely what this "self" was, but I had a feeling that there was something in me that, though still undeveloped, would eventually blossom, until one day I would do something very special. . . . We were taught that the true way to start on the revolutionary path was through self-abnegation. The first political term we learned was *bourgeois ideology*, which we were told was synonymous with *individualism*—although nobody could ever explain to me where natural self-interest ends and selfishness begins.[15]

The rest of Liu Binyan's autobiography is a documentation of his slow discovery that the Party's attack on what he called the "original sin" of individualism was directed at keeping the masses in line so that the leadership would be free to advance its interests, which could be quite personal and not necessarily in the national interest.

This peculiar combination of idealizing self-sacrifice but also seeking recognition through achievement, and linking these apparent opposites to the essence of heroism, was repeatedly exploited in the stories of the model heroes of the Mao era. Lei Feng embodied that combination, but what is culturally significant is that the Chinese people generally accepted as plausible that this "model" soldier would have left behind not just a diary, which was the sole source of evidence of his good deeds, but also glossy print photographs of himself in action, new ones to accompany the fresh stories in each new campaign. For a people to be able to suspend disbelief to such a degree suggests that they must have been presented with material which conformed to their social expectations.

The tension at the basis of self identity is made more complex in Chinese

Taoist Values (Ann Arbor: Center for Chinese Studies, University of Michigan, 1985). Especially noteworthy are the various works of Francis L. K. Hsu, including "The Self in cross-cultural perspective," in Anthony J. Marsella, George De Vos and Francis L. K. Hsu (eds.), *Culture and Self: Asian and Western Perspectives* (New York & London: Tavistock Publishers, 1985); "Eros, affect, and Pao," in Francis L. K. Hsu (ed.), *Kinship and Culture* (Chicago: Aldine Publishers, 1971); and *Americans and Chinese: Passages to Difference* (Honolulu: University of Hawaii Press, 1985).

15. Liu Binyan, *A Higher Kind of Loyalty* (New York: Pantheon Books, 1990), p. 16. Italics in original.

culture by a further source of fundamental ambivalence: the individual is expected to be selfless in sacrificing for the collectivity, but in return the collectivity provides only limited rewards. The group rarely stresses emotional support, only material well-being. There is little sense of team spirit or warm intimacy in any of the collectivities which define the individual's identity. Individuals are, of course, given a degree of security through association with the group which establishes their sense of identity. Their rewards are, however, primarily of a symbolic or ritualistic nature, while their reciprocating demonstrations of proper selflessness are expected to be quite materialistic. Consequently the individual learns early to be content with getting relatively little out of what is often a very unfair exchange. Chinese children also learn through the disciplining effects of socialization the necessity of controlling their emotions. To act properly is not to follow one's feelings but to conform to standards, and one should not expect emotional returns just for doing what is right. When emotions do surface, they tend to be destructive and not constructive, for there are few acceptable ways of displaying one's feelings.

The traditional inhibitions about expressing warm emotions toward the members of the very group that provides one's identity, and the taboos about admitting to having private interests, created in Chinese culture an unresolvable problem of craving for intimacy, of idealizing warm relationships in the abstract but in practice finding them unobtainable.[16] The arranged marriages of the past and today's numerous obstacles to easy and open ways of courting have made self-discovery through intimacy a difficult and often frustrating matter. Moreover, individuals have generally not been encouraged to seek out kindred spirits and to build webs of strong emotional ties with people with like private interests. The rules of *guanxi* hold that these relationships should have as their basis shared particularisms that are objectively defined, such as a common place of origin, the same school or class, the same unit, but not shared private interests. Even the lubricating spirit of *ganqing* generally lacks the emotionally intense feelings of personal indebtedness and obligation of, say, the Japanese bonds of reciprocity which are built upon their powerful sentiments of *on* and *giri*. The tacit understanding in Chinese culture is that people may be driven to using *guanxi* for materialistic reasons but not generally to fulfil an emotional need for belonging. The popular appeal of the Robin Hood band in the *Water Margin* novel and the poems about the fellowship of drinking companions stemmed in part from the fact that they responded to the tension between the idealization of intimacy and the recognition that it was a forbidden goal, involving what was probably improper if not illegal behaviour.

16. Many Chinese have informed me that the discussion of the problem of intimacy in *The Mandarin and the Cadre* (ch. 2) spoke to something very real in their lives, and that they wished it was a topic that could be more frankly discussed by Chinese.

In short, the problem of individualism in Chinese culture is one in which form and ritual call for conformity, humility and selflessness, but the urge for assertiveness and for being seen as special is not entirely dampened. Conformity may be widespread, but the emotions of a team spirit are rarely experienced. The Chinese craving for the unobtainable ideal of intimacy makes people believe that true comradeship should be possible, but experience teaches that it is unrealistic, indeed dangerous, to let go of their emotions and openly trust others. Thus while behaviour must deny the legitimacy of individualism, under the cultural constraints there are strong urges toward individual autonomy. This suggests that should structural circumstances change there could be a strong potential for greater self-orientated rather than group-orientated behaviour. We can see this potential, and its limitations, in the Chinese tradition of belonging to associations but not making heavy demands on the group's policies.

Passive Participation and the Absence of Voluntary Associations

From early times a remarkably high proportion of the Chinese elite belonged to private societies or associations in which they could find personal security and well-being just from belonging while having little say in the group's policies. In a literal sense the Chinese had a higher level of "participation" than was found in most traditional societies, but it was essentially a passive form of participation in which individual self interest was not openly asserted.[17] In the Qing dynasty, as James Townsend has observed, ". . . virtually every Chinese was thoroughly experienced in the benefits, problems, and adjustments of cooperative and associational life as a result of membership in small-scale social units. . . . The Chinese citizen found his social identity, his security, and his hopes for advancement in his local associations and not in the wider political community."[18] Indeed, beyond the family and clan there were in traditional China a great variety of associations ranging from lineage societies, benevolent associations, occupational guilds and provincial associations to the secret societies which helped to provide identity and security for their members. In most cities there were *huiguan* or "Landsmann halls" where people originating from the same province or region could meet and gain a sense of collective security. As Ping-ti Ho has noted, "While all these organizations tran-

17. The added theoretical dimension to the essentially structural–functional approach which made Franz Schumann's *Ideology and Organization in Communist China* (Berkeley: University of California Press, 1966) such a classic study was the historical recognition of continuity and change with respect to organizational membership in Chinese society.

18. James R. Townsend, *Political Participation in Communist China* (Berkeley: University of California Press, 1967), p. 19.

scended biological ties, they nevertheless offered their members a face-to-face intimacy that usually characterizes primary social associations."[19]

Beyond providing their members with a sense of belonging, the traditional association and societies also performed a variety of public functions. The leadership could be quite public-spirited, and as a local elite they would make voluntary contributions in answer to community concerns, such as helping to maintain water control, public works, schools, and other charitable and benevolent activities. Mary Backus Rankin, after detailed studies of such associations, has concluded that it is helpful to think of state–society relations in the late imperial period in terms of three spheres: the state sphere (*guan*), the private sphere (*si*), and a distinctive public sphere (*gong*) which included the public-spirited dimensions of the various associations and societies.[20] In a sense the associations were performing functions which properly belonged to the Chinese state but which the state was unable to carry out because of its limited effectiveness. What is significant for state–individual relations is that the associations and societies did not advance the private interests of citizens, for that would be seen as selfishness. The only ideology available was that of benevolent rule, and hence the "public" sphere was not a challenge to the state but rather an ally in support of a system of group memberships in which participation was essentially passive.

There are several features of this tradition of passive participation that are relevant for understanding state–individual relations in contemporary China. First, the group identities established by the societies and associations (*she* and *hui*) tended to be intense and generally undiluted because individuals usually belonged only to one, and thus they did not experience the cross-pressures common to organizational membership in modern societies. At the most, people might belong to their lineage association and one other, but since the same people would generally belong to both, the likelihood of cross-pressures was minimized. Therefore people were generally exposed only to the views of like-minded individuals and hence the pressures for conformity were constantly reinforced. Martin C. Yang describes how the introduction of Protestants and Catholic churches into a Shandong village simply reinforced the existing group divisions and thereby intensified conflicts in a community in which people were already divided into their separate associations.[21]

19. Ping-ti Ho, "Salient aspects of China's heritage," in Ping-ti Ho and Tang Tsou (eds.), *China's Heritage and the Communist Political System* (Chicago: University of Chicago Press, 1968), Vol. I, p. 32.

20. Mary Backus Rankin, "The origins of a Chinese public sphere: Local elites and community affairs in the late imperial period," paper presented to New England China Seminar, Harvard University, 27 November 1990. See also her *Elite Activism and Political Transformation in China* (Stanford: Stanford University Press, 1986).

21. Martin C. Yang, *A Chinese Village* (New York: Columbia University Press, 1945), chs. 12–13.

Secondly, there tended to be little connection between personal motivation for participation and the ostensible objectives of the group or association. Individuals might have their private needs for belonging which were in no way related to the policy goals of the leadership. Consequently the membership did not feel itself critically involved in either making or evaluating policy decisions. This tradition meant that there was considerable tolerance for whatever the leadership wanted to do. The lack of rigour in distinguishing policy, ideology and private motives and purposes contributed to a blending of what some might feel should be separated but which the Chinese captured with their once-popular phrase of *sanjiao heyi* (the three teachings [Confucianism, Taoism and Buddhism] united into one).[22]

Thirdly, individuals were not only expected to be passive in following the guidance of the group but they were also essentially passive in coming to their associations, in that membership tended to be essentially ascriptive. Birth determined one's geographical association and membership in secret societies tended to be a family matter. Thus, even though there might be initiation rites, one generally had little choice about whatever association one was expected to join. This was a critical feature in the organization of Chinese society since it meant that there was no tradition of people forming voluntary associations spontaneously in response to their private interests. One of the striking features of Chinese social and economic history is that from dynasty to dynasty the societies and associations remained the same and there were astonishingly few innovations.

Thus, although people had a recognized basic need to belong to groupings, the culture did not encourage the creating of new groupings in response to new interests. Before the rise of the Chinese Communist Party little attention was given to designing and executing strategies to attract members to groups, so in spite of the group-oriented character of Chinese society people showed little inclination or skill in seeking out others with like interests to form new associations. It was this difficulty in getting people to join voluntary associations that made Sun Yat-sen characterize the Chinese people as a "plate of sand." Fears and suspicion that one might be taken advantage of were easily heightened by the common notion that there was something improper about forming new voluntary associations. Evidence of the essential illegitimacy of such groups can be seen from the fact that historically the most successful ones were usually gangs formed by criminals.

In modern times the tradition of having to participate socially and politically according to one's assigned group identity, and of being unable to form more personally meaningful associations, has no doubt contributed to

22. Richard J. Smith, *China's Cultural Heritage: The Ch'ing Dynasty, 1644–1913* (Boulder, Colorado: Westview Press, 1983), p. 100.

rising levels of discontent and frustration. The group identity tradition made people feel that it was natural and acceptable for the Party to assign them to their respective units or *danwei*, and thereafter to mobilize them to participate in mass campaigns. Yet such group identities failed to answer the desire for more complete personal fulfilment which might have been satisfied by a greater variety of voluntary associations. Even when things are going well the individual may gain little emotional satisfaction from his assigned group, and when things go badly demoralization tends to spread quickly. During the Mao years the state had the institutional arrangements to command mass participation, but with limited individual initiative; and when setbacks occurred, as with the Deng reforms, the mood in China could quickly become depressed.

Collective Responsibility and State Control of the Individual

The character of state–individual relations takes on additional dimensions when the focus of attention is shifted from the individual's identity to the state's attitude towards the individual. Historically the fact that the individual was inexorably bound to a collectivity—the family, clan or village—simplified the state's tasks of maintaining order. Operating according to the tradition of collective responsibility, officials did not have to deal with separate individuals but only with the responsible figures of each collectivity. When a crime was committed it was not necessary to apprehend the actual culprit; it was only necessary to identify his family or clan and then approach the patriarch to deliver up the person, or whoever else might serve the purposes of punishment. Since fathers had no desire to suffer for the misdeeds of their sons, they tended to be stern in inculcating both filial piety and correct behaviour. Filial piety was not just a matter of ancestor worship and respect for one's parents, it was honoured as a guarantee that offspring would not bring down upon their parents the anger of the state. Similarly the Confucian state, in extracting resources from society in the form of taxes and corvée labour, delegated responsibilities for reaching the individual by dealing with community leaders who in turn would call upon the family or clan heads to provide what was required.

A key institution for maintaining order in imperial China was the *baojia* system which was based on a pyramid ordering of households. In each district the magistrate was expected to organize all the households into, first, units called *pai*, consisting of 10 or so households, then the *jia* of 100 households, and finally the *bao* of 1,000 households. The system provided a police network without the need for policemen. Heads of households kept their own members in line and neighbours looked in on each other. T'ung-tsu Ch'u notes that, "Consequently, the principal task of the heads of *pao-chia* was to watch the local residents and report any unlawful activities in the various families (gambling, religious heterodoxy, selling unlicensed salt, illegal coining of money, harbouring of fugitives or other criminals), and to keep an eye on suspicious strangers."[23] The system has also had the positive function of providing care for the needy. The Kuomintang revived the *baojia* system, and used it also for political and ideological control.[24] Interestingly, during the Sino–Japanese war the Japanese in many ways invigorated and administratively improved upon the *baojia* institutions in the areas under their control by instituting regular reporting procedures.

Although the *baojia* system both facilitated state control of individuals and reinforced their ties to a larger group, it also, on the positive side, gave them a limited shield against having to have direct dealings with the state, thus sparing them many of the troubles of citizenship. This degree of marginal security for the individual in relations with the state became dramatically significant under the new system which came with the establishment of the People's Republic.

The PRC Redefines the Status of the Individual

One of the sharpest breaks with China's political traditions brought about by communist rule was the radical change in the basis of the individual's group identity. It might have been easier and more efficient for the Party to have imposed its authority upon the Chinese people by simply relying upon the established institutions of collective responsibility. Indeed, during the civil war the communists did make use of the authority of village leaders and the heads of families and clans. Yet, with the establishment of the People's Republic, a direct assault was made on precisely those institutions. Indeed, the family system was one of the first institutions targeted for destruction, initially by a new marriage code and then by encouraging children to report on their parents' beliefs and actions.[25] In driving out the

23. T'ung-tsu Ch'u, *Local Government in China Under the Ch'ing* (Stanford: Stanford University Press, 1962), pp. 150–1.
24. Under the Kuomintang the system involved 10 households for each *jia*, and 10 *jia* for each *bao*. Hsu, *Under the Ancestors' Shadow*, p. 111.
25. It would be hard to overstate the appeal of radicalism for young Chinese in the 1920s and 1930s which stemmed from their dissatisfaction with the traditional family system. Writers such as Ba Jin and Ding Ling were popularly described as radicals largely because they wrote stories about unhappy family life. Historically there probably has been no greater disfunction between private cause and public effect than that of the radicalized Chinese youth who wished to get rid of arranged marriages, concubinage, and the absolute authority of grandfathers and fathers, and who ended up with the totalitarian controls of a Confucian Leninist party—a party which professed that it was seeking to raise political consciousness and make more modern many of those radicalized writers by sending them to the countryside to live with traditional peasants who believed in the old family system. To add insult to injury such writers were required to idealize such peasants in their writings while attacking as evil "rightists" enlightened individuals with modern skills and knowledge, that is, people who were like what they themselves had aspired to be. Ding Ling seemed to believe until the day she died that 22 years

old the Party introduced new units of collective identity which were more administratively binding and less rewarding than those of the traditional society. In the urban areas it was the work unit, the *danwei*, and in the rural areas the production brigades.[26]

There were several reasons why the Party chose to abandon the conventional Chinese institutions for collective responsibility. The Party distrusted the *baojia* system because it had been used by the Kuomintang to capture undercover communists. In addition, however, there was the objective of not just controlling the population but changing people's thinking. The leadership was alert to the probability that under the old system of collective responsibility it would have been much too easy for people to engage in feigned compliance and to practise the art of what James Scott has called "everyday forms of resistance."[27]

During the Mao era the state went beyond placing individuals in small group organizations (*xiaocu*) by forcing the population essentially into a caste system by giving everybody a class label according to the status of the head of the household at the time the PRC was established. From 1951 the Party used the traditional family for its household registration book (*huji bu*), in which a page for each member of the family recorded basic biographical data, including the "place of the family's ancestral origin, family origin, and class status."[28] In the 1960s class labelling became an increasingly important element in every individual's life. Those who were fortunate enough to be classed among the "five red types" (*hong wu lei*) could hope for upward mobility while those in the "five black categories" (*hei wu lei*) or worse were designated as "bad elements" (*huai fenzi*) and had no future at all. Intellectuals, of course, were denounced as being of the "striking ninth category."

The public reaction to the policy of placing people in work units, maintaining secret dossiers, and giving "class" labels reflected the fundamental Chinese cultural ambivalence about individualism. Initially the people were surprisingly docile, accepting as almost normal and useful the idea that everyone should belong to some group and have a classification which reflected moral goodness and badness. In time, however, as Lynn White has

---

of rustication at labour reform in the countryside, topped by three years of solitary confinement, was a price worth paying for getting rid of concubinage and the authority of Chinese fathers.

26. These organizational arrangements are well described in Martin King Whyte, *Small Groups and Political Rituals in China* (Berkeley: University of California Press, 1974). The dependence of the individual on the *danwei* was in some respects more complete than the traditional dependence upon the family, for the *danwei* controlled one's career, housing, rationing, marriage decision, and even when to have a child. Moreover, through the institution of the personal dossier, the *danan*, the work unit knew things about individuals that were kept secret from them.

27. James C. Scott, *Weapons of the Weak* (New Haven: Yale University Press, 1985).

28. Lynn T. White II, *Policies of Chaos* (Princeton: Princeton University Press, 1989), p. 88.

shown, the policy of labelling became the cause of deep and angry frustration which helped to fuel the violence of the Cultural Revolution,[29] and Richard Kraus has documented how Mao Zedong transformed the Marxian class categories into a host of additional "classes," and then made "class into caste."[30]

On balance what is most significant for understanding the relationship of the state and the individual is the passive spirit with which the Chinese public initially accepted the Party's use of group identities for controlling individuals.[31] People seem to have taken it as normal that there should be neighbourhood committees, with old "Aunties" keeping an eye on everyone's movements, and that the *danwei* should have such extensive command over so much of one's life. It is surprising, but significant, that the protests for democracy in the late 1980s involved almost no complaints about the *danan* files. The idea that the state should keep such secret dossiers, which would horrify people in western cultures, has not been the focus of complaints by even liberal Chinese. The critical writer Liu Binyan complained that he had been unjustly classified as a "rightist," but until Tiananmen he seemed to accept it as quite natural that people should be classified and that there should be a system of secret files on all urban people. Indeed, one of the most striking features of post-Cultural Revolution behaviour has been the passion with which so many Chinese tried to rectify their class classifications. In spite of the horrors of a system of labelling people, few who suffered from it were immediately ready to denounce the practice and many were interested only in correcting their personal classification.

Yet there remains a fundamental difference between the traditional basis of group responsibility and the communist system of classification and group belonging which has added to popular frustrations. In traditional China the "Other" which helped to define the self was a permanent institution which played a central role in childhood socialization and the adult life cycle. In contemporary China individuals are forced into the *danwei* long after their personalities are formed, and thus there is a greater urge to avoid what can be seen as a form of entrapment. Conformity with the group norms of the traditional family was a part of the individual's basic culture and personality; conformity with the norms of the *danwei* is an outside imposition of control. This suggests that the psychological intensity of the group's control may be less today, and that with any further weakening of the *danwei* system there may be significant signs of greater individualism.

29. Lynn T. White II, ch. 1.

30. Richard Curt Kraus, *Class Conflicts in Chinese Socialism* (New York: Columbia University Press, 1981), ch. 6.

31. The ways in which Chinese have responded to the *danwei* system have been well analysed in Andrew G. Walder, *Communist Neo-Traditionalism* (Berkeley: University of California Press, 1986).

Cracks in the Structure

Forty years of erratic PRC rule has seriously strained both the image of an omnipotent state and the cellular groupings basic to the individual's identity. The zig-zags of policy over the decades has raised widespread doubts as to whether the leadership has the answers to the country's problems. Ideology has been stretched to breaking-point and both leaders and followers talk of a "crisis of faith." The violent turmoil of, first, the Great Leap, then the Cultural Revolution, and then the unexpected openings of the Deng reforms, followed by the repressive closings after Tiananmen, have all combined to weaken the security of group-based identity and compelled people to worry more about themselves as individuals.[32] Change, however, has been checked by the inertia of the past, and thus the system of state–individual relations holds, but with increasingly large cracks.

The erosion of the moral authority of the Chinese state, and the failure to create a modern system of legitimacy based on a political order shaped by the competing interests in society, has left the regime inordinately dependent upon repression. But the legacy of the decade of reforms has also left the state incapable of terrorizing the people to the degree it once could. In the post-Tiananmen environment people are demonstrating once again their mastery of the Chinese art of dissembling. As the Chinese state has become weaker and its legitimacy has been brought into greater question there seems to be a dual process of ritual behaviour: the state's actions have become more formalistic and less substantive, while the people's response to the state's authority has become increasingly cynical, with general acceptance on the surface, but private reservations, combined with a touch of anger.

The change in the character of the post-Tiananmen Chinese state involves more than just a question of legitimacy; it involves a confusion about state purposes to a degree that the government seems paralysed midway between its Confucian and its Leninist traditions. The leadership still seeks legitimacy by claiming to be the upholder of a moral order, and it pretends that its ranks are filled with morally exemplary cadres whose superior attributes justify their domination over mere subjects. But the more the state asserts its claims to moral superiority, the more it is seen as corrupt, and so the disease of cynicism spreads. The state's power, however, is not trivial. The official Beijing *Evening News* reported that during the Asian Games 650,000 people were involved in security work and surveillance in the capital alone.[33] It also has more than just the powers of coer-

---

32. For an excellent discussion of the rediscovery of personal relationships in the post-Mao era, see Thomas B. Gold, "After comradeship: personal relations in China since the Cultural Revolution," *The China Quarterly*, 104 (1985), pp. 657–75.

33. Nicholas Kristof, "From China's provinces, rare voice of dissent," *New York Times*, 12 November 1990, p. 5.

cion; it has in its favour fear of chaos and the inertia of habit, which in the realm of government is easily translated into the potency of ritual and formality. And as Clifford Geertz has documented, a state devoted to ritual can be a stable and enduring institution.[34] The ritual state, of course, has an easier time if its subjects are believers, but it can still preserve its critical element of dignity if the people are willing to go along in order to get along.

Today the Chinese rulers have had to abandon many of the activist ambitions of their Leninist tradition. The Party can no longer mobilize the masses as it did during the campaigns of the Mao era.[35] Instead, officialdom in Beijing, as it awaits the succession to Deng's rule, goes through the motions of governing, not wanting to check too carefully on how thoroughly its orders are being carried out—particularly in the coastal provinces where not only citizens but also local officials pretend that the era of economic liberalization is not over.[36] Half-hearted commands are reciprocated with half-hearted obedience. The words of government have lost much of their substantive meaning, as they have at best only symbolic significance—often as code words which stand for the opposite of their literal meanings.

Beijing officials have become increasingly aware of their impotence in controlling the provincial authorities. Chen Yun has been quoted as criticizing the "traffic-light philosophy," which he says originated in Guangdong, where the localities treat the centre's policies in three ways: "When the red light is on, they make a detour and proceed as they were going; when the yellow light is on, they ignore it and keep going at the same speed; and when the green light is on, they rush ahead at full throttle."[37] The central authorities in Beijing have sought to strengthen the state by transferring provincial and local officials and rotating the governors of such key provinces as Liaoning, Henan and Hebei in the hope of preventing them from consolidating their independent power bases. As the *People's Daily* editorial of 4 August 1990 said of the shuffling, its aim is to "free cadres from being plagued with various complicated relations . . . [an] unfavourable position caused by their long tenure in one locality."[38] But this attempt to revive the

34. Clifford Geertz, *Negara* (Princeton: Princeton University Press, 1986).

35. Tyrene White argues that the practice of the Maoist mobilization campaigns is not entirely dead in the post-revolutionary Deng era, as can be seen in her case study of the one-child policy. But she admits that "Mobilization of some sort may not necessarily remain a permanent feature of Chinese politics." Indeed so, for to call, for example, the 1990 blowing of bugles against pornography a mobilization campaign is to make a mockery of the concept. Tyrene White, "Postrevolutionary mobilization in China: The one-child policy reconsidered," *World Politics*, Vol. 43, No. 1 (1990), pp. 53–76.

36. Although Ezra Vogel's research was done before Tiananmen, his findings about Guangdong's economic progress are still largely valid. See Ezra Vogel, *One Step Ahead in China* (Cambridge, Mass.: Harvard University Press, 1989).

37. "Guangdong does it own way, the centre reproaches," *Chung-yang ribao* (*Central Daily News*), 23 October 1990, p. 4.

38. Cited in Ann Scott Tyson, "China rotates leaders to cut local power," *Christian Science Monitor*, 14 November 1990, p. 4.

Qing dynasty "rule of avoidance" in assigning officials only accentuates the extent to which the central authorities are ruling more in form than in fact.

The character of the Chinese state is thus reverting back to the traditional and highly ritualized Confucian state. The Ming state, which Ray Huang has so vividly described, was a hierarchy of officials who were much too wise to advance policy alternatives with vigour and earnestness, for they knew that policies rarely succeeded and therefore advocacy would only reveal impotence.[39] It is better to uphold stability by concentrating on the rituals of governance, arguing about orthodoxy, and scheming to ensure that any misguided attempts at a policy by another faction will be doomed. This is the direction in which the post-Tiananmen Chinese state seems to be heading as the Beijing leaders try to mask the degree of paralysis that their factional differences have created.[40] The PRC state has a long way to go before becoming a Ming state, but it has already gone a long way from its Leninist tradition.

Signs of Increased Individual Autonomy

The drift toward a more ritualized state has been facilitated by the skills of the public (and of local officials) in practising feigned compliance. People have been quick to learn the limits of obligation in obeying the state's will and the areas where lip-service is enough to do the trick. Intellectuals and students know what can and cannot be said in different contexts.

The combination of the shocks and disillusionments of the Cultural Revolution and the fresh air that came with the decade of "opening" to the outside and the liberalizing reforms may have done more to inspire a spirit of individualism among modernizing Chinese than any development in Chinese history, with the possible exception of the May Fourth movement. A generation of former Red Guards has seemingly taken to heart Mao's message of distrusting authority, and they are now directing their suspicions toward the current rulers. The new ideas that came with the opening of China in the 1980s have transformed a still younger generation into non-believers in the jargon of revolution which was the faith of their fathers. Older people react passively as they face the fact that all the heroic efforts of 40 years produced little progress toward their goals of Utopia, for it is too late for them to seek new beliefs.

39. Ray Huang, *1587, A Year of No Significance: The Ming Dynasty in Decline* (New Haven: Yale University Press, 1981).
40. Although it has become conventional to picture the Chinese leadership as paralysed because of the divisions between "hardliners" and "reformers," the actual factional divisions are more complex and less vividly determined by policy alternatives. For a good identification of four factional groupings, see David Shambaugh, "China in 1990: The year of damage control," *Asian Survey*, Vol. XXXI, No. 1 (1991), pp. 36–49.

In this situation leaders of what were once the disciplining collectivities—the small group, the *danwei*, the rural brigade—are torn between accepting the feigned compliance posturing of their members and trying sternly to implement the spirit of the orders from above. It is normally easier to side with those one has to live with day by day, and the result is an ever-increasing institutionalization of a ritualized state. As individuals learn what the leaders of their *danwei* will let them get away with, the unit they are obliged to belong to turns into a shield against the possibility of the state's acts becoming substantive rather than just tolerable rituals. This has been particularly true since Tiananmen.

More than just opening the door to outside influences, the decade of reforms institutionalized changes of a modern nature which have strengthened the position of the individual in Chinese society. A potentially significant development associated with the decade of reforms which in time may give greater protection for the individual was a series of steps taken to establish a more comprehensive legal system. The discovery that foreign investors were unhappy with the protection provided by Chinese legal practices resulted in improvements in the civil code which made it possible for private parties to sue each other and the government for breach of contract. Then on 1 October 1990 there came into effect the new Administrative Litigation Law, which specifies how citizens can sue officials who have wrongfully treated them. Although not many citizens have been so foolish as to try to take to court any senior cadres, there have been a few publicized cases of citizens suing manifestly corrupt local officials. The pride the government seemed to take in the new laws helped to give the idea that people should have rights that go beyond the traditional practice of simply publicly bewailing mistreatment. The efforts by the two lawyers defending the Tiananmen protester Wang Juntao to use the Criminal Procedure Law also suggests that enacted laws are not entirely meaningless. Although the government steamrollered over the attempt, it was still significant that the lawyers stood up in a Chinese courtroom and appealed to the text of that law. Just as hypocrisy is the compliment that vice plays to virtue so the Chinese state's acknowledgement of certain legal maxims does suggest that individuals have rights, at least in principle if not always in practice.

In more general terms the greater opportunities for individual self-expression and initiative inherent in the reforms have provided scope for the latent cravings for more autonomy and more wilful action. As the obligations for conformity are weakened the balance between group-orientated and self-orientated behaviour is slightly changed so that the former is less unchallenged. The speed and the enthusiasm of young Chinese in picking up the fashions and the popular culture of the outside world, particularly that of Hong Kong and Taiwan, is evidence of a new state of mind. Conformity is still extremely important but it is now tempered by a willingness to strive to be somewhat different, to stand out as an individual.[41]

This process of individuals becoming more autonomous has not, however, brought unmixed pleasure to most Chinese. Ingrained feelings and expectations linger on, and consequently there is widespread cynicism about the faltering Chinese state and anger because the Chinese do want an omnipotent authority as their benevolent protector.[42] Moreover, there is discomfort in living in a society in which it is normal and essential to dissemble much of the time. Thus the increasing ritualization of state–individual relations has produced a general feeling that the state has become more corrupt and that citizens in general have to tell lies in many situations. On both sides of the relationship there is a sense of increased immorality, especially in contrast to the supposed puritan standards of the Mao era.[43] Objectively measured, the level of corruption may not be much worse than is the norm for Third World countries, but subjectively legitimacy in China is still tied to the idea that the government should be the defender of a moral order. Therefore, if there is a decline in moral standards, the state is directly at fault.

The Individual as Part of a Lonely Crowd in a Floating Population

Structurally the most dramatic change in state–individual relations since the mid-1980s has been the rapid growth of a floating population of rural people coming into China's larger cities. These people are totally unattached to any collectivity and are in theory an illegal population. Estimates suggest that there may be as many as 100 million such "blind migrants." One tabulation suggests that every day as many as 10 million people are moving in and out of the 23 cities with a population of over one million.[44] Beijing has as many as 1,300,000 "blindly migrating" people, and nearly a quarter of Canton's population is in that category.[45] Xinhua News Agency reported on 6 August 1988 that nearly one in every 20 people in China is

41. Possibly the most vivid description of how young Chinese in particular have enthusiastically sought to find themselves by seeking out the fads and fashions of modern youth culture is Orville Schell's *Discos and Democracy* (New York: Pantheon, 1988).

42. I have analysed the psychological bases for why disappointment with authority produces the reaction of anger in *The Spirit of Chinese Politics* (Cambridge, Mass.: MIT Press, 1968).

43. Even during the Mao period citizens had to engage in deception and questionable strategies to get ahead. For an excellent study of how that system forced people to act in immoral ways see Susan Shirk, *Competitive Comrades: Career Incentives and Student Strategies in China* (Berkeley: University of California Press, 1982).

44. Lin Wei, "Mangliu shehui dongluan de zhengzhao?" ("'Blind migration,' is it an omen of social upheaval?" *The Nineteen Nineties* (April 1989), pp. 53–5.

45. Deng Xinwei, "Zhonggong renkou zhengce yu dalu renkou wenti" ("The CCP's population policy and the population problem on the mainland"), *Zhongguo dalu* (*China Mainland*), No. 274 (August 1990), p. 20.

involved in the great population movement from the rural areas to the cities, and the daily numbers going in and out keep rising; in the case of Shanghai there were 700,000 in 1984, 850,000 in 1985, 1,346,000 in 1986, 1,900,000 in 1988 and 2,000,000 in 1989.[46]

The increasing numbers are easy to understand. First, the loosening of state controls—the household registration system, the personal dossiers and the rationing system—allowed Chinese peasants to flock to the cities to seek their fortunes wherever they heard that life was better. Secondly, the credit-tightening that came with the general austerity policies after 1988 caused many rural industries to close which pushed more people toward the cities. The rural unemployment problem was further compounded by the suspension of large-scale construction projects, and agricultural developments reduced the demand for field workers, liberating peasants from bondage to the land.[47]

This huge mobile population is seen as a threat to stability. They participated in the 1989 Tiananmen demonstration. They continue to be a major source of violation of the one-child policy, with over 1,200,000 babies being born to migrants outside the plan. They are also said to have been identified with the spread of contagious diseases. Above all, however, they are seen as a potential criminal element. It is estimated that 25 per cent of the major crimes in Shanghai, such as murder, rape, robbery and prostitution, are committed by migrants; and in Guangzhou 90 per cent of the prostitutes are migrants.[48]

In the context of the Chinese tradition of collective responsibility it is understandable that not only the authorities but citizens in general have been frightened by such an influx of unaffiliated people and suspect that they are criminally inclined. It is assumed that without the constraints of a bonding group people will act in anti-social ways. The fear is not without some foundation in fact. Crime has risen in Chinese cultural areas whenever controls are relaxed. In Taiwan, for example, there was a rise in crime with the ending of martial law which was only brought into check with the appointment as prime minister of the tough-minded general Hua Pei-tsun. Initially his appointment was greeted with fears that he was too close to the Old Guard of the Kuomintang, but after his anti-crime campaigns he was seen even by opposition leaders as a necessary law enforcer.[49]

An Upside-Down Safety Net

Although many of the Chinese are troubled by their floating population, it does not follow that they will turn out to be a source of serious social unrest.

46. Shi Lei, "Renkou da liudong de chongji" ("The impact of the great population movement"), *Zhongguo zhi chun* (*China Spring*) (April 1989), pp. 47–8.
47. Lin Wei, "Blind migration," pp. 54–5.
48. Shi Lei, "The impact of the great population movement," p. 48.
49. *New York Times*, 29 October 1990, p. 15.

The rural people who have gone to the cities are individualists who are willing to take the initiative in looking after themselves. They are ready not only to take jobs without the benefit of the "iron rice bowl," but also to start their own services and even small enterprises, and so they become peddlers, cobblers, repairmen, tailors and the like.

The fact that China has been able to absorb such a huge number of essentially unemployed people without any substantial demands for new state services may be a source of stability rather than unrest. In a peculiar way in the topsy-turvy world of Chinese official practices, the government seems to have built for the country an upside-down safety net, in that it is the large, established state enterprises, with their "iron rice bowls," which cannot survive in a competitive world and are receiving massive subsidies; while the truly unemployed migrant individuals have to make it on their own, without any state help. This combination of unemployed and self-employed individuals looking after themselves and large, inefficient state enterprises getting government subsidies may turn out to be a formula for many years of stability for China. It could give China the same surface appearance of stability that the Soviet Union had during the Brezhnev era. But under the surface the strain of the subsidies and the distortion of the irrational price system will certainly produce eventually a crisis comparable to the one Gorbachev inherited.

The situation is made more troublesome because it is the migrants, with fewer skills and less education and technical competence, who have the greatest initiative, while those with the security of the subsidized state enterprises, who do not have to take initiative, have more technical competence. This mismatch of competence and initiative cannot help but work against China's modernization efforts. The same mismatch can be found in the activities of former Red Guards who missed out on schooling but are boldly ambitious.

The dramatic increase in the flow of rural people to the cities obscures to some degree the fact that throughout Chinese society there has been a steady increase in people seeking greater autonomy. It is, of course, not just rural migrants but also city people who are striking out on their own in greater numbers. The increase in the number of small individual enterprises (*getihu*) and the somewhat larger individual enterprises (*siren qiye*) has continued in spite of the austerity programme of the state which began in late 1988.[50] In the post-Tiananmen state of national uncertainty in which the economy is partly centrally planned and partly responsive to market forces, it is possible to speak of China as having, like many semi-socialist Third World countries, a primary or formal economy under the control of the state, and a secondary or informal economy involving individuals struggling on their own to advance themselves. Whereas in the earlier days of the

---

50. See Thomas B. Gold, "Urban private business in China," *Studies in Comparative Communism*, Vol. 22, No. 2–3 (Spring–Summer 1989), pp. 187–200.

People's Republic everyone sought the security of the "iron rice bowl" of the state enterprises, it is now the independent entrepreneurs who are often the envy of others. The Chinese press is filled with complaints about the corruption of officials, particularly the sons and daughters of high cadres who use their status to make money in the private sector. Furthermore, since the enterprises in the informal economy generally do not pay all of the heavy surtaxes levied on them, it seems that increasing numbers of state enterprises feel that they too should try to avoid their taxes, to the extent that Chinese officials report that in 1989 tax evasion and under-reporting exceeded 80 billion *yuan*.[51] Thus the increasing initiative of Chinese individual citizens has affected the behaviour of officials so that cadres at all levels are manifesting more "individualism." Many people living on fixed incomes—such as scholars, doctors, scientists and other professional people—find that they are making far less than those in the market economy, and they complain that it is unreasonable that the more knowledge one has, the less money one earns; a state of affairs they characterize as *gongzi daogua* (wages are hanging upside down).[52]

Efforts to Build a New Relationship

The dual erosion of both state authority and the primary group identity structures could bring about a radical transformation in the long-standing character of the relationship of the state and the individual in China.

There is accumulating evidence that individuals are increasingly shaping their own identities less in terms of their primary group, whether the family or the *danwei*, and more in terms of the broad strata of society, such as workers, migrants, students, intellectuals and the like. If this is the trend of the future it would represent for the individual a half-way point between the tradition of being a passive, parochial participant in face-to-face group structures and being an autonomous citizen capable of political relationships with the Chinese state. The blossoming artistic and literary creativity in the 1980s testifies to the straining in Chinese culture for greater individual self-expression. The "poisonous weeds" of early periods were allowed to reappear, and a whole generation of new voices was heard.[53] The Xi'an Film Studio produced works of exceptional artistic and intellectual creativity, such as Chen Kaige's *Yellow Earth*, Zhang Yimou's *Red Sorghum Well*; and there was the extraordinarily frank self-criticism of

51. "Top-to-bottom tax evasion," *Ming Pao Monthly* (December 1990), pp. 8–10; translated in *Inside China Mainland*, Vol. 13, No. 2 (February 1991), pp. 15–16.
52. Personal communication from senior Chinese scholar.
53. Much of the best of the new writing has been translated in Geremie Barme and John Minford, *Seeds of Fire: Chinese Voices of Conscience* (New York: Hill and Wang, 1988); Helen Siu and Zelda Stern, *Mao's Harvest* (New York: Oxford University Press, 1983).

Chinese traditional culture, the six-part television documentary *River Elegy* (*He Shang*).[54]

A very significant but little noted feature of the democracy movement of spring 1989 was the informal associations that became the basis for mobilizing the students. Prior to the earlier democracy demonstration of 1986–87 there had been no significant informal clubs or societies on the various campuses, and thus the move toward political activism was disjointed, nearly leaderless, and guided by improvised strategies. After the return to normality following the purging of Hu Yaobang, Fang Lizhi and Liu Binyan, a significant development quietly took place among the students. While the government was absorbed with its "anti-spiritual pollution" rhetoric, the students at the leading Beijing universities began to create a variety of informal discussion groups according to their academic interests. Shen Tong, who was to become a major leader in Tiananmen Square, tells of how the biology students at Beijing University formed their meeting groups to advance their academic interests.[55] Then, when the situation was ripe for political action, the various groups were easily mobilized and the students knew they could trust the others because they had a more fundamental, non-political basis for associating with each other. The discussion groups were formed not solely with ulterior political purposes in mind but in part in the spirit of like-minded people seeking the personal advantages of association.

If in the future it becomes easier and more natural for the Chinese to come together to advance their shared private interests it will be the beginning of a true civil society. As they begin to build voluntary associations, the Chinese will develop the strength not only to check the state but to make effective demands on state policies. The result will be a strengthening of both the autonomy of individuals and the authority of the state. If this were to happen the state would no longer be just a tool of a ruling elite with its own values and interests, but would become an institution responsive to the political preferences of society. And these preferences would represent the genuine interests of free individuals.

Such a development, however, is not likely to be a smooth one because the ambivalence about autonomy and dependence is too fundamental a feature of Chinese culture to be resolved so easily. As much as people may crave freedom, there remains the deep longing for the security of dependency. As an abstraction the picture of the lonely figure is attractive for the Chinese, but in practical terms their desire is more for the protection and support of a collectivity. The Chinese need for belonging is likely to create an even greater problem about individual freedom than the one Eric Fromm described for the Germans in his classic *Escape from Freedom*. For

54. For a discussion of the significance of this outburst of artistic creativity for state–society relations in China, see Gold, "Party-state versus society," pp. 143–5.
55. Shen Tong, *Almost a Revolution* (Boston: Houghton Mifflin, 1990).

individual Chinese there are two levels of ambivalence that need to be resolved. In addition to the political ambivalence about freedom and dependency there is the more basic conflict between conforming and self-assertion. In short, the issue of individualism has yet to be resolved in Chinese culture. In the meantime the problem of human rights will continue to play an important part in the relations of the United States and some other countries with China. The process of working toward a new equilibrium in state–individual relations is certain to be filled with tensions, especially as officials sense the weakening of state authority and the increasing role of the people. It is an unfortunate but undeniable fact that the *modus operandi* of Chinese leaders, both traditional and contemporary, is to treat manifestations of individualism as obstreperous acts of disorder and a threat to legitimacy, and therefore cases for repression. Their basic distrust of individualism is reinforced by their conviction, strengthened by what they see happening in the Soviet Union, that it should be possible to have economic development without individual freedom. They seem to be blind to the fact that in their own country economic progress has been consistently correlated with a rise in individualistic tendencies. Thus progress, if it comes, will reduce the gap between state and individual in Chinese culture.

Postscript

In the mean time, however, the mystique of the omnipotent state will surely continue its hold on the Chinese imagination, based as it is on even more deeply ingrained sentiments about authority. The mystique endures in spite of internal contradictions. For example, Chinese intellectuals in the first decades of the century saw nothing illogical in simultaneously believing that China needed a stronger state while being themselves totally impotent in affecting the actions of whatever state did exist. The main response of the Chinese to the horrors of the Mao era was the essentially passive classical Confucian remedy for bad government: a call for "better", that is, more "virtuous" rulers. They failed to see that the system itself might need to be changed.

Thus, while Western observers since Tiananmen tend to see ominous cracks in China's Leninist state, the prospects for systemic change remain uncertain. This is especially so given the Chinese artistry in feigned compliance and in dissembling toward government. Away from the centre local authorities, from the provinces to the townships, are enthusiastically embracing the spirit of entrepreneurship, but this should not be mistaken for the death-knell of the Leninist state. Even the most secular of Western scholars, possibly unconsciously reflecting their religious heritage, tend to attach inordinate importance to the question of whether people "truly

believe" in their professed ideologies. Consequently they have little understanding of cultures in which the degree of belief is less important than
ritualized actions and practices. Lip-service, if carefully and uninterruptedly
practised, can serve the purposes of authority quite as well as internalized
convictions. In Chinese culture praxis has generally been more important
than ideology.[56] Therefore as long as the Chinese continue to act as though
they believe in the Four Cardinal Principles, the Leninist state can endure,
and the depth or strength of ideological conviction will matter little.

Western cultural biases can also cause China-watchers to exaggerate the
delegitimizing effects of corruption, which some Chinese say, with their
customary tendency to political hyperbole, is today as bad as it was in the
last days of the Nationalists. Yet in most of history, corruption has supported rather than undermined legitimacy. Today party membership is
growing at an amazing rate for a supposedly dying institution, as single-
minded opportunists are joining it in the spirit of Deng's dictum that "To
get rich is glorious."

Thus, for all the signs of regime decay there remain powerful
counterforces, not the least of which is the unshakeable consensus of
Chinese of all political persuasions that the supreme value of the day is
unquestionably stability. The Chinese with one voice sing their mantra to
stability, rejoicing in self-congratulation for their wisdom in having gradual
reforms, and they happily shudder in feigned horror at what they believe
are Russia's disastrous mistakes.[57] The Chinese state may appear to outsid-
ers to be losing its grip, even to the point of faltering in its capacity to raise
revenue, which is presumably an ultimate test of governmental effectiveness, but still systemic political change may be slow in coming. China
endured long as a "Phantom Republic", and it may do the same as a
"Phantom People's Republic".

Moreover, when change does come it may not be gradual or just a
continuation of current trends, but rather it could be dramatic and extreme.
The problem of prediction based on the playing out of latent tensions is
for the social sciences very much like that of the physical sciences in fore-
seeing the consequences of stress. Earthquakes are long in building up but
sudden in happening; bridges do not collapse gradually and airplanes do not
fall slowly from the sky because of the prolonged stresses of metal fatigue.
And so, as much as we may wish that China will have a gradual transition to

56. For an insightful discussion of the importance in Chinese culture of the ritualizing of
everyday practices rather than belief, see James L. Watson, "Rites or beliefs? The construction
of a unified culture in late imperial China," in Lowell Dittmer and Samuel S. Kim (eds.),
China's Quest for National Identity (Ithaca, NY: Cornell University Press, 1993), pp. 80–103.

57. The Chinese have been so intense in their worshipping at the altar of stability that they
seem blind to the fact that after Deng's reforms had been running for a decade and a half
Russia was barely four years into Yelsin's reforms, and therefore it is not unlikely that after
another decade Russia will be more advanced, both politically and economically, than China
was in 1993.

a new balance between the individual and the state, the change may be delayed but then sudden in the event, if and when it does come. In sum, we need to suppress our impatience as we try to forecast how China's irreversible reforms may change the historic relationship between the Chinese state and the individual Chinese subject. Before jumping to premature conclusions about where China's reforms are heading we might do better to remember that when Zhou Enlai was asked what he thought of the French Revolution he said, "It's too soon to tell."

Workers, Managers, and the State: The Reform Era and the Political Crisis of 1989

Andrew G. Walder

In May of 1989 urban workers burst suddenly onto the Chinese political scene. They marched by the tens of thousands in huge Beijing street demonstrations, in delegations from hundreds of workplaces—acts repeated on a smaller scale in cities throughout the country. While organized strikes were rare, small groups of dissident workers formed dozens of independent unions and other political groups from Sichuan to Shanghai, and from Inner Mongolia to Guangdong. The most visible, the Beijing Workers' Autonomous Union, set up in mid-April, had an organized presence on Tiananmen Square beginning in the week of the student hunger strike, claimed thousands of members, published dozens of handbills and political manifestos, and played an important role in organizing demonstrations after the declaration of martial law. The workers' unprecedented political response helped transform a vibrant student movement into the most severe popular challenge to Communist Party rule since 1949.

Why such a political awakening among workers in 1989? This is something of a puzzle, because the 1980s have been viewed widely, despite inflation, as a period of unprecedented rises in worker living standards, and also because an equally vibrant student movement at the end of 1986 did not elicit such a large response. Many observers have quickly focused upon levels of worker dissatisfaction as the key to this puzzle. The post-1986 inflation is commonly singled out, and this certainly was among the grievances mentioned first and most often by workers during the movement. Such inflation is often asserted either to have led to a rapid rise in the level of worker dissatisfaction or, more generally, to have led to a frustration of material expectations stoked by a decade of material progress.

Yet an aggregate rise in worker dissatisfaction or in levels of frustration due to dashed expectations, real as both may be, will take us only part of the way towards an understanding of what happened in 1989. Popular dissatisfaction with incomes and prices is merely one plausible source for workers' political motives. But motives are only part of the picture: they do not help us to understand how and why workers were able to act on their motivations. China's system of work unit control failed to prevent dissatisfaction from turning into widespread popular protest, as it had despite prevalent dissatisfaction and scattered labour protest during the mid-1970s and early 1980s. Moreover, knowledge about motive does not help us to understand why wage issues would become so widely expressed in the form of a *political* critique of corrupt officialdom, and as a demand for greater democracy. Clearly, some other changes must have taken place in the 1980s to make workers more responsive to student political appeals, and to make work units less effective in averting collective protest. This article is about the changes, their consequences in 1989, and their implications for the future.

Factory Politics on the Eve of the Reforms

Those inclined to attribute 1989 to widespread worker discontent with material conditions and government performance would do well to recall the end of the Mao era and the beginning of Deng's. By 1976 real wages for urban wage earners were some 20 per cent lower than they had been two decades before. The wages of the labour force had been frozen since 1963. By 1978 average housing space in China's cities had shrunk to only 3.6 square metres per person, down from an already-crowded 4.3 metres in 1952. Housing conditions were abysmal and had not improved for many years: much of the urban housing stock was in severe disrepair; modern indoor plumbing was rare. Basic foodstuffs were distributed through a spartan system of rationing; such primitive consumer goods as were available were rationed and scarce. Spot shortages of such daily necessities as matches and toilet paper were very common.[1]

These conditions, combined with the arbitrary and sometimes brutal victimization of workers typical of the campaigns and searches for political enemies in the preceding period, bred widespread worker demoralization and political cynicism. The abuse of power and special privileges of factory officials who put on a public face of extreme political rectitude, and the favouritism they showed towards their loyal followers in the workforce, led to a pronounced feeling of "us" versus "them" in the attitudes of workers toward the Party. Periodic slow-down strikes, inattention to quality, breakdowns, absenteeism and pilfering of supplies prevailed in factories.[2]

This dissatisfaction periodically erupted into major strikes and street protests in many industrial cities. In 1975, a late spring strike wave in Wuhan paralysed public transport and closed the massive Wuhan Steel Corporation, and workers staged a large-scale sit-down demonstration in front of the Hubei Provincial Government headquarters.[3] The railway sys-

1. See Andrew G. Walder, *Communist Neo-Traditionalism: Work and Authority in Chinese Industry* (Berkeley: University of California Press, 1986), ch. 6.
2. *Ibid*. chs. 4 and 6.
3. This is based on a report by Gong Xiaoxia, now a graduate student in sociology at Harvard University, who was at that time working as a Guangzhou textile worker, and who witnessed these events while travelling through Wuhan. She reports that the streets were littered with abandoned buses, some being driven along haphazard routes by citizens. Two friends of hers who worked at the Wuhan Steel Corporation told her that the strike was motivated by pay and working conditions, even though the protests became part of factional

tem also suffered periodic disruption in many locations.[4] In the best-known labour event of the period, political unrest in several large Hangzhou industrial plants crippled production for much of the summer and was eventually quelled only after the intervention of the armed forces.[5] The next year, workers were well-represented in the Tiananmen Square events of April 1976 and associated protests in Nanjing and elsewhere. And in the summer of 1976, Xi'an was paralysed for weeks by street barricades and worker pickets as a "worker rebel movement" comprised of a collection of groups from separate factories cordoned off and held large sections of the city.[6]

These outbursts, however, were short, isolated, and quickly repressed, even if they were sometimes large and threatening. This is to a great extent due to the fact that the central authorities in those years, with the exception of such localities as Hangzhou whose administrations were thoroughly racked with factionalism, could rely upon the integrity of their systems of repression and control, both police and workplace. Professional managers were politically isolated and demoralized, and had little effective authority. Factories had very little autonomy in the conduct of business. The political officials who ruled factories were firmly subordinated to political officials in the state structures above them. Labour discipline may have been lax, but the Party and security organs of the factory and local government reacted swiftly to acts of overt protest or collective insubordination. Emigrés of the late 1970s told of extensive security investigations touched off by political graffiti in their factories, and of harsh reprisals against workers absent from work on the days of the April protests of 1976. And the strict controls over travel and information of those years prevented widespread and

politics in the city. She had also heard, from people directly involved, of similar labour protests in Sichuan province during the same period.

4. Li Minghua, "Observations on recent labor unrest in mainland China," *Issues and Studies*, Vol. 11, No. 10 (October 1975), pp. 2–15, at p. 9.

5. See Keith Forster, *Rebellion and Factionalism in a Chinese Province: Zhejiang, 1966–1976* (Armonk, New York: M. E. Sharpe, 1990), pp. 214–28. Forster makes clear that the Hangzhou outbreak was closely tied to factional divisions dating back to the Cultural Revolution.

6. This is based on a report by Søren Clausen, now teaching at Aarhus University, who witnessed these events while travelling as a Beijing University student at the end of July. The movement had originated among workers in the city power plant over the persecution of a young couple who worked there. According to a wall poster read by Clausen, in 1974 the young couple had been discovered while engaged in sexual activity in the plant. Party cadres sought to make an example of such blatant bourgeois immorality by ordering a severe administrative punishment. When co-workers protested, the cadres took the case to court and had the man convicted of rape and sentenced to 10 years. When co-workers protested further that it had not been a rape, the woman was given two years of labour reform as an accomplice to a criminal act. Thus began a long struggle against the plant cadres that would blossom when factional divisions split the national and local leadership. While the protests were expressed as opposition to Deng Xiaoping's "revisionist line," each group within the larger coalition had specific grievances against their factory leadership. Corruption, abuse of power, and living conditions were common complaints. I would like to thank Professor Clausen for providing me with a translation of some of his notes in Danish.

accurate knowledge of events in different parts of the country. Despite widespread worker disaffection, and occasional opportunities for collective action provided by factional strife among national or local leaders, the structures of the state could still effectively contain and isolate workers' collective action.

China's leaders in the late 1970s were acutely aware of widespread worker discontent and its potential political consequences. It is no coincidence that shortly after leading Maoists were deposed in 1976, the new leaders announced the first general round of wage increases since 1963, and the first of any kind since 1973. Reminders of the urban workers' conditions emerged in 1980 and 1981, just as Deng's reforms got under way. After widespread and objective reporting in the Chinese media of the Solidarity movement in Poland, China experienced a small wave of work stoppages and several local attempts to form independent trade unions.[7] A small group of working class dissidents, exemplified by Shanghai's Fu Shenqi, stood up to speak on behalf of workers and promptly disappeared into China's labour camps.[8] These events reinforced the characteristic Dengist urge both to improve worker living standards through vigorous economic reform, and to repress firmly any stirrings of independent political activity.

Workers' Material Lives in the 1980s

By the end of the 1980s many urban workers had come to feel that they had benefited little from the reforms. However, the 1980s appear to have been a decade of rapid growth of income and rising living standards for urban residents. In the decade after 1978, average nominal wages in state and collective sectors almost tripled.[9] There was a virtual consumer revolution: ownership of electric fans grew 12-fold; television sets 38-fold; refrigerators 131-fold; and the number of washing machines in households grew from around 1,000 to 5.7 million.[10] Average housing space in urban areas more

7. See Jeanne L. Wilson, "'The Polish Lesson': China and Poland 1980–1990," *Studies in Comparative Communism*, Vol. 23, Nos. 3/4 (Autumn/Winter 1990), pp. 259–80.

8. Fu Shenqi was a factory worker who had been active in Shanghai in the 1978–79 "democracy wall" movement, and who in 1980 sought election to the local People's Congress as a representative from his factory. One of the main planks of his platform was improvement of workers' housing. See the materials collected in Xianggang zhongwen daxue xueshenghui (Student Association of Chinese University of Hong Kong) (ed.), *Minzhu zhonghua: Zhongguo dalu minjian minzhu yundong beibuzhe wenji* (*Democratic China: Collected Writings of People Arrested in the Popular Democracy Movement on the Chinese Mainland*) (Hong Kong: Xianggang zhongwen daxue xueshenghui/Yuandong zhiwu pinglunshe, 1982), pp. 350–2, 358–61, 370–7.

9. In 1978 average state sector wages were 644 *yuan*, in the collective sector, 506. In 1988, the respective figures were 1,853 and 1,426 *yuan*. Guojia tongji ju, *Zhongguo tongji nianjian 1989* (*Statistical Yearbook of China, 1989*) (Beijing: Zhongguo tongji chubanshe, 1989), p. 138.

10. Guojia tongji ju, *Zhongguo tongji nianjian 1988* (Beijing: Zhongguo tongji chubanshe, 1988), p. 804.

than doubled, from slightly over 4 square metres per person in 1978 to 8.8 square metres in 1988.[11]

The impressive progress portrayed in official data makes it difficult to understand how workers could be anything but profoundly grateful for the Deng reforms. Inflation, however, cut deeply into the large increases in nominal incomes. The cumulative increase from 1978 to 1988 in the official cost of living index for urban residents was 88.7 per cent.[12] In official terms, therefore, the tripling of nominal wages becomes instead a still-impressive increase of 50 per cent over 10 years.[13] Very important for subsequent worker perceptions, however, is the fact that inflation accelerated sharply from 1985. Between 1978 and 1984, inflation averaged only 2.8 per cent a year, but from 1985 to 1988 the average rate jumped to 12.1 per cent, the highest year by far being 1988, at 20.7 per cent.[14] By *official* standards, in other words, real incomes in the state and collective sectors overall fell slightly between the end of 1986 and the end of 1988.[15]

This picture, however, is based upon aggregate national data that merge the effects of many different processes: large scale retirements from and entries into the labour force, the creation of new enterprises in rapidly developing regions of the country, and possibly widening income gaps between regions or economic sectors. It would be more relevant to the question of how workers have experienced income changes in the era of reform to be able to trace a representative sample of individuals through time, and measure changes in their incomes, adjusted for inflation. Such data, of course, are not widely available. However, we do have data for a representative sample of 740 employees in the city of Tianjin, and they help us to explore this question in an admittedly less than comprehensive fashion.[16] Tianjin is by no means representative of urban China as a whole, although it is one of the large industrial cities in which worker protest emerged in 1989. The sample, moreover, consists solely of people who were already in the labour force in 1976. Such a sample therefore can tell us little about aggregate trends, but it may provide us with some insight into the varied impact of wage trends on different urban sub-populations. For this sub-population, nominal wage increases were large, but they barely

11. *Zhongguo tongji nianjian 1989*, p. 719.

12. Calculated from *Zhongguo tongji nianjian 1989*, pp. 687–8.

13. In constant 1978 *yuan*, average state sector incomes rose from 644 to 982 *yuan*; collective sector incomes from 506 to 756 *yuan*. Calculated from *Zhongguo tongji nianjian 1989*, p. 138.

14. *Zhongguo tongji nianjian 1989*, pp. 687–8.

15. *Ibid*. p. 138.

16. The source is a 1986 survey of 1,011 urban households conducted in collaboration with the Institute of Sociology, Tianjin Academy of Social Sciences, and the Bureau of District Affairs, Municipal Government of Tianjin. See Andrew G. Walder, *et al.*, "The 1986 survey of work and social life in Tianjin, China: Aims, methods, and documentation," Working Paper No. 25, Center for Research on Politics and Social Organization, Harvard University Department of Sociology, 1989.

outpaced the rate of inflation for the decade after 1976. The blue-collar workers in the sample fared only slightly worse than the work-force as a whole; instead of a 50 per cent increase in nominal wages, incomes rose in real terms by only 6.5 per cent between 1976 and 1986, less than one per cent a year. These figures are sobering if we keep in mind that the survey was conducted in October 1986, *before* the period during which real wages fell according to official statistics. While it is impossible to generalize from these data, a sub-sample of this kind reminds us that variations in wage trends among cities, occupations and age cohorts are still very poorly understood. Aggregate trends may mask important variations that bear on the experiences and political motivations of key sub-groups in the urban labour force.

However important real incomes are in evaluating living standards, other direct measures are available. Housing and commodity ownership are also important physical indicators. Here, the presence of a commodity in the household and the actual amount of living space for family members need not be adjusted for inflation. Do aggregate national data significantly overstate improvements actually enjoyed by blue-collar workers? The Tianjin survey, which gathered data on commodity ownership and housing conditions, offers some insight into this question. Tianjin's blue-collar workers do indeed appear clearly to have benefited from the consumer revolution of the 1980s. Some 26 per cent of working class households owned a colour television set (compared to 30 per cent of the entire sample); 76 per cent a black and white television set (74 per cent for entire sample); 18 per cent had a refrigerator (21 per cent); and 62 per cent had a washing machine (64 per cent). These are striking improvements from the late 1970s, when only a tiny percentage owned black and white television sets, and washing machines, colour televisions and refrigerators were almost unheard of. The reforms of the 1980s appear clearly to have brought a new generation of consumer durables into ordinary working-class households.

National data on urban housing space, however, probably overstate improvements in the larger cities. Rural and small-town housing has long been less crowded than in the larger cities, and there was a large reclassification of formerly rural areas into the "urban" category in the 1980s.[17] In the Tianjin survey, which sampled only the urban districts of the municipality, the respondents lived in households that had an average of only 5.7 square metres per person, or 2.3 persons per room. Only 15 per cent said they were satisfied with their housing, and 52 per cent said they were dissatisfied (the rest in between), while 35 per cent said that they had no hope of getting a larger apartment (blue-collar workers in the sample fared only slightly worse than these averages).

17. For example, in 1984, average per capita housing space was 25% higher in county towns than in municipalities. See State Statistical Bureau, *A Survey of Income and Household Conditions in China* (Beijing: New World Press/China Statistical Information and Consultancy Service, 1985), p. 140.

In sum, the reforms improved workers' material lives primarily by making widely available a new generation of consumer goods and more plentiful, varied, and higher quality foodstuffs. There were impressive increases in purchasing power, but these increases mainly took place before 1986. After that year, real wages began to decline under the impact of inflation, and workers found it progressively more difficult to sustain the patterns of consumption they enjoyed in the middle of the decade. Finally, housing conditions, long the most acutely-felt source of dissatisfaction for urban wage earners, appear to have improved somewhat in the larger industrial cities, but dissatisfaction with housing and despair over future improvements nevertheless remain deeply ingrained features of the urban experience. The record of the 1980s was one in which sustained—even unprecedented—material progress was mixed with continuing disappointment over housing and rising dismay over inflation. Yet one would not be able to predict workers' political response in 1989 solely on the basis of this information. Clearly, workers' perceptions mediate between the conditions and political action. To understand the sources of these changing perceptions—and workers' willingness and ability to act on them in the ways they did—we might profitably examine changes in factory institutions and the experience of work in the decade of reform.

The Changing Politics of the Factory

The reforms of the 1980s also appear to have affected workers' interests and perceptions by transforming politics within factories. Managers have been released from the tight restrictions of the past system of central planning and Party supervision, and they are now increasingly responsible for the performance of their firm and the welfare of their employees. The Communist Party's formerly central role in the enterprise has declined significantly, especially the politicized reward system that characterized Chinese enterprises in the 1960s and 1970s. In place of the mass campaigns of the past, practical issues of pay and benefits have come to dominate factory life, and workers have developed newly effective means to influence managers over these issues. Managers, still unable freely to lay off or fire significant numbers of workers, have been forced to develop new ways of punishing those who fail to perform, or who challenge their authority, by transferring them to lower-paying jobs inside and even outside the factory. In so doing, they have begun to encroach upon workers' formerly sacrosanct job security in threatening ways; and the issue of job tenure and punishments has become a new source of tension. In such an atmosphere, management–labour antagonisms have sharpened over the past decade, enmeshing many factories in endless rounds of slowdowns, concessions, and lingering animosities.

The essential first step in the emergence of heightened labour contention was introduced by the planning and financial reforms of the first half of the 1980s. While these reforms arguably have not achieved their aim of creating truly autonomous firms with sufficiently hardened budget constraints, they have detached industrial enterprises from the structures of the state in two highly visible and politically important ways.[18] First, managers' former role as disciplined agents of Party and state organs has been exchanged for a new role as representatives of the interests of their enterprise including, to a considerable extent, the interests of their employees. Secondly, these reforms have shifted the determination of wages and other benefits away from national ministries and local planning bureaus and placed them firmly at the level of the enterprise. These changes have had a series of political consequences within the firm.

The decline of the Party organization

The first of these consequences has been to detach the enterprise from Party discipline. The 1980s have marked the progressive erosion of the authority and organizational integrity of Party branches within factories, and of the responsiveness of enterprise Party organs to their superior organs in local and central government. The new profit retention schemes, tax obligations, and loan repayment contracts have made clearly visible to all parties concerned—local government agencies, banks, managers, and their employees—the respective costs to all of the Party's political interference and of politicized reward systems. This is one important reason why the several political campaigns of the 1980s have reverberated only weakly, if at all, within enterprises. Local government revenues, the liquidity of the financial system, enterprise profit, and employee pay and benefits are all visibly harmed by political interference, and this has strengthened managers' hands in resisting contrary directives from above.

As enterprises have become detached politically from the structures of Party and state, Party organizations within them have withered into a shadow of their former selves. The beginning of this withering was already evident in the early 1980s,[19] but has now progressed much further, as reflected in interviews with managers in China in the middle years of the 1980s, and with a small group of emigré workers interviewed at the end of the decade.[20] This withering is evident in two ways. First, factory Party

---

18. This account of the altered position of firms and managers draws on two of my earlier papers, "Wage reform and the web of factory interests," *The China Quarterly*, 109 (1987), pp. 22–41; and "Factory and manager in an era of reform," *The China Quarterly*, 118 (1989), pp. 242–64.

19. Walder, *Communist Neo-Traditionalism*, ch. 7.

20. See the 1984–86 interviews cited in Walder, "Factory and manager." The emigré workers were interviewed in mid-1990 in Cambridge, Massachusetts, and are cited individually below. Three were production workers, one a ticket seller on a bus, and another had advanced from repair worker to manager over an 18-year career. They all left China after October 1989.

organizations have largely abandoned their former political presence on the shop floor, even to a great extent their still-sanctioned vestigial role of engaging in "thought work" (*sixiang gongzuo*). The testimony of two recent emigrés summarizes accurately the conclusions one may draw from a number of sources:

The work groups hardly ever have meetings for politics or anything else. Sometimes they will have a meeting to greet the New Year or something like that. Other than that, we only have meetings if there is an important document or speech to be covered, or if there is some kind of political crisis, like 4 June. The time for criticism and repudiation meetings has long passed. Workers think that sort of thing is laughable now. They were still trying to do this in the early '80s, but even then it was superficial and formalistic. Workers didn't absorb it, just got it over with and it had no effect on them at all.[21]

There is no longer any political study for the masses, only for Party members themselves. People are more realistic (*shiji*) these days. There is no more spiritual (*jingshen*) goal now, no more slogans.[22]

Secondly, this decline in the Party's political role has led to a greatly-reduced prominence of Party loyalists and activists on the shop floor, and a decline in the prestige and value of Party membership. As two Beijing production workers put it,

The Party doesn't have much of a role in the workshop. They still have activists, but not like before. They want to enter the Party—mainly it's just a matter of developing *guanxi* with the shop leaders. . . . The only real advantage is to become a cadre later on. That's the only advantage I can think of. . . . Party members are just average people, nothing outstanding about them. They aren't any smarter, they don't work any harder. They're just people who want connections with leaders, maybe they want to become cadres, and get some security for themselves. Their quality is not that high, just average.[23]

In the past advanced producers could enter the Party, and people wanted to get in. Now they don't really have high standards to enter the Party any more. People have an attitude toward the Party and the behaviour of its members, the corruption. They don't want to be Party members these days, and they don't have a lot of respect for the Party. To enter the Party today, you have to have a good work attitude, good work ability, willingness to take responsibility. Political thought means something different now. It means generally that you respect the Party, have a proper under-standing of its task. Now you just fill out an application form if you're interested. If they think you are qualified, or are close to being qualified, they will try to develop you.[24]

This represents a striking depoliticization of the "activist" role. In the past, these Party loyalists took unpopular public positions; they were the most vocal and orthodox in meetings; and they would sometimes criticize and

21. Interview no. 140, former fitter in a Beijing machinery plant.
22. Interview no. 137, production line worker in a Beijing electronics factory.
23. *Ibid.*
24. Interview no. 140.

inform on their more "backward" co-workers. For this they earned the enmity of their co-workers in the Mao era, and many of the animosities workers felt toward the Party and factory leaders were directed towards them.[25] Now one gathers a contrary impression of the Party loyalist as simply an obedient and reliable worker, someone who, quietly and unobtrusively, seeks to improve his or her career prospects by gaining the approval of leaders. This appears to have blurred the prominent cleavage between activists and non-activists on the shop floor that characterized factories in the Mao era: "There is no real contradiction between Party and non-Party people now. The Party people don't stand out like they used to. All of us are workers, no more activists like in the past. There are no big conflicts and contradictions [among workers] on the shop floor anymore."[26]

The rise of pay and equity issues

As the politicized reward system operated by the Party branches of the Mao era shifted decisively to production bonuses at the outset of the reforms, China's industrial enterprises quickly became engulfed in a new wave of conflict over issues of pay and equity. By what criteria are salary rises and large money bonuses to be distributed? Initially, China's managers attempted to use the methods of the Mao era: laborious collective work group evaluations whose results could be manipulated by factory leaders. No method could have been calculated to generate more discord on the shop floor, and many factories became paralysed by emotional arguments and work slow-downs touched off by dissatisfaction with the process.[27] These conflicts helped spawn a wave of strikes and several attempts by dissident workers to form independent labour unions.[28]

Managers adopted a different strategy after this experience and for the rest of the decade sought to keep differences in bonuses to a minimum and keep them and pay rises linked only loosely to individual and group performance. Instead, they sought to win the co-operation of labour by bringing about steady increases in compensation and benefits. Workers, in turn, came to expect such increases and these expectations were construed by

25. See Walder, *Communist Neo-Traditionalism*, ch. 5.
26. Interview no. 137.
27. See Susan L. Shirk, "Recent Chinese labour policies and the transformation of industrial organisation in China," *The China Quarterly*, 88 (1981), pp. 575–93, and Walder, "Wage reform."
28. See Jeanne L. Wilson, "Labor policy in China: Reform and retrogression," *Problems of Communism*, Vol. 39, No. 5 (September–October 1990), pp. 44–65, at p. 54; and a statement in an unofficial publication by a Changsha worker and democratic activist (arrested shortly thereafter) that attacked the wage readjustment process: Zhang Jingsheng, "Baifenzhi sishi de zhigong zengjia gongzi he gongzi zhidu gaige" ("Raises for 40% of employees and the reform of the wage system"), *Zhongsheng (The Clarion)* [Wuhan], No. 4 (1980), reprinted in *Minzhu zhonghua*, pp. 473–5.

managers as pressures from below.[29] This appears to have quelled the wave of conflict that accompanied the first years of reform. However it did not put an end to issues of equity in pay and benefits.

As the reforms began to lead to wider differences between enterprises in various sectors, and especially as private entrepreneurs visibly amassed remarkable sums, the equity issue was reborn as a feeling that the average worker was falling behind, which led in turn to heightened discontent and to increased pressures upon managers to deliver more benefits. By the late 1980s, most workers could claim personal knowledge of individuals who were reaping enormous incomes in other sectors, or of enterprises in their city rumoured to pay much more than their own. In Beijing, it is widely believed (and perception, not fact, is crucial here) that workers at such enterprises as Capital Steel or Beijing Jeep may make two or three times as much as workers of the same pay grade at poorer enterprises, and it is also general knowledge that joint venture enterprises and "people-run" (*minban*) enterprises such as the electronics companies in the Haidian district, pay considerably more than the average state factory.[30] One former Beijing worker could name five people who had left his factory in the early 1980s and were now private entrepreneurs, and he felt certain that they averaged 1,000 *yuan* per month (compared to his 120).[31] Truck drivers in a freight-hauling company made an average salary, with bonus, of 150 *yuan*, but averaged 500 *yuan* per month in illicit tips.[32] In addition, many state enterprises today will allow workers to become independent entrepreneurs under the guise of working for their "labour service company" (*laodong fuwu gongsi*), or by taking a leave without pay (*tingxin liuzhi*); workers pay a negotiated fee to the company, and in return they keep their housing and state benefits. Some of them reap large net incomes as a result.[33]

Knowledge of these opportunities appears to have affected the thinking of workers in urban enterprises in two opposing ways. On the one hand, many workers are deeply envious of these incomes and feel left behind by the reforms. On the other hand, they are usually unwilling to take the risk of leaving their jobs: they do not want to leave their factory apartment; they

29. The process of reaching a new accommodation is described in Walder, "Wage reform," and Walder, "Factory and manager."

30. Interview no. 137. There is some factual basis for such beliefs. In 1988 the average annual wage in ownership forms other than the state and collective sectors (excluding private entrepreneurs) was 2,382 *yuan*, and in joint state–private enterprises 3,229 *yuan*, compared to a national average of 1,747 *yuan*. The number of enterprises in these special ownership forms are, however, very small. *Zhongguo tongji nianjian 1989*, pp. 139, 143, 146 and 149.

31. Interview no. 137.

32. Interview no. 142, a repair worker promoted gradually to director. The workers demanded the tips from customers before picking up the job, "in order to make sure the goods got there, and in good shape." Customers rarely refused, though they sometimes would complain afterwards to the company.

33. Many, however, make little money, making a transfer to a "labour service company" a new and pernicious form of punishment (see below). This new informal practice was described in all the 1990 interviews with workers.

do not want to risk their steady income; they feel they do not have market-able skills, or start-up capital, or connections with important people in enterprises or government who can bestow success upon them.[34] This in turn causes heightened dissatisfaction with the job assignment system and the dead-end nature of jobs in urban China: "This leads to imbalances in people's minds (*xinlu bu pingheng*). Because you know that others have better work, better wages and benefits. They have left and you are still stuck in the old job. It affects your performance on the job, you become less active at work, you become very passive and lack initiative."[35]

The issue of job security

While managers still find it very difficult to dismiss individual workers or to reduce unilaterally the size of their labour force by laying off workers, the reforms have created new threats to worker job security. The chief mecha-nism appears to be the "labour service companies" that have been formed by large numbers of urban enterprises. In the early 1980s, these companies were organized in order to provide jobs for children of employees. Some-times these jobs were favours granted to the academically indifferent chil-dren of factory employees: they became service personnel in guest houses, or drivers of factory cars and buses. Employees who wanted to become private entrepreneurs were also transferred to these companies and al-lowed to ply their trades in return for a monthly fee, often around half their former salary, that maintained their benefits.

By the later 1980s managers discovered that these labour service compa-nies could be used to punish recalcitrant or rebellious workers, or reduce the size of the wage bill without actually laying off workers. One worker described a new "system of job appointments" (*pinren zhi*) whereby shop directors had the power to expel a worker from the shop. If no other workshop head wanted the worker, he or she would be sent to the labour service company. If the labour service company did not have a job for the worker, which was common, he or she would be sent home at 60 per cent of the normal salary and no bonus—a cut of more than 50 per cent in the worker's original earnings.[36] One manager reported that it became common practice in the later 1980s to send "those who had a bad attitude, poor health, or low skills" to the labour service companies, where they would get full salary but lose their bonuses (which averaged around 30 per cent of total compensation). In a variation on this practice in the same firm, women who took maternity leave were required to take 18 to 24 months leave

34. These are the reasons mentioned in interview nos. 137, 140 and 142. In a large national survey in 1986, 83% of the respondents specified a preference for a state sector job. "Gaige de shehui huanjing: bianqian yu xuanze." ("The social environment of reform: Changes and choices"), *Jingji yanjiu*, 12 (1987), pp. 52–62, at p. 61.
35. Interview no. 140.   36. Interview no. 137.

(instead of the state-mandated 56 days) at 80 per cent of their salary (again, no bonus). Workers who refused the deal and insisted on their state-mandated rights would be assigned to a more arduous, lower-paying job on their return.[37]

In addition to these new threats to job security within enterprises, the 1980s have also seen some lay-offs in financially-troubled firms or sectors that have been targeted by planners for contraction. The lay-offs are characteristically given such euphemistic names as "improvement and reorganization" (*youhua zuhe*) or "selective reductions" (*caijian*). Workers are typically sent home on a living stipend set at a percentage of their former salary (again, no bonus). These lay-offs began in the early 1980s, but they appear to have increased in the last half of the decade, although no hard data are available about their scope. Knowledge of such measures, coupled with reformers' constantly repeated desire to close unprofitable firms, reportedly led to a "job security panic."[38]

Cadre power and privilege

In view of the rise of many new issues about pay, equity and job security, it is remarkable that there have emerged no new means of negotiating labour issues, either collectively or individually. China's enterprises ended the 1980s with the same powerless trade unions and workers' congresses with which they began them. Workers speak of these organs in the same way they spoke more than a decade before about their Mao-era predecessors: "The representative committee of workers and staff is not really representative. It's just like the National People's Congress. . . . There are a lot of middle-level cadres in it. It's an empty shell (*kong jiazi*). Workers still don't really dare raise serious opinions. Still they are a little afraid of cadres."[39] In view of the new labour issues created by the reforms, the failure to devise some means of interest representation and grievance resolution would appear to risk chronic dissension and deliberate slow-downs and sabotage on the shop floor. Left unresolved in factories that still have very low rates of turnover, such issues deepen collective antagonisms toward those cadres who abuse their power and position and, perhaps, towards all factory cadres as a group. Some evidence suggests that this is precisely what has happened.

37. Interview no. 142. This is one example of a widespread pattern of infringement on the rights of female workers; see Wilson, "Labor policy," pp. 50–1.

38. *Jingji ribao*, 16 May 1989, as cited in Shaoguang Wang, "Deng Xiaoping's reforms and the Chinese workers' participation in the protest movement of 1989," unpublished paper, Department of Political Science, Yale University, 1990. This paper contains a long and well-documented account of the kinds of worker dissatisfactions publicized by Chinese social scientists and newspaper reporters.

39. Interview no. 137. The problem was so self-evident that leaders of the All-China Federation of Trade Unions admitted their failure with surprising frankness at their 1988 congress. Wilson, "Labor policy," pp. 55–6.

While in the 1980s managers sought to keep pay differentials among workers small, and to link them rather loosely to performance, the largest pay differences in the factory have become those between cadres and workers. These pay differentials are in fact quite low by international standards, but by the standards of the Mao era they are large. A worker in an electronics plant described a typical situation: despite the fact that cadres had significantly higher salaries than workers, they gave themselves larger monthly and year-end bonuses by a fixed formula: 1.7 times the average bonus of workers for shop directors, and 2.2 times for plant directors. In addition, cadres allotted themselves monthly "work post supplements" (*gangwei jintie*): 50 *yuan* for plant directors and 30 *yuan* for shop directors. Given out quite openly (in this case they were ratified at a meeting of the congress of workers and staff), these new pay advantages appear to invite enhanced collective antagonisms towards cadres.[40]

The allocation of factory housing has become easily the greatest source of conflict in factories in the 1980s, and as such it throws into bold relief the way in which the abuse of power and privilege by even a small minority of factory cadres can create seemingly insoluble conflicts and deep-seated antagonisms. In the Mao era, housing assignments were often given preferentially to cadres and their loyal followers in the factory, but the decisions were made behind closed doors, one at a time, and were not announced publicly. In the reform decade, however, managers commonly sought to defuse conflict over housing allocations by creating more "democratic" forums to make even-handed decisions based on such "hard" criteria as years on the waiting list, seniority, and metres per person in the current apartment. The members of these "housing allocation committees" (*fenfang weiyuanhui*) are chosen in a wide variety of ways, and the proportion of workers and managers who sit on them, and the criteria they employ to allocate new apartments, also vary considerably. However, the new committees have instead often heightened worker anxiety over housing allocations and their awareness of cadre privilege. This is so for two reasons. First, the committees have turned the periodic allocation of apartments into a public spectacle, in which the attention of the majority of the workforce is for several weeks focused firmly on the decision-making process and the name list that results. Secondly, regardless of the integrity and good will of some cadres, there seem always to be others who cannot resist manipulating the process to the advantage of their families and friends. The consequence, of course, is to make cadre privilege and abuse of power more transparent than before, and since this is open subversion of the democratic process promised by the committees, it may make cadre privilege appear to be even more illegitimate and intolerable than in the past.

In one characteristic case, a Beijing worker reported that his factory built

40. Interview no. 137.

a new housing block in the late 1980s and created a committee to assign the apartments. The committee created an elaborate point system, which considered the metres per person in the current apartment, whether three generations lived under one roof, whether the employee's spouse had a work unit that distributed housing, the employee's seniority, whether both spouses worked in the unit, and the "importance" of position in the unit (cadres, of course, got more points). After the committee deliberated, the final decisions were made by the factory director personally, in consultation with one or more of the vice-directors. Despite the fact that rank was only one of many criteria, most of the apartments went to middle-level cadres. When the results were announced a number of distraught workers whose applications had been denied ran immediately to the director's office to scream and plead, while others simply became depressed and angry. The director finally extricated himself from the throng at his door by quietly allocating to several of them an apartment to be vacated by one of the middle-level cadres.[41] Another worker, after relating a similar story, observed, "There are always conflicts after they make the decision. This is the most important thing in people's lives, the most sensitive of all social issues."[42]

One individual, who rose through the ranks to director during the 1980s, described his struggle to reduce labour discontent by making housing distribution more open and fair. The enterprise had three distributions in the 1980s. In the first, the committee members were pressured by cadres, and new apartments were given to several of their young relatives. When the list was released, a wave of anger swept through the unit. Several years later the informant was elected by the employees of his team to sit on the next housing committee, and the committee members elected him head. Wanting to avoid the problems of the last time, he laid down two conditions to all the cadres in the enterprise: they could not come to him with special requests for themselves or anyone else, and they could not talk to him privately about housing matters. He was relieved to find little objection from the officials, and the committee distributed 50 apartments strictly according to the regulations, with only three cases near the bottom of the list causing extended debate. He later discovered, however, that before turning over the 50 apartments to the committee, the cadres had kept six for themselves to solve "special cases." When the third committee was formed in 1987, the informant, now director of his enterprise, was soon to be transferred. One of the more venal vice-directors took over the committee, and forced through allocations to two young sons of officials in the company and bureau above their enterprise. The outraged committee members held their tongues in the meeting for fear of retaliation, but reported fully to their co-workers. The result:

41. *Ibid.*
42. Interview no. 140. Many managers interviewed in China in 1986 gave identical accounts.

When the drivers heard about this, there were about three days or so when no work was done at all. The unit was thrown into confusion. Everybody did nothing except talk about the housing decisions, from the top of the unit to the bottom. The two vice-directors had a lot of people run to their office to complain and yell, cry, and try to reason with them. About six or seven got really angry and yelled. The two cadres said it wasn't their decision, it was the committee's, and they couldn't interfere in the committee's decision. No one listened to me, or came to complain to me, because they knew I was almost gone. After I left, the unit began to lose money for the first time, and I think this was mainly because of the cadres' workstyle problem and the workers' anger about it. . . . This is also a major reason why the drivers began to demand tips all the time from the customers.[43]

In the same unit, workers had long been angry about one of the older cadres, a corrupt character who obtained jobs for his wife, other relatives and friends, and got better housing for all of them. Many workers found this intolerable, and wrote letters under assumed names to the discipline inspection commission of the company informing them of what was going on ("If they signed their names, of course, they would certainly suffer revenge"). The old cadre, however, had strong relations with other cadres in the company, so nothing was ever done. Attempts to complain within the unit earned only retaliation. One worker complained to other cadres that the man's wife used the unit's vehicles for her personal errands, and routinely came to work late, left early, or never turned up at all. Moreover the man himself came to the unit storeroom regularly to pick up items for his home, and would always hug the women there and behave in an inappropriate and impolite fashion. The woman who complained was transferred from the storeroom to a repair garage. "This shows that workers are unable to take direct criticisms to leaders, they can't bring things up to their faces without fearing revenge. These are things that cadres should know, they would be able to improve the unit if they could hear these things . . . but revenge is so common workers don't dare. . . . Workers were upset because nothing was ever done about it. Workers are just as upset about these things as the students [who demonstrated in 1989]. This is a very serious problem and they have not yet found a way to control it."

All the changes in the political life of the factory described here—the erosion of the Party, the rise of new issues of pay and equity, the new threats to worker job security, and heightened sensitivity to cadre privilege and abuse of power—have contributed to one very important change in industrial politics. During the Mao era workers were effectively divided among themselves, constantly monitored, rewarded and punished according to their loyalty, and competed with one another for advantage while devising strategies to escape the intrusion of Party politics into their lives. Over the era of reform, however, antagonisms formerly focused on the Party and its activists appear to have become focused increasingly upon factory cadres as

43. Interview no. 142.

a group, and workers have developed a heightened awareness of their collective interests and the ways in which the actions of factory cadres affect them directly. Quietly but surely, this has helped to lay a foundation for group-based identities and antagonisms among workers, just as it creates a heightened interest in legal procedure and other "democratic" reforms within the enterprise. When in 1989 university students marched on the streets of Beijing to denounce special privileges and corruption among national leaders, and to demand greater "democracy" and legal protections for citizens, many workers drew direct analogies to their own lives in the factory. One worker articulated a connection likely to have been evident to a great many: "Why do a lot of workers agree with democracy and freedom? . . . In the factory the director is a dictator, what one man says goes. If you view the state from the angle of the factory, it's about the same, one man rule . . . we want rule by laws, not by men. . . . In work units, it's personal rule."[44]

Managers and Work Units in the Democracy Movement

When the student movement emerged in the spring of 1989, it quickly struck a responsive chord among workers. Many had concluded that the reforms largely benefited other groups—private entrepreneurs, suburban peasants, and especially cadres and their families—while leaving the ordinary workers to cope with dead-end jobs, inflation and declining real incomes.[45] Workers' homes were adorned with new consumer goods, but these homes were still overcrowded and poorly equipped. Heightened perception of job insecurity, and the chronic dissatisfaction evoked by the privilege and abuses of some factory cadres, intensified awareness of how vulnerable workers were, and how undemocratic their workplaces.

The impact of the student movement in factories

Throngs of workers lined the streets, cheered on the student marchers, and helped clear police barriers in the pivotal and defiant demonstration of 27

44. Interview no. 141, a former ticket seller for the Beijing Public Bus Company who later became active in the Beijing Autonomous Workers Union.

45. The survey data reported in "Gaige de shehui huanjing," pp. 60–2, suggest that inequality of opportunity was the main source of dissatisfaction with reform, something confirmed repeatedly in my recent interviews. It was clear well before 1989 that there was widespread discontent about inflation and corruption. A series of public opinion polls illustrated this dramatically. The 1986 survey just mentioned found inflation to be second only to official corruption as the matter about which citizens were most dissatisfied, and both issues far outpaced all others. An internal Tianjin city government survey in the fall of 1987 found that 98% of the respondents named inflation as their primary concern, and that almost 80% considered their income to be either unsatisfactory (26%) or barely adequate (52%). Wang Hui, "Municipal administration in China and sociological studies," unpublished paper, Tianjin

April. Workers performed the same roles, while also donating money and food to students and joining in behind the student ranks, in the huge march of 4 May.[46] But factories were not greatly affected by the movement until after 4 May, the day that Zhao Ziyang declared the student demands "patriotic," permitting national newspapers and television stations to broadcast objective (and later openly sympathetic) accounts of the student movement. At this point workers began to receive abundant information about the student protests and their aims.

The first response among many workers was sympathy, a feeling that was intensified by the nature of the media coverage. "A lot of workers supported the students, almost all of us sympathized with them, even if we never went out on the streets. . . . Workers thought that inflation was caused by corruption, and that if there was more democracy, there would be less corruption. That's why workers supported the students; the students' slogans appealed to them. In our unit, workers didn't really participate until the newspapers and TV came out to support the students. Then we really got involved."[47] Much of the sympathy workers felt for the students was not only because the students appeared to articulate workers' feelings; it was also because workers felt that with families and jobs, they could not afford to risk all to protest the way the students were. This led to gratitude toward the students, a feeling reinforced after 13 May by the media portrayal of student hunger strikers as risking themselves for the good of the nation.

Of course the workers were interested in the movement. . . . We all talked among ourselves, and said that the students were representing our own inner thoughts and desires. On corrupt officials, the students were calling for an end to it and the workers agreed very much with that. We wanted the situation to change. But workers are not the same as students. We have families, a steady job, social relationships. . . . Workers always have a burden on their minds: work, family, and so forth. So we aren't willing to stick our necks out against the government. But we were happy to see the students speak up against the things we opposed too.[48]

A second worker response, common especially after the beginning of the hunger strike on 13 May, was surprise and wonder at the spectacle unfolding on the square. "All the workers were very dissatisfied, so when the movement first began they realized it was necessary and weren't surprised. But we never expected that it would develop so fast or so far. So the workers all

Academy of Social Sciences. And a large 1988 survey by the Sociology Institute of the Chinese Academy of Social Sciences and State Statistical Bureau found inflation to be by far the most serious problem in people's social lives, with 94% of respondents mentioning it. Zhu Qingfang, "Yijiubajiu nian dalu chengshi zhigong xintai lu" ("The state of mind of mainland urban workers in 1988"), *Liaowang* (haiwai ban) 2, 1989, pp. 7–8, at p. 7.

46. See Andrew G. Walder, "The political sociology of the Beijing upheaval of 1989," *Problems of Communism*, Vol. 38, No. 5 (September–October 1989), pp. 30–40. The account here will trace events in Beijing since the movement there was by far the best-documented case.

47. Interview no. 137.   48. Interview no. 140.

stood around to talk about what the students were saying, demanding and doing. We talked during work, after work, all the time. . . . We paid very close attention to developments and we were very interested."[49] As May progressed, work slowed as workers talked excitedly in groups about what was going on. As many of the former pillars of Party rule—newspaper and television stations, retired generals, university presidents, members of the National People's Congress and the democratic parties, and even the All-China Federation of Trade Unions—expressed public sympathy for the student demands for negotiation, or donated money to the student hunger strikers, groups of workers in hundreds of workplaces throughout the city began to form "sympathy delegations" (*sheng-yuan tuan*), make up banners, collect donations, and request that their factory directors lend them trucks to drive to the square in a show of support.[50]

The response of managers to the movement

Some managers publicly supported the student demand for negotiation and urged moderation on the part of both the government and protesters. Ten directors of large enterprises in Beijing published an appeal to this effect in *Guangming ribao*.[51] Managers of at least one Beijing factory—the Beijing Coking Plant—personally led the entire work-force out to march on the square.[52] And the Beijing workers I have interviewed all relate that many of their managers, from shop director up, expressed sympathy for the students in unmistakable ways, and would often permit groups of workers to use factory vehicles and supplies for their activities, although they cautiously refrained from taking any open public stance or organizing any activities themselves.

This is the point at which the gradual relaxation of bureaucratic controls over factories, and the weakening of factory Party organizations, played an important role. Once it was clear that a major popular challenge was under

49. *Ibid*. The impact was felt immediately after the large demonstration of 27 April. At a 28 April meeting called by the Municipal Trade Union headquarters of Beijing, a cadre from Guanghua Lumber Company complained that all workers wanted to do as soon as they arrived at work was to talk about "rumours." Xuan Yan (ed.), *Jingdu xuehuo: xuechao, dongluan, baoluan, pingbao quan guocheng jishi* (*The Capital in Blood and Flames: A Factual Record of the Entire Process of Student Movement, Turmoil, Rebellion, and Pacification*) (Beijing: Nongcun duwu chubanshe, 1989), p. 62.

50. The All-China Federation of Trade Unions donated 100,000 *yuan* to the Beijing Red Cross for the hunger-striking students. Guojia jiaowei sixiang zhengzhi gongzuo si (Political–Ideological Work Office of the State Education Commission) (ed.), *Jingxin dongpo de 56 tian* (*A Soul-Stirring 56 Days*) (Beijing: Dadi chubanshe, 1989), pp. 131–5. On 14 May a delegation from the union marched to the square in support of the students. Li Yun *et al*. (eds.), *Diankuang de shenian zhi xia* (*The Tumultuous Summer of the Year of the Snake*) (Beijing: Guofang keji daxue chubanshe, 1989), p. 114.

51. Wu Mouren *et al*. (eds.), *Bajiu zhongguo minyun jishi* (*A Record of the 1989 Chinese Democracy Movement*) (New York: n.p., 1989), p. 251, which reprints the appeal.

52. Interviews no. 138 and 141, both of whom were active in the autonomous union.

way, and that sectors of the Party and state sympathized with the students and dissented from the elders' hard line, many managers prudently stepped aside to await the outcome.[53] They did so despite a prior series of Beijing municipal government regulations strictly forbidding any factory personnel to participate in demonstrations or show any other expressions of sympathy, and despite Li Peng's personal visit of 13 May to Capital Steel to ensure that workers remained at their posts.[54]

The cadres didn't know what to do once the newspapers came out this way. Should they support the students or not? After 4 May, when the newspapers changed, they were not sure what to do. In our unit they neither prevented people from going, nor encouraged them to go. They just said, "if you want to go, go." . . . Cadres let them go because they weren't sure what to do. If they acted to stop them, they might get in trouble later on.[55]

Nobody stopped the workers from going down to the square. Nobody tried to control them. . . . A lot of factories would send representatives and a truck to express their support. Our factory sent down a truck with some representatives, only about 30 in all. They had a banner with the factory's name on it. This was just to express support. The leader said you can go, but not everybody, just a few representatives, and he let them use one truck. This was for two days.[56]

It is not possible to characterize the political attitudes of managers as a group. Whether sympathetic to the student movement or fearful of its impact on Party unity, factory managers in Beijing appear commonly to have reacted with instinctive caution. However, just as it was evident that many Party and government officials sympathized openly with the students' aims and dissented from the direction taken by the Party leadership, there were certainly many factory managers who harboured serious doubts about the direction the Party had been taking the country. One manager I interviewed clearly fell into this category.

Cadres' thinking is even more complicated [than the workers']. They have more information, can think things through more. They almost all realize that if we continue to do things in the way we do now, we'll never get anywhere. Everyone has their own point of view, but there's a general feeling that the current way of doing things won't work. When we get together to talk, we often talk about our worries for the country, the problem of corruption, the fear of a political campaign from above. . . . So many people don't trust the Party, or any party, any more. The Party can't handle China's problems, but I don't think any other party can either. Look at the fact that so many of the children of high level cadres are in America. . . . What

53. The same thing occurred in the early stages of the Cultural Revolution, allowing rebel factions very quickly to disrupt factories. See Andrew G. Walder, *Chang Ch'un-ch'iao and Shanghai's January Revolution*, Michigan Papers in Chinese Studies No. 32 (Ann Arbor: University of Michigan Center for Chinese Studies), ch. 2.

54. Wu Mouren, *Bajiu Zhongguo minyun*, p. 267; Jingji ribao (ed.), *Jieyan ling fabu zhiqian: 4.15–5.20 dongluan dashi ji* (*Before Martial Law was Declared: Major Events during the Turmoil of 15 April to 20 May*) (Beijing: Jingji ribao chubanshe, 1989), pp. 131–3.

55. Interview no. 137.   56. Interview no. 140.

are the people back in China supposed to think about this? With one side of your mouth you talk about Marxism–Leninism and socialism, yet your children are all abroad! . . . Every country has its problems, but China! Unless things change, this country will get nowhere.[57]

Factories as organizing centres for protest

By mid-May, the support for students evident in the news media and among other government institutions, combined with factory cadres' general hesitance to enforce standing orders not to permit workers to demonstrate, allowed workers in Beijing and many other cities to stage a massive show of support. Long the lynchpin of social and political control in urban China, in mid-May 1989 work units suddenly became centres of political organizing and protest. The characteristic form of protest in the week preceding the declaration of martial law was the organized work unit delegation. As hundreds of such delegations from factories and other work units filled the streets in the huge demonstrations of 14 to 18 May, the student protests were transformed into a broad popular movement.

According to official accounts published after 4 June, over 700 work units sent delegations into the streets that week, at least 160 of which were industrial plants or other enterprises.[58] In the demonstrations of 17 and 18 May, both of which were estimated to number more than a million people, Beijing Jeep Corporation sent over 3,000 workers in identical uniforms, all marching and shouting slogans in a co-ordinated fashion.[59] Beijing No. 2 Chemical dispatched a huge delegation riding in 60 trucks, all the same colour.[60] Among the factories that sent large delegations were some of the city's largest heavy industrial concerns: Beijing Crane, Beijing Construction Machinery, Beijing Internal Combustion Engine, Beijing Electrical Machinery, Beijing No. 2 Computer, Beijing No. 3, 4, and 5 Construction Companies, and (on several occasions) the Capital Steel Corporation. As heavy rain began to fall during one of the demonstrations, employees of the Municipal Bus Company drove 90 buses to the square for the students to use as shelter; the Beijing Plastics Factory sent dozens of rolls of plastic sheeting; and the Beijing Oxygen Bottling Plant sent tanks of oxygen with which to revive hunger strikers.[61]

The Beijing scenes of mid-May were repeated, albeit on a smaller scale, in other large cities throughout the nation. On 18 May alone, over 50,000 people marched in Shanghai and Xi'an, with delegations of factory workers prominently represented. Marches of around 10,000 people, with prominent worker representation, were reported in Tianjin, Hangzhou and

---

57. Interview no. 142.
58. Guojia jiaowei, *Jingxin dongpo de 56 tian*, p. 137.
59. Wu Mouren, *Bajiu zhongguo minyun*, p. 251.
60. *Ibid.*   61. *Ibid.* p. 264.

Lanzhou, and demonstrations of comparable size also took place in Wuhan, Nanjing, Shenyang, Changsha, Harbin, Lhasa, Changchun, Chengdu, Nanning, Huhehaote, Fuzhou, Kunming, and elsewhere.[62]

These work unit delegations were expressly political. They marched to the square in support of students, not as workers with separate grievances of their own. They demanded that the government negotiate student demands, and expressed the heartfelt support of the "elder brothers." They repeated student slogans that called for an end to official corruption and speculation, and called for greater democracy and freedom. In light of the evident sympathy expressed by the mass media, some Party leaders, officials in the planning and trade union structures, and often their own managers, these workers must have felt that their actions were supported from above and therefore had a real chance of success.

Workers in the Democracy Movement

As work unit delegations filled the streets, other workers were already busy organizing independent associations that brought together people from different places of work. One typical kind of organization was the "workers' support team" (*gongren shengyuan tuan*) or "city people's support team" (*shimin shengyuan tuan*). These were loosely-defined associations whose purpose was to mobilize workers into marches and demonstrations. Another kind of common organization was the "workers' picket team" (*gongren jiucha dui*) or "city people's picket team" (*shimin jiucha dui*), usually a few dozen workers who policed demonstrations and marches, seeking to maintain public order and protect student protesters. After martial law in Beijing and other cities, they manned barricades to prevent the advance of troops. A third type of organization was the "dare-to-die corps" (*gansidui*). Similar in some respects to the picket corps, these groups of young male workers had sprung up mainly in response to the declaration of martial law, were quite numerous, though small and informal in nature, and travelled widely throughout the city or even to different provinces. They were mobile, and travelled to wherever action or violence was reported in order to block troop movements.

The most important of the independent groups, and certainly the most threatening to the authorities, were independent associations that aspired to represent workers' interests. A preliminary survey of public arrest reports yields the names of close to 30 "illegal organizations" that evidently made an effort to form an independent union or workers' association. They emerged in virtually every corner of the country. Beijing (several), Shang-

---

62. These reports were all from official sources, and published after 4 June. Guojia jiaowei, *Jingxin dongpo de 56 tian*, pp. 135–7.

hai (at least two), Hefei, Lanzhou, Guangzhou, Guizhou, Harbin, Wuhan, Zhengzhou, Changsha, Nanjing, Shenyang, Huhehaote, Xi'an Jinan, Tianjin, Hangzhou, and Nanchang (the only one to name itself "Solidarity Union," *tuanjie gonghui*).[63] Very little is known about most of these groups, but many of them are known to have printed hand bills, making demands that typically included the right to represent workers in negotiations with managers.

A profile of known independent workers' organizations in Beijing will give a sense of the variety of such political activity. There were at least two organizations of the "picket corps" variety, both with a continuous presence on Tiananmen Square from mid-May onward. The Beijing Workers' Picket Corps (*Beijing gongren jiucha dui*) was a quasi-independent offshoot of the Beijing Workers' Autonomous Union (see below), and was made up almost entirely of factory and construction workers. The Capital Workers' Picket Corps (*shoudu gongren jiucha dui*) was formed at the apparent instigation of teachers at the Workers' Movement Institute under the All-China Federation of Trade Unions, and included workers and other urban wage earners.[64] There were several organizations of the "dare-to-die corps" variety, primarily the Beijing Workers' Dare-to-Die Corps, and the Beijing City People's Dare-to-Die Corps, both of which mainly comprised ordinary wage earners. In this category should also be included the large motorcycle brigade of some 300 known as the "Flying Tigers" (*feihudui*). Headed by a worker from Beijing Jeep, it consisted primarily of young workers and private entrepreneurs who owned motorcycles. They rode prominently and loudly in the many street demonstrations of May; after martial law, they formed smaller teams of messengers that helped co-ordinate the blockade of army trucks; on at least two occasions they clashed with the security forces, and one afternoon invaded the grounds of the Capital Steel Corporation in an effort to call the workers out on strike.[65] Beijing also teemed with small dare-to-die corps of unknown origin, for example, the "Manchu-

63. These names were culled primarily from the following sources: Xianggang gonghui jiaoyu zhongxin (Hong Kong Trade Union Education Centre) (ed.), *Gongren qilaile: Gongren zizhi lianhehui yundong 1989* (*The Workers Have Arisen: The Autonomous Union Movement of 1989*) (Hong Kong: Xianggang gonghui jiaoyu zhongxin, 1990); Zong zhengzhi bu xuanchuan bu, Jiefang junbao bianjibu (Propaganda Office of the General Political Department, Editorial Office of People's Liberation Army Daily) (eds.), *Hanwei shehui zhuyi gongheguo* (*Protecting the Socialist Republic*) (Beijing: Changzheng chubanshe, 1989); Xuan Yan, *Jingdu xuehuo*; and Guojia jiaowei, *Jingxin dongpo de 56 tian*.

64. Xianggang gonghui jiaoyu zhongxin, *Gongren qilaile*, pp. 152–4; and a hand bill issued by the Institute of the Chinese Workers' Movement Committee to Support the Students, and Temporary Headquarters of the Capital Workers' Picket Corps, "Zhi shoudu gongren shu" ("Letter to the workers of the capital"). Undated wall poster, but contents establish date as 13 May 1989. Reprinted in *Zhongguo minyun yuan ziliao jingxuan (1)* (*Selected Source Materials from the Chinese Democracy Movement*) (Hong Kong: Shiyue pinglunshe, 1989), p. 31.

65. Interview no. 141, and Li Yun, *Diankuang de shenian zhi xia*, pp. 189–93.

rian Tigers" (*dongbei hu gansidui*) and the "Long White Mountain Dare-to-Die Corps" (*changbai shan gansidui*).[66]

There were also efforts to organize at least three independent labour unions in Beijing. A group from Capital Steel attempted to form a Beijing Steel Workers' Autonomous Union (*Beijing gangtie gongren zizhihui*) in order to represent steel workers at the industry level. They marched at one major demonstration under a banner that said "Beijing Steel Workers," and made contact with the organizers of the Beijing Workers' Autonomous Union, but little is known of how far their organization developed.[67] A second organization, the All-China Urban Construction Workers Autonomous Union (*Zhongguo chengjian gongren zifa lianhehui*), announced their desire to represent construction workers and established a presence at the eastern reviewing stand of Tiananmen, after a number of their members broke away from the Beijing Workers' Autonomous Union.[68] Little is known of any activities they may have organized.

The Beijing Workers' Autonomous Union (hereafter *gongzilian*) is by far the best-documented such organization in the country, and probably the largest and most active.[69] It originated in the activity surrounding the revolutionary heroes' monument on the evening of Hu Yaobang's death, and issued its first two formal declarations on 20 April. By the week of the student hunger strike it had almost 200 full-time activists, the vast majority of whom worked for state enterprises, and maintained a continuous presence at their headquarters at the western reviewing stand of Tiananmen. By the end of May it claimed to have registered around 20,000 members, although it had established no branch organizations in places of work. The union had a picket corps, several "dare-to-die" teams, a broadcasting station on the square, and a printing press and other duplication equipment, with which it issued over 25 printed statements and a long list of demands. It marched prominently in each of the large demonstrations of mid-May. Its broadcasts on the square satirized the government, revealed official wrongdoing, articulated citizen demands, and attracted large and appreciative audiences. It promulgated a formal programme and a charter. After the

66. Interview no. 141.
67. *Ibid.*
68. *Ibid.*, and Zhongguo chengjian gongren zifa lianhe hui zonghuizhang, "Chengjian gongren zifa lianhe hui de zongzhi" ("Aims of the urban construction workers' autonomous union"). Wall poster dated 21 May 1989. Reprinted in *Zhongguo minyun yuan ziliao jingxuan (1)*, p. 32.
69. The organization used several variations of its name, causing some observers to believe at the time that there was more than one such union. In its various written pronouncements it took the names *Beijing gongren zizhi lianhehui*, *Beijing gongren zizhi hui*, and *Shoudu gongren zizhi lianhe hui*. This account of *gongzilian* draws from a paper that is based on several dozen hand bills and interviews with two of the organization's activists: Andrew G. Walder and Gong Xiaoxia, "Workers in the Beijing democracy movement: Reflections on the brief history of the Beijing workers' autonomous union," paper presented to the Berkeley China Seminar, 15 November 1990.

declaration of martial law, as work unit delegations ceased to march, it appeared to grow stronger and bolder, organizing large protest marches, forging closer ties with student organizations, successfully confronting the Beijing Bureau of Public Security over the arrest of three of its leaders, and issuing two (largely unheeded) calls for general strikes.

The orientation of the autonomous union movement

This profusion of independent organization among workers is remarkable more for its variety and vitality than its political effectiveness. All these organizations were quite small and loosely organized. Within a very short period of time, and under chaotic circumstances, the Beijing Workers' Autonomous Union was able to develop a respectable organization and marshall significant resources, but at the beginning of June it was more threatening as a portent of things to come than as an effective political organization. The independent organizations are more significant for their aspirations and, in the case of *gongzilian*, for the political positions and specific grievances they articulated.

Even before the student movement had developed into a significant off-campus force, the workers of *gongzilian* set out a number of economic grievances and political demands. Early and repeatedly, they demanded price stabilization and wage rises. They demanded an end to the forced sale of state treasury bonds to workers, an accounting of how these funds were used, and the immediate redemption of all outstanding bonds, with interest.[70] They demanded the right to change jobs freely, the indexing of wages by age and family burdens, and an end to discrimination against women in hiring and benefits. As students would later do in May, *gongzilian* demanded an investigation of all top officials, starting with those who lived in state villas, an accounting of all such state residences, their total revenues and costs, and the publication of the incomes and expenditures of all top officials and their children.

While it made these demands from the outset, *gongzilian* appeared more interested in establishing its right to represent workers' interests than in immediately pursuing specific demands. In most of its pronouncements during May, it declared that it was engaged in a "fight for democracy" and a struggle to "bring down dictatorship," and that it was established to "correctly lead the democratic patriotic movement." Some observers have criticized the student movement for having vague conceptions about democracy. *Gongzilian*, however, had a clear and concrete definition of the term. It wanted to take over the task of representing workers at the national

---

70. This demand referred to involuntary sales of state treasury bonds to workers. A large percentage of one month's wage was issued not in cash but in the form of a state treasury bond redeemable with interest at some future date. Interviews with workers in 1990 suggest that this had been common every October for a number of years.

level from the All-China Federation of Trade Unions, which it asserted did not fulfil this task. It wanted to represent workers in policy-making at the national level and exercise "supervision" over decisions made by the Communist Party that affected workers. It wanted to establish within all enterprises union branches endowed with the right to negotiate with management and represent aggrieved individuals, and "take any legally sanctioned steps" to pursue their interests within the framework of plant-level negotiation. This trade unionism responds directly to the developments of the 1980s, and there is every reason to expect that such efforts will re-emerge in the future and, if conditions permit, on a larger scale.

Conclusion: Some Implications of 1989

It is hard to avoid the conclusion that 1989, with regard to labour as in other respects, signified the unravelling of the Deng strategy for reform. Economically, workers now appear to be as much if not more concerned with their economic situation than on the eve of reform. Politically, workers appear to have a heightened awareness of their common interests as a group, and to be increasingly aware that such issues as democracy and legal reform affect their condition directly. Moreover, they appear to be more willing than a decade ago to assert their rights as Chinese citizens along with other groups. While 1989 did not reveal a strong capacity of workers to organize independently and lead a major political movement—such political activity that occurred was clearly dependent upon the division of the leadership and the temporary paralysis of its formidable apparatus of repression—it certainly did show that there exist throughout the country small groups of committed workers who already contemplate doing so. The memory of 1989 will persist, and it is hard to imagine any future movement of students or intellectuals that will not draw workers once again into collective action. It remains to be seen whether these students and intellectuals will welcome the participation of a self-conscious workers' movement, or whether they will continue to prefer that the "city people" play their assigned roles as compliant cheering section and human shields.

Even should no political upheaval occur in the years ahead, workers' participation in the 1989 events laid bare the weaknesses of the reform strategy of the 1980s, and underlined the difficulties yet to come. The reforms have heightened factory disputes over pay, benefits, housing and job tenure, while at the same time weakening the political institutions used in the past to suppress conflict and collective action. These things have occurred despite the fact that the decontrol of prices, cuts in subsidies of urban living standards, and the shake-out of inefficient and obsolete plants—all anticipated components of a more effective economic reform—have yet to be carried out. The political lessons of 1989 are likely to be more than obvious to China's future leaders, whoever they may be. Whether such changes will be contemplated by a revitalized reform wing of the Party, or by a post-communist government that enjoys (at least initially) greater popular support, they will be fraught with enormous political risks. The growing political relevance of urban labour is one of many factors that will make China's future course of economic and political change an arduous and unpredictable affair.

The Peasant and the State*

Robert F. Ash

Introduction

The institutional framework of agriculture defines the context in which the relationship between the peasant and the state is enacted. In China from the mid-1950s until 1979 that framework was characterized by a collectivist and interventionist ethos. The state–peasant relationship weighed heavily in favour of the state. The three tiers of agricultural organization—commune, brigade and production team—facilitated control of the economic activities of individual peasants by the government, whether at central or local level. Individual initiative was largely limited to those activities which could be carried out in spare time or on private plots. The relationship between effort and reward was frequently tenuous and distribution was guided by egalitarian principles.

The inherent disadvantages of such a system from an individual's point of view had to be set against undoubted benefits which accrued to the state. The collective framework conferred upon the state great economic power in both the day-to-day running of agriculture and the formulation and implementation of longer-term planning. The system facilitated the fulfilment of goals set by the state, even when these conflicted with the self-interest of peasant producers.[1] It is true that in the early 1960s the retreat from the more radical phase of the Great Leap Forward was accompanied by decentralization of decision-making and an extension of private economic activities in the countryside (including the introduction of contractual arrangements with individual households). Such initiatives were, however, short-lived and although the reaffirmation of the pre-eminent role of the production team as the basic unit of production and accounting was maintained throughout the second half of the 1960s and the 1970s, claims of lasting institutional stability need to be set in the context of

* I am indebted to Professor Y. Y. Kueh for his detailed and helpful critique of an earlier version of this paper.

1. The overwhelming emphasis on the achievement of grain self-sufficiency during the Cultural Revolution decade (1966–76) is a good example of such tension. This policy, which was implemented at a local level throughout China and ignored the dictates of the principle of comparative advantage, compelled farmers to engage in unprofitable activities. Thus, data suggest that the cultivation of cereals was not only less profitable than that of other food and cash crops, but often yielded a *negative* return per unit of sown area (Planning Department of Ministry of Agriculture, *Nongye jingji ziliao, 1949–83* (*Materials on the Agricultural Economy, 1949–83*), hereafter *NYJJZL* (1983), pp. 456–71).

the increasing average size of each of the three levels of agricultural organization.[2]

The nature, economic rationale and impact of the institutional changes which took place after 1978 have been analysed elsewhere[3] and this article does not seek to add to such analysis. These initiatives sought to reinvigorate agricultural production and productivity by returning decision-making powers to individual peasant households and simultaneously stimulating enterprise through renewed emphasis on material (especially price) incentives. The promotion of various forms of responsibility system—often sanctioned by the central authorities only after the peasants' own spontaneous actions in setting them up had presented a virtual *fait accompli*—epitomized the early approach towards institutional reform in the countryside. It is worth recording that these early changes were designed explicitly to enhance the functioning of the existing system of collective agriculture. There was no hint of *anti*-collectivism in the early policy documents. To this extent, these institutional reforms may be seen as an attempt to realign, but not re-define, the relationship between peasant and state.

After 1982 the situation changed in a more fundamental way that had not been envisaged by the planners. First, the communes themselves were rapidly disbanded—and with them, the entire collective system of agricultural organization. Further, in the wake of a series of record harvests and in the face of what the central government mistakenly regarded as unmanageably large surpluses of basic agricultural products (including grain), the decision was taken largely to abandon the monopoly procurement system for agricultural and sideline products which had existed for more than 30 years.

These later initiatives represent a watershed in the evolution of a new peasant–state institutional relationship. If the reintroduction of contractual arrangements between individual households and the economic representatives of the state pointed to a new production relationship between the state

2. The trend is reflected in the following data, which show the average number of member households at each level of organization:

	Average number of households:		
	Commune	Brigade	Production team
1962	1,793	191	24
1965	1,810	209	25
1970	2,948	236	33
1975	3,126	243	34
1978	3,287	251	36

Source:
  NYJJZL, pp. 82–3.

3. See, for example, Y. Y. Kueh and R. F. Ash (eds.), *Economic Trends in Chinese Agriculture: The Impact of Post-Mao Reforms* (Oxford University Press, 1993).

and the individual farmer, the dismantling of the collective system seemed to presage a more fundamental loss of control over many other aspects of the farm economy. Subsequent appeals to peasants to market signals and the attempt to replace mandatory quotas for grain and cotton in favour of an acceleration of market transactions and contracts[4] apparently signified an even greater abrogation of the state's involvement in the direction and disposal of agricultural production.

The performance of agriculture in the first half of the 1980s was interpreted as a triumphant vindication of the measures adopted after 1978. With hindsight, such an interpretation looks a little simplistic, although it undoubtedly also contains some truth. But agriculture's performance in the second half of the 1980s highlighted some of the very real contradictions between the economic motivations and activities of peasant and state which had emerged in the wake of decollectivization and the move towards a more demand-orientated system of agricultural production and distribution. In a situation in which the economic goals of state and peasant do not coincide, a shift of power from one constituency to the other is bound to create tensions. In China after 1978 reforms gave peasants much more control over production decisions than they had enjoyed since the early 1950s. Encouragement to sell more through markets and the institution of supposedly voluntary contracts for the delivery of grain and cotton no doubt reinforced peasants' sense of independent decision-making. In so doing, it led them, in their search for income maximization, towards a structure of agricultural production which threatened to undermine the fulfilment of certain key *state* goals, such as the maintenance of grain supplies for urban consumption and industrial use. As early as 1986 the government was in retreat and had effectively re-introduced mandatory quotas for grain. By 1990 "contractual procurement" (*hetong dinggou*) of grain had given way to "state procurement" (*guojia dinggou*),[5] in apparent recognition of the failure of the 1985 initiative to generate adequate food supplies for the cities.

Meanwhile the abandonment of the collective framework had robbed the government of a means of control and a mechanism for the allocation of investment funds and other scarce resources. With state investment in decline and no surge in voluntary investment by peasants, infrastructural decline (especially the deterioration of irrigation systems) became a serious problem. Against this background it is not surprising that some have looked for a new institutional framework—one which will provide for integration of a degree of planning and co-operation with continuing household-based farming. Experience suggests that finding such a formula will be very diffi-

4. *Hetong dinggou.*
5. British Broadcasting Corporation, *Summary of World Broadcasts, Part 3: The Far East*, hereafter *SWB*, Weekly Economic Report, FE/W0155, A/2, citing Xinhua (New China) News Agency, Beijing, 10 November 1990.

cult. Peasants' suspicion of co-operation is coloured by their fear of a return to the old collective system of agriculture. Advocacy of a "two-tier operational structure"[6] has been the most recent way of achieving the desired integration. To what extent such a structure has been set up in China is not clear, and it is in any case too early to assess its impact upon the agricultural sector.[7]

The existence of such tensions, arising out of institutional initiatives in China's rural sector since 1979, may be taken as clear evidence of the difficulty of accommodating the two sides of the peasant–state relationship simultaneously.[8]

These introductory remarks are intended merely to suggest the changing facets of the institutional relationship between peasant and state which evolved out of post-1978 reforms. They also serve to highlight some of the tensions which those reforms engendered. In what follows, no further reference will be made to the rural institutional changes of the 1980s. But they provide the backcloth against which the subsequent analysis is set.

The changing relationship between the peasant and the state in China most readily lends itself to the analysis of its political economy dimensions. This is certainly the area which has been most written about by Western scholars and there now exists a rich literature on the subject.[9] By contrast, the more purely economic aspects of the relationship have attracted less attention, even though they have obvious implications—sometimes conflicting—for government agricultural policy and peasants' standard of living. It is these economic aspects, or some of them, which are the focus of the rest of this article. In particular, it seeks to examine the changing nature and direction of key financial and real resource flows between the two parties in the wake of post-1978 rural reforms. The flows embrace investment, credit and other forms of support afforded the agricultural sector by government; and tax remittances and procurement requisitions made available by farmers. Brief consideration is also given to changes in the inter-sectoral terms of trade between agriculture and industry.

6. *Shuangceng jingying tizhi.*
7. One argument is that the new structure seeks to bring the household level of operations under the guidance of the collective tier and so reimpose government control over households' farming activities. See You Ji and Wang Yuesheng, "China's agricultural development and reform in 1990" in Kuan Hsin-chi and Maurice Brosseau, *China Review* (Hong Kong: The Chinese University Press, 1991), pp. 12.15–12.17.
8. The reluctance of the government to de-regulate retail prices of basic foodstuffs is another factor which has limited the scope of rural price reform and severely drained budgetary resources. As this article goes to press, it has been announced that urban subsidies for basic rationed foodstuffs are to be reduced from 1 May 1991 (*SWB*, FE/1058, 29 April, B2/1).
9. The most notable recent addition to this literature is Jean C. Oi, *State and Peasant in Contemporary China: The Political Economy of Village Government* (University of California Press, 1989).

Fiscal and Financial Support for Agriculture

One of the most notable features of the farming scene in China during the 1980s was the continuous decline in state agricultural investment. *A priori*, savings out of rapidly rising agricultural incomes[10] should have provided the wherewithal for significant rises in investment by the peasants themselves, thereby offsetting the reduction in central budgetary allocations. The implied equation is, however, not so simple. State investment has mostly been used for large-scale capital construction (especially of irrigation and water conservancy projects), which lies beyond the scope, or horizons, of peasants—particularly when they are acting as individual producers. Even if peasant accumulation is, in physical terms, sufficient to finance large-scale projects of this kind, an appropriate framework is needed to make such investment feasible and worthwhile. One of the ironies of developments in the 1980s is that de-collectivization, which played an important part in releasing peasant initiative, may also have left a void, still unfilled.

In any case, the state's financial role in the agricultural sector has traditionally extended beyond direct budgetary allocations for capital construction. Additional budgetary assistance has been forthcoming on a significant scale in support of other aspects of agricultural production. The banking system too has been the source of substantial credit to farmers. Finally, the state has favoured peasants with a variety of generous subsidies—in some cases to finance living expenses, but also for productive purposes. The changing relationship between peasant and state in terms of each of these flows is considered below.

Table 1 shows the changing pattern of state investment for agricultural capital construction[11] since the early 1950s. The atypical figures for 1963–65 can be ignored. They reflect the impact of a profound agricultural crisis, which forced the government to increase dramatically, albeit temporarily, agriculture's share of a significantly reduced capital construction project in order to generate recovery from severely depressed levels of production associated with mismanaged policies during the Great Leap Forward. These apart, the data reveal a fairly stable relationship between agricultural

10. For example, between 1978 and 1984 the savings ratio out of per capita net income increased from 13.1 to 22.9 per cent. See Y. Y. Kueh, "Food consumption and peasant incomes in the post-Mao era" in *The China Quarterly*, No. 116 (1988) (Special Issue on Food and Agriculture in China During the Post-Mao Era), p. 641.

11. That is, *nongye jiben jianshe touzi*. This provides a measure of the volume of work accomplished in capital construction, expressed in monetary terms, and is a comprehensive indicator which reflects the scale and progress of construction within a certain period of time. It is calculated on the basis of actual progress made and the original budget price. "Accomplished investment in basic capital construction" is to be distinguished from "financial expenditure on capital construction" (*caiwu zhichu*)—the latter reflecting the amount of money spent on capital construction projects. See State Statistical Bureau (SSB), *Zhongguo tongji nianjian, 1989* (*China Statistical Yearbook, 1989*), hereafter *TJNJ* (Beijing: Zhongguo tongji chubanshe, 1990), p. 564.

TABLE 4.1. Investment by the State in Agricultural Capital Construction, 1953–89

	Average annual level of agricultural investment (mill. yuan)	As percentage of overall capital construction investment
1953–57	837	7.1
1958–62	3,114	11.3
1963–65	2,482	17.6
1966–70	2,085	10.7
1971–75	3,461	9.8
1976–80	4,922	10.5
1981–85	3,436	5.0
1986–89	4,350	3.1

Sources:
Appendix A, Table A1; and Statistical Office for Fixed Capital Investment of the SSB, *Zhongguo guding zichan touzi tongji ziliao, 1950–85* (*Statistical Materials on Fixed Capital Investment, 1950–85*), hereafter *ZGGD* (Beijing: Tongji chubanshe, 1987), p. 43. The averages for 1966–70 and 1971–75 are available in *TJNJ 1990*, p. 166.

and total state investment between the First and Fifth Five-Year Plans (1953–57 and 1976–80). By contrast, a sharp decline then ensued. Between the Fifth and Sixth FYPs the proportion of the investment budget allocated to the agricultural sector halved, and it continued to fall, hardly less dramatically, thereafter. The *absolute* level of agricultural investment recorded a decline of 44 per cent between 1980 and 1981. Although recovery has subsequently taken place, in 1989 basic capital construction in agriculture was still more than 12 per cent below its 1979 peak (during the same 10-year period the overall capital construction investment budget has risen by 193 per cent).[12] This record is far removed from the CCP Central Committee's undertaking of 1979, which spoke of agriculture's share in the construction budget rising to 18 per cent within three to five years![13]

The precipitate decline in agricultural capital construction investment during the 1980s has been the source of serious concern amongst Chinese commentators.[14] Comparison of this trend with those of other sectors is also

12. See Appendix A, Table A1.
13. "Zhonggong zhongyang guanyu jiakuai nongye fazhan ruogan wenti de jueding" ("Decision of the Central Committee of the CCP on some questions concerning the acceleration of agricultural development"), He Kang (General Editor), *Zhongguo nongye nianjian, 1980* (*Chinese Agricultural Yearbook, 1980*), hereafter *NYNJ* (Beijing: Nongye chubanshe, 1981), pp. 56–62.
14. Two representative articles are: Liu Qiusheng, "Woguo nongye touzi wenti he duice" ("Problems of agricultural investment in China and remedial measures"); and Lei Xiaoming, "Nongye touzi: weiji, yuanyin, chulu" ("Agricultural investment: Crisis, causes and solutions") in He Kang and Wang Yuzhao (eds.), *Zhongguo nongcun gaige shinian* (*Ten Years of Rural Reform in China*), hereafter *ZGNCGGSN* (Zhongguo renmin daxue chubanshe, 1990), pp. 473–7 and 484–91.

instructive. Between the Fifth FYP (1976–80) and the first four years of the Seventh Plan (1986–89), average annual construction investment by the state in agriculture fell by 11.62 per cent, compared with increases of 233.66 and 180.8 per cent for light and heavy industry.[15]

Most state investment in agriculture was used for large-scale construction projects. In particular, available evidence indicates that between the 1950s and the 1970s (the period of Maoist ascendancy) about two-thirds of capital construction funds in this sector were used for water conservancy and irrigation purposes.[16] Bearing in mind that labour mobilization for purposes of agricultural capital construction had fallen from an average of 30–40 days per household per annum during the 1960s and 1970s to no more than three or four workdays in the 1980s (in some places it was eliminated altogether),[17] it is hardly surprising that rural infrastructural decline should have become the focus of anxiety in recent years.

The declining share of the agricultural sector in total capital construction investment was complemented by an increasing allocation to industry. But an assessment of the adequacy of state investment flows to peasant farmers based on a simple comparison of agricultural and industrial rates of investment may be misleading to the extent that part of heavy industrial investment is used for the development of agriculture-support industries. In China the most important areas of such support have been production of farm machinery and chemicals (especially fertilizers). Table 2 presents official estimates of construction investment in these sectors. These figures reinforce the earlier findings and indeed mirror the estimates of state agricultural construction investment closely. Until the second half of the 1970s investment allocations to these two key sectors show a rising trend. But thereafter the trend was reversed. In particular, the period of the Sixth FYP (1981–85) witnessed a dramatic decline, in both absolute and relative terms, in the level and proportion of heavy industrial funds received by these agriculture-support industries. It is worth recording that after the Great Leap Forward an increasing share of these funds was directed towards fertilizer and pesticide production. This orientation was reinforced after 1980—a reflection perhaps of the declining role of agricultural mechanization in the wake of a return to household-based farming.[18]

15. These figures are available in *ZGGD*, pp. 43 and 97; and *TJNJ 1990*, p. 166. Other comparative indicators can be found in "Tigao nongye zonghe shengchan nengli; wujia nongye chixu wending fazhan" ("Raise the comprehensive production capacity of agriculture; promote the continued stable development of agriculture") in *Nongye jingji wenti* (*Agricultural Economic Problems*), hereafter *NYJJWT*, No. 3 (1990), p. 9.

16. Only in 1963–65 did the allocation of capital construction funds to irrigation fall significantly below two-thirds. See *NYJJZL*, p. 303.

17. "Yindao nongcun zijin; zengjia nongye touru" ("Give direction to rural capital and increase allocations to agriculture"), *NYJJWT*, No. 4 (1990), p. 22.

18. During 1981–85 88.6% of agriculture-support industrial investment was allocated to chemical fertilizers and pesticides (85% for fertilizers alone). The corresponding figure for the previous (Fifth) FYP period was 77.7%. See *ZGGD*, p. 103. The decline in the rate of

Table 4.2. State Investment in Two Agriculture-Support Industries, 1953–85

	Investment in chemical fertilizers and other agricultural chemicals	Investment in agricultural machinery	Total investment in both industries	As % of overall construction investment in heavy industry
1953–57	465	270	735	3.45
1958–62	2,139	1,517	3,656	5.61
1963–65	1,315	571	1,886	9.74
1966–70	3,293	1,189	4,482	8.98
1971–75	7,226	2,352	9,578	10.95
1976–80	8,347	2,391	10,738	9.98
1981–85	3,975	513	4,488	3.42
1953–85	26,760	8,803	35,563	7.38

Note:
   The figures, in million *yuan*, show the cumulative investment for each period.
Source:
   ZGGD, pp. 97 and 103.

Funds made available through the state budget for capital construction purposes are not the sole source of budgetary support for the agricultural sector. Other forms of revenue support have been important and relevant data are set out in Table 3. The data here overlap with, but are also more all-embracing than, the estimates of agricultural investment shown in Table 1.[19] The most important addition is the category "spending in support of production and various operational expenses" (*shiyefei*). This includes spending on a wide range of activities, such as reclamation, crop farming, animal husbandry, forestry, aquatic production and management of farm machinery, as well as small-scale water conservancy and soil conservation work.[20] The distinction between such spending and basic capital construction investment is probably best understood in terms of scale and time-horizon: the latter refers to fixed capital formation, whereas the former is more concerned with the day-to-day operation and management of agricultural facilities.

   Overall, as the figures in the final column indicate, the pattern of change

agricultural mechanization in China in recent years is highlighted in the finding that in 1988 the mechanically-cultivated area was more than 1.25 million hectares less than in 1979. In many areas, practices of ploughing and digging by hand, and even slash-and-burn cultivation, had reappeared. See Liu Qiusheng in *ZGNCGGSN*, p. 476.

   19. The activities subsumed under "basic capital construction" are the same in the two tables. The slightly different measures of these activities merely reflect the conceptual distinction rehearsed in n. 11.

   20. For full details see *TJNJ 1990*, p. 246.

TABLE 4.3. State Budgetary Expenditure in Support of Agriculture

| | Total state budgetary expenditure in support of agriculture (average spending per annum) | of which: | | | | | Spending on agriculture as percentage of state budgetary expenditure for all purposes |
		Spending in support of production and various operational expenses	Spending on basic agricultural construction	Revolving capital	Spending on science and technology	Other	
1953–57	1,817	570	818	58		371	6.75
1958–62	5,714	2,308	2,532	300		574	12.48
1963–65	5,925	2,013	2,272	303	95	1,241	14.75
1966–70	4,622	1,578	1,969	259	79*	785	9.18
1971–75	8,024	3,220	3,495	280	9	1,021	10.24
1976–80	13,871	6,917	4,761	502	112	1,579	13.22
1981–85	13,170	8,744	3,171	165**	165	990	9.47
1986–87	18,983	12,923	4,534		249	1,290	5.52

* Average for 1966–67
** Average for 1981–83
Note:
   All figures in million *yuan*, unless otherwise stated.
Source:
   Appendix A, Table A2.

observable here is similar to that shown in Table 1. In particular, state spending on agriculture as a proportion of gross budgetary outlays for all purposes is shown to have declined sharply during the Sixth and into the Seventh FYPs. But at the slightly more disaggregative level, while capital construction investment was falling during the 1980s, other forms of agriculture-support spending (including operational expenses) rose in both relative and absolute terms.[21] Stated differently, the ratio of funds used for longer-run, fixed capital formation to those absorbed for shorter-term uses was falling.[22]

Funds for agriculture-support and operating expenses were destined for a variety of agricultural uses. What is interesting is that during the early period of rural reform, the share of irrigation and water/soil conservation fell off sharply, as allocations to crop farming, husbandry, reclamation, forestry and fisheries all rose. The same pattern is observable from an examination of the uses to which capital construction funds were directed.[23] Such changes help explain the deterioration of China's agricultural infrastructure in the 1980s.

A final comment relates to the "other" category. This consists overwhelmingly of emergency assistance to poor and disaster-hit regions, as well as expenditure incurred through the "sending down" to the countryside (*xiafang*) of urban inhabitants. The periods of the greatest spending on these items were those associated with severe economic depression (the Great Leap Forward) and large-scale rustication campaigns (the Cultural Revolution). But such essentially non-productive spending still absorbed 10 per cent or more of total budgetary outlays on agriculture in the early 1980s.[24]

Traditionally, investment needs for *local* agricultural capital formation requirements and the dissemination of scientific information and techniques were the responsibility of collective and local financial departments. In theory, declining state allocations during the 1980s might therefore have been offset by increases in agriculture-support spending from these sources—and supplemented by further assistance from town and village enterprises (the most rapidly growing sector of the Chinese economy). In fact, this did not happen, not least because of higher and swifter returns that were available from investment outside agriculture. Between 1981 and 1987 local budgetary allocations to agriculture rose by only 53.5 per cent (by significantly less than spending through the central budget) and agricul-

21. As a proportion of total budgetary expenditure (for *all* purposes), agriculture-support spending was just about maintained during the Sixth and Seventh FYPs (1.32% and 1.26% respectively) and during 1986–87 it rose to 5.41%.

22. The ratio fell from 1.03:1 (1953–78) to 0.41:1 (1979–87).

23. Such disaggregative data are available in *NYJJZL*, pp. 308–11, but unfortunately only up to 1982.

24. *Ibid.*

ture's share in this expenditure fell from 18.87 to 10.89 per cent.[25] Meanwhile, notwithstanding an increase in overall rural collective fixed investment of almost 250 per cent during 1982–87, collective agricultural capital formation *declined* by 18 per cent (from 39.6 to just 9.4 per cent of the total).[26] As for help from rural enterprises, a similar picture emerges: between 1979 and 1988 agriculture-support capital from this source fell precipitately (by 72 per cent). The average annual level of such funding declined from 4,190 to 1,360 million *yuan* between the first and second halves of the "decade of reform."[27]

As a supplement to funds entering the agricultural sector through central and local budgets, credit made available through the banking system (the People's Bank and Agricultural Bank) and rural credit co-operatives (*nongcun xinyongshe*) has been very important. Until the early 1980s the most common destinations of agricultural loans were communes and state farms, most of the credit being used for the short-term financing of production and the purchase of working capital. Thereafter individual peasant households became beneficiaries of such loans at the expense of the contracting collective sector (state-run agricultural units' share of loan funds meanwhile continuing to grow). The need to pay for credit makes assistance from this source different from that available through the central budget or other revenue-support mechanisms. Interest charges on most short-term loans were, by the early 1980s, significantly higher than the rate of return on private savings, although preferential terms were offered on credit extended to purchase agricultural equipment.

Data relating to the deposit and loan portfolios of China's three major financial sources of agricultural credit are presented in Appendix A. Table 4 is a summary of some of the information presented there.

Sources of information on rural deposits and agricultural loans are not entirely consistent and there are considerable difficulties in interpreting available data. It is a pity too that there is little information on the historical background of post-1978 developments.[28] Nevertheless, the general picture which emerges for the 1980s is clear enough and it is substantiated in a wide variety of Chinese sources.

During the reform decade the volume of both rural deposits and agricultural loans grew very rapidly (on the evidence of Table 4, by about 20 and

25. Zhang Zhongfa *et al.*, "Woguo nongye fazhanzhong de zichan wenti" ("Problems of capital in China's agricultural development"), *Zhongguo shehui kexue* (*Social Sciences in China*), No. 1 (1991), pp. 37–8.
26. *NYJJWT*, No. 4 (1990), pp. 20–1.
27. *Ibid.* Also see Liu Qiusheng in *ZGNCGGSN*, p. 474.
28. Estimates of rural deposits in the People's Bank for every year from 1953 can, however, be found in *NYJJZL*, p. 321. And Nicholas R. Lardy has data on the volume of agricultural loans going back to 1950 in his *Agriculture in China's Modern Economic Development* (Cambridge: Cambridge University Press, 1983), p. 141. Note, however, that before 1979 the Agricultural Bank operated as a separate administrative entity during 1951, 1953–57 and 1963–65 (*ibid.*).

TABLE 4.4. The Volume and Structure of Rural Deposits and Agricultural Loans of
the People's Bank, Agricultural Bank and Rural Credit Co-operatives, 1979–88

A. Deposits

| | Total volume of rural deposits (m. yuan) | of which, contributions from each source (%): | | |
		People's Bank	Agricultural Bank	Rural credit co-operatives
1979	71,761	28.39	41.53	30.09
1980	90,714	26.44	43.54	30.02
1986	274,594	20.38	44.57	35.04
1987	334,850	18.70	44.71	36.59
1988	379,815	17.63	45.57	36.80

B. Loans

	Total volume of agricultural loans (m. yuan)			
1979	27,430	49.87	37.55	12.58
1980	33,388	52.68	36.54	10.78
1986	110,797	51.48	21.21	27.31
1987	141,583	48.44	22.46	29.10
1988	163,011	49.99	22.39	27.66

Source:
  Appendix A, Tables A3 (i)–(iii).

22 per cent per annum respectively). But the underlying structure of credit
changed significantly during this period. Between 1979 and 1988 the People's Bank's share of all rural deposits declined, whilst that of the Agricultural Bank and rural credit co-operatives increased. By contrast, the
Agricultural Bank's share of *agricultural loans* fell sharply, leaving the
credit co-operatives to make up the difference[29] (the relative contribution
of the People's Bank in the meantime remaining largely unchanged). Given
that the Agricultural Bank had a special responsibility for credit extension
for agricultural development, its loan performance was disappointing.

In any case, against the physical expansion of agricultural loans through
the two banks and the credit co-operatives must be set the serious decline
in the *share* of agriculture in loans from these sources. There can be no
doubt that in the 1980s rural credit was directed increasingly towards
non-agricultural uses (pre-eminently rural industrial and commercial development). For example, during 1981–88 the share of village and town

29. The relationship—indeed rivalry—between the Agricultural Bank and credit co-
operatives is explored in Lu Jianxiang, "Tan nongcun xinyongshe gaige" ("A discussion
of the reform of rural credit co-operatives"), *NYJJWT*, No. 8 (1986), pp. 38–40.

enterprises in all rural loans increased from 14.9 per cent to 22.1 per cent (in the case of rural credit co-operatives alone, from 28.6 to 50 per cent), whilst that of agriculture fell from 27.6 to 21.5 per cent.[30] Between 1979 and 1988 total loan disbursements made by the Agricultural Bank rose by 387 per cent: the increase for individual sectors was 1,465 per cent [sic] for rural enterprises; 387 per cent for commercial enterprises; but only 254 per cent for agriculture.[31] It was also revealed that in 1988 only 14.2 per cent of loans made through the same bank were directed towards agriculture—and a mere 7.1 per cent for crop farming.[32] It was only because of the disproportionate share of credit capital held in the People's Bank that credit assistance to the agricultural sector was not more severely affected.

A feature of post-1978 developments which deserves to be highlighted is the increasingly important role played by the private savings of rural households as a source of credit. There had already been a rapid expansion of such savings during the 1970s (the average annual rate of growth for 1970–79 was around 20 per cent), but in the 1980s the rate of increase accelerated to a remarkable 35 per cent per year. By 1988 private savings deposits constituted a third of all rural deposits held in the People's and Agricultural Banks and the credit co-operatives—sufficient to finance almost three-quarters of agricultural loans from these sources!

Although banks and credit institutions did undoubtedly discriminate against farmers during the 1980s, the greater relative decline in other forms of agriculture-support funding seems to have enhanced the role of the banks and credit co-operatives as the single most important source of financial assistance to the agricultural sector (see Table 5).

At the beginning of the reform period the contribution of credit institutions to the financing of agricultural operations and development already outweighed, in purely value terms, that of central budgetary allocations.[33] By 1988 agricultural loans accounted for almost 90 per cent of all funds from these sources. The estimates highlight the decline in agricultural fixed capital formation and underline the finding that an increasing share of financial resources flowing into the farm sector was dedicated to short-term uses, to be set against production expenses or the purchase of working capital. This was a further reflection of the changing economic relationship

30. Zhang Zhongfa et al., "Problems of capital," p. 38.

31. NYNJ 1989, p. 113. See also Song Zuanming, "Tanlun muqian woguo nongye zijin touru de niuquxiao ying ji duice" ("Trying out the idea that the present vagaries of capital allocations to China's agriculture are in need of urgent counter-measures") in ZGNCGGSN, p. 480.

32. Liu Qiusheng in ZGNCGGSN, p. 473. For further supporting evidence see Lei Qiaoming; and Tian Ming, "Gongxu zhiyue: nongye xindai touru de kunjing yu chulu" ("The interaction of supply and requirements: the difficult circumstance of agricultural credit and possible solutions," both in ZGNCGGSN, pp. 484–91 and pp. 536–42.

33. Official data for the period of 1958–78 indicate that only during the first half of the 1970s was this relationship reversed. See NYJJZL, p. 321.

TABLE 4.5. Changing Sources of Agricultural Funding: 1979–80 and 1986–87 compared

	Construction investment	Other central budgetary assistance	Agricultural loans	Total
	Value, and % contribution, of each funding category:			
1979	62.41	111.92	274.30	448.63
	(13.91%)	(24.95%)	(61.14%)	(100.00%)
1980	48.59	101.36	333.88	483.83
	(10.04%)	(20.95%)	(69.01%)	(100.00%)
1986	43.87	140.33	1,107.97	1,292.17
	(3.40%)	(10.86%)	(85.74%)	(100.00%)
1987	46.81	148.65	1,415.83	1,611.29
	(2.91%)	(9.23%)	(87.87%)	(100.00%)

Note:
  All value figures in million *yuan.*
Sources:
  Appendix A, Tables A2 and A3 (i)–(iii).

between the peasant and the state in the wake of post-1978 reforms and the process of de-collectivization.

The analysis to this point has taken no account of the impact of subsidies granted to agricultural production. Table 6 indicates the wide variety of such subsidies and provides a measure of their value to peasants in the early years of rural reform. The figures show that the benefits which accrued to farmers from production subsidies were considerable, especially in the supply of key inputs such as chemical fertilizers, diesel oil and electricity (these three items accounting, on average, for almost 60 per cent of all subsidies during the period shown). Tax concessions were also important, particularly between 1979 and 1982. But what is most striking is that, paralleling the other financial flows in support of agricultural production, the farm sector's share of total subsidy benefits declined sharply in the early stages of reform, falling from 21 per cent in 1978 to a mere 6 per cent five years later. In absolute terms too, there was a falling-away after 1981, so that the level in 1983 was 13 per cent lower than that of the year immediately preceding the institution of rural reform.

The decline in production subsidies to the agricultural sector should, however, be set against the finding that in both absolute and relative terms, subsidies designed to improve peasants' *living standards* increased steadily during the same period—from 11.75 to 13.58 per cent of the total value of all such subsidies between 1978 and 1983.[34]

34. *NYJJZL*, p. 104. Most of the benefit from this source derived from the subsidized provision of grain and oil crops. Between 1978 and 1983 the ratio of production to consumption subsidies to peasants fell from 1.81:1 to 0.45:1.

TABLE 4.6. State Subsidies in Support of Agricultural Production, 1978–83

	1978	1979	1980	1981	1982	1983
Total value of production subsidies to agriculture	3,398	4,697	4,916	6,098	4,918	2,947
(As % state subsidies for all purposes)	(21.23)	(16.99)	(14.53)	(13.82)	(11.81)	(6.04)
of which, subsidies associated with supply of:						
(1) chemical fertilizers	589	732	1,266	2,248	1,946	1,292
(2) other agricultural chemicals	106	149	116	110	134	146
(3) agricultural machinery	402	278	153	241	185	69
(4) electric power	610	610	650	680	671	643
(5) diesel oil	834	861	795	687	482	52
(6) plastic film	51	50	50	49	54	50
(7) small farm tools	50	50	50	23	25	23
(8) credit via tax reduction/exemption	—	1,191	1,198	1,180	880	270

Note:
All figures in million *yuan*, unless otherwise stated.
Source:
NYJJZL, p. 101.

It is unfortunate that such detailed information on agricultural production subsidies is not available for the years after 1983. Official estimates of
the value of price subsidies on agricultural inputs do, however, exist for
every year from 1978 to 1987.[35] Not only do they corroborate the picture
shown in Table 6, but they also suggest that the same trend continued into
the second half of the 1980s.

The level of financial flows made available to peasants through the central budget and financial institutions, as well as the benefits accruing from
various production subsidies, provide a measure of the economic assistance
afforded to agricultural production. In a real sense they reflect a crucial
aspect of the economic relationship between peasant and state. The picture
which emerges from the foregoing analysis is a consistent one. Where long-
run data are available, most of the indicators suggest that before the late
1970s financial support for agriculture was generally stable—and occasion-

35. *TJNJ 1989*, p. 673.

ally even rising. By contrast, the reform initiatives of 1979 and the early 1980s seem to have coincided with a falling-off in such support. Most striking was perhaps the decline in allocations for infrastructural maintenance and repair and net farmland construction. One result of this neglect was a decline in the effectively-irrigated area; another may have been to increase the impact of natural disasters.[36]

But there is a final qualification. The decline in the state's financial involvement in the agricultural sector occurred, whether coincidentally or not, at a time when peasant incomes were rising faster than ever before. A glance at the remarkable increase in peasants' personal savings deposits during the second half of the 1970s and throughout the 1980s is testimony to the enormous capacity for increases in agricultural investment from within the rural sector (including by farmers themselves).

The reality has, however, been otherwise, and peasant households' personal investment in agriculture has not kept up with the expansion of this obvious potential. There is, it is true, some evidence that peasants responded positively to early institutional and economic reforms in the countryside. For example, between 1981 and 1984 peasant investment in agricultural fixed capital formation increased from 2,000 to 13,973 million *yuan*.[37] But from 1985 this rising trend was reversed and in 1988 the level of such investment by farmers was still 11.25 per cent below that of 1984.[38]

Farmers' failure to assume their investment responsibilities appears to have been the product of various forces. One was no doubt a long-held belief that such matters fell within the remit of the state. Uncertainty over land use rights and a lack of confidence in the permanence of land policies, as well as a blurring of the nature of the contractual relationship between themselves and the state, were other more tangible factors. In any case, the evidence is that peasants increasingly directed their spending away from production towards consumption (between 1984 and 1987 productive spending by peasant households increased by only 15.7 per cent, compared with 37.7 per cent for consumption).[39]

Peasants' investment behaviour can also be interpreted as a rational response (in terms of profit maximization) towards the opportunities facing them. The returns from investing in industrial manufacturing and commerce were much higher than those which agriculture offered. Moreover, within crop farming itself the least profitable occupation was the cultivation

36. The case is rehearsed and developed in an unpublished paper, "The analysis of agricultural economic reform in China," by Chen Qiguang. I am indebted to Dr Chen for showing me a copy of this article. Claude Aubert takes a more complicated view: see his "The agricultural crisis in China at the end of the 1980s" in Jørgen Delman *et al.* (eds.), *Remaking Peasant China* (Aarhus: Aarhus University Press, 1990), p. 18.

37. *NYJJWT*, No. 4 (1990), p. 21.

38. *Ibid.* Between 1984 and 1986 there was a decline of almost 50%. Notice that during 1984–88 peasant income rose on average by over 53% (*TJNJ 1989*, p. 743 and *TJNJ 1990*, p. 313).

39. Zhang Zhongfa *et al.* in *Zhongguo shehui kexue*, No. 1 (1991), p. 38.

of food grains. It is not surprising that a feature of evolving peasant investment patterns during the 1980s was a re-orientation of funds towards non-
agricultural uses.[40]

Flows out of Agriculture: Taxes and Procurement

Since 1949 agricultural taxes in China have overwhelmingly been paid in
kind.[41] The most important of these has been the grain tax, although its role
has been overtaken since 1953 by that of compulsory sales to the state at
fixed prices. The relative importance of these two categories will be considered below.

Table 7 provides a measure of the financial burden upon peasants, arising
from the payment of the agricultural tax. At face value, the figures in the
first column point to a major increase in the tax burden upon farmers during
the reform period. Reference to Appendix B (Table B1) shows that from
the mid-1960s until the early 1980s the absolute level of the agricultural tax
remained stable within a 10 per cent margin. By contrast, between 1982 and
1987 it increased by almost 80 per cent, and during 1988–89 by a further 60
per cent! But such findings need to be interpreted with caution. The estimates shown above are expressed in terms of current prices, whereas the
prices of many agricultural products (including grain) rose sharply after
1978. The *real* level of the tax is therefore exaggerated.

TABLE 4.7. The Burden of the Agricultural Tax

	Average annual value of agricultural tax (mill. yuan)	*As % of value of all taxes*	*As % total state revenue*
1953–57	3,013.60	22.32	11.12
1958–62	2,762.60	15.07	6.53
1963–65	2,522.33	13.74	6.23
1966–70	3,001.20	13.32	5.93
1971–75	2,985.20	8.57	3.81
1976–80	2,881.00	5.75	2.90
1981–85	3,351.60	3.29	2.45
1986–89	6,330.50	2.71	2.49

Source:
   Appendix B, Table B1.

40. For supporting evidence see *NYJJWT*, No. 4 (1990), p. 21.
41. At least until 1985, when the state moved from an agricultural tax collected in kind to
one collected in cash. See Li Bingkun and Tang Renjian, "Gaige nongyeshui zhidu de
shexiang" ("Some thoughts on reforming the agricultural tax system"), in *NYJJWT*, No. 3
(1986), pp. 22–6.

In any case, the *relative* burden on peasants is seen generally to have been in decline since the early 1950s. Whether expressed as a proportion of the overall value of state taxes or total budgetary revenue, tax remittances fell steadily until 1985–86, thereafter recovering marginally. Perhaps most telling of all is the finding that the value of the agricultural tax as a proportion of agricultural gross value output (GVO) was almost halved between 1978 and 1986. For the period 1979–88 it averaged a mere 1.22 per cent.[42] No wonder that some commentators have spoken of China's "chronically low rate of agricultural taxation" and called for urgent reforms.[43]

There is, however, a caveat. The light, and declining, tax burden described above may be a reflection of the changing economic relationship between peasant and state in China. But it has not been an unqualified benefit, for in recent years many departments and regions have taken advantage of the low tax rate to impose many different kinds of levies upon peasants.[44] Such levies have added anything from 20 to 100 *yuan* to the "official" tax burden and it has been estimated that the total, national extra-tax burden has been as high as 16,000 million *yuan*.[45] Given that these resources have often been embezzled by local cadres, the effect of such additional expropriations has merely been to deprive agriculture of funds and further dampen farmers' enthusiasm.

In any case, as a proportion of the total value of purchases by the state of all farm and sideline products, the tax contribution was of minor importance. Data suggest that in 1978 it constituted 5 per cent of such purchases and by 1982 had fallen to 2.7 per cent. By far the heaviest burden on farmers arose from enforced sales of grain to the state. Estimates of physical requisitions are reproduced in Appendix B and show that in both gross and net terms the procurement ratio (i.e. sales as a proportion of annual production), having remained fairly stable throughout the 1950s, 1960s and much of the 1970s, thereafter rose sharply to reach 35 per cent (gross) and 27 per cent (net) in 1987. As a measure of the impact of reform, the net procurement ratio increased from 18.13 to 31.58 per cent between 1975–78 and 1979–84.

Such figures would appear to suggest that the implementation of rural reform was accompanied by an increasingly onerous extractive burden on farmers. But this is not the case. Between 1978 and 1984 at least, grain output rose rapidly and although procurement increased even more quickly than production, the residual amount of grain in peasant hands (total output less gross procurement plus re-sales to the rural sector) also increased.

---

42. Agricultural GVO estimates can be found in *TJNJ 1990*, p. 335.
43. Li Bingkun and Tang Renjian in *NYJJWT*, No. 3 (1986), p. 22. The burden of taxation is also unbalanced between different regions and different crops and activities.
44. That is, in addition to local surtaxes, which have traditionally—and legally—been a means of funding public welfare facilities (e.g. the construction of schools and transportation).
45. *Ibid.*

The peak level of per capita grain availability was in fact reached in 1985, when some 386.56 kilograms of unhusked grain were available, on average, to each peasant. The reality was that under the impact of reform, with total grain production rising fast and with purchase prices also increasing (including more opportunity to sell more at "above-quota" and "negotiated" prices), there was added incentive for peasants to release more of their output to the state, without fear of jeopardizing their own consumption standards.

A detailed statistical breakdown of grain acquisitions by the state during the 1970s and early 1980s, as shown in Table 8, supports such an inference. Table 8 contains information on procurement sales at three different prices: *tonggou* refers to the basic "list" price, set by the State Price Bureau; *chaogou* is the "above-quota" price—30 per cent above the list price before 1978, and 50 per cent higher thereafter; and *yigou* is the "negotiated" price, which seems to have been close to the free market price.

The data reveal much about the impact of early economic reform measures, designed to enhance material incentives amongst peasants. They show that in contrast to the remarkable stability which had obtained before 1978, the late 1970s and early 1980s witnessed striking changes in the composition of grain tax and procurement.[46] First, the relative importance of tax levies (*zhengshou*), which had fluctuated within a small band, fell steadily after 1978, in both absolute and relative terms. More significant, however, was the more than doubling of physical sales at above-quota prices in the four years between 1978 and 1982, to account for about half of all the grain collected through taxes, list-price and above quota-price sales (*cf.* a figure of less than a quarter before 1979). In addition, for the first time since the immediate post-Leap agricultural crisis, sales at *negotiated* prices assumed a significant—and increasing—role. Indeed by 1982 grain purchased at these near-market prices constituted a fifth of total tax and procurement acquisitions. For more than a decade before 1978 they had been negligible.[47]

46. The impact of early reforms is brought out in the following comparison of the composition of total grain requisitions between 1974–78 and 1979–82:

	Taxes, tonggou and chaogou sales	of which:			Yigou sales
		Taxes	Tonggou	Chaogou	
1974–78	93.97	(22.79)	(48.20)	(23.85)	2.05
1979–82	83.58	(14.94)	(29.98)	(35.47)	16.44

47. Between 1963 and 1965 *yigou* sales accounted for almost 5% of total grain requisitions. Thereafter they declined rapidly and between 1967 and 1978 they never exceeded 1% of the total. *NYJJZL*, p. 339.

TABLE 4.8. Grain Procurement and Tax Levies, 1971–82

| | Total requisitions (grain tax + procurement) | Taxes; tonggou+ chaogou sales | | Tax levies | | Tonggou sales | | Chaogou sales | | Yigou sales | |
	Volume	Volume	as % total requisitions	Volume	as % total requisitions	Volume	as % total requisitions	Volume	as % total requisitions	Volume	as % total requisitions
1971	44.04	43.63	99.07	11.70	26.57					0.41	0.93
1972	39.64	39.29	99.12	10.75	27.12					0.35	0.88
1973	47.06	46.67	99.17	11.29	23.99					0.39	0.83
1974	48.90	48.42	99.02	11.92	24.38	24.31	49.71	10.74	21.96	0.48	0.98
1975	51.49	51.11	99.26	11.43	22.20	25.16	48.86	13.04	25.33	0.39	0.76
1971–75 av. p.a.	46.23	45.82	99.11	11.42	24.92					0.40	0.87
1976	49.29	49.09	99.59	11.74	23.82	23.63	47.94	12.17	24.69	0.20	0.41
1977	47.37	47.16	99.56	11.30	23.85	24.10	50.80	10.15	21.43	0.22	0.46
1978	51.10	47.83	93.60	10.91	21.35	23.13	45.26	12.16	23.80	3.27	6.40
1979	59.25	54.01	91.16	10.52	17.76	22.59	38.13	19.13	32.29	5.25	8.86
1980	58.83	50.23	85.38	9.60	16.32	18.69	31.77	20.29	34.49	8.60	14.62
1976–80 av. p.a.	53.17	49.66	93.40	10.81	21.77	22.43	45.17	14.78	29.76	3.51	6.60
1981	62.56	52.10	83.28	8.99	17.26	15.63	30.00	23.83	45.74	10.46	16.72
1982	73.68	56.20	76.28	8.88	15.80	19.33	34.40	26.95	47.95	17.48	23.72
1981–82 av. p.a.	67.62	54.15	80.08	8.94	16.51	17.48	32.28	25.39	46.89	13.97	20.66

Note:
All procurement estimates in million tonnes of commercial (*maoyi*) grain.
Source:
NYJJZL, pp. 339 and 341.

It will be recalled that average net per capita grain availability within the rural sector was rising steadily through these years. That this occurred at a time when farmers were releasing a rising share of total output—and at a rising average unit price—suggests that it was the peasants who benefited most from procurement policies implemented in the early reform period. What is more, the figures shown in Table 8 underestimate peasant financial benefits by the amount of grain which they sold at free market prices. Relevant data do not appear to be readily available and although it has been estimated that market transactions in grain rose from 1.2 to 6.3 million tonnes between 1978 and 1986,[48] the likelihood is that much of the expansion took place in 1985 and 1986, following the attempted abandonment of the monopoly procurement system.

At a more aggregative level, however, the expanding role of free market transactions during the early reform years emerges clearly in the statistical analysis of the composition of sales of *all* agricultural and sideline products as shown in Table 9.

Despite the different coverage of the two tables, these figures underline the findings of Table 8 in pointing to a rapid decline in the importance of list-price sales in favour of those at above-quota and negotiated prices. But they also highlight the emergence of free markets as an increasingly important vehicle of commercial transactions in agricultural and sideline products after 1978.

TABLE 4.9. Breakdown of Sales of Agricultural and Sideline Products by Price Categories, 1978–83

	Value of sales in each price category as percentage of total sales value of all agricultural and sideline products:			
	List price	*Above-quota price*	*Negotiated price*	*Market price*
1978	84.7	7.9	1.8	5.6
1979	71.7	16.7	4.9	6.7
1980	64.4	17.9	9.5	8.2
1981	58.2	20.9	11.5	9.4
1982	57.5	20.8	11.5	10.2
1983	48.0	28.1	13.4	10.5

Source:
    SSB, *Zhongguo maoyi wujia tongji ziliao, 1952–83* (*Statistical Materials on China's Commerce and Prices, 1952–83*) (Beijing: Tongji chubanshe, 1984), p. 112.

48. Robert Michael Field, "Trends in the value of agricultural output," *The China Quarterly*, No. 116 (1988), pp. 564–5.

It is true that incremental income accruing to peasants as a result of increasing sales of grain at higher prices did not constitute a *net* gain. Rather, it had to be set against the cost they incurred as a result of buying back some grain from the state. Available evidence suggests that in the first half of the 1980s re-sales were rising: between 1976–80 and 1981–85, for example, the volume of re-sales doubled, the ratio of annual re-sales to gross procurement increasing from 31.4 to 36.8 per cent. To the extent that re-sale prices in the countryside were tied to procurement prices, the net benefit to farmers was correspondingly reduced. The relationship between the two price categories may, however, have been more complex. In the four years 1979–82, on average about 14 million tonnes of grain a year (just over half of annual re-sales) was made available by the state to peasants who were short of grain either for reasons of inherent resource deficiencies or because of the effect of natural disasters, or who were engaged in non-grain farming (for example the cultivation of economic crops and vegetables, or the pursuit of animal husbandry, fishing or forestry—all areas of high state priority).[49] It is possible that the re-sale price charged to such peasants was set at a nominal or subsidized level—in the case of peasants in city suburbs, perhaps close to the retail price paid by urban residents. If this is so, the erosion of peasants' incremental income resulting from the re-sale of grain to the rural sector was less serious.

From the state's point of view, higher procurement did give it greater access to and control over an increasing volume of grain and so made it possible to raise consumption standards in the urban sector. But committed, as at this stage it still was, to a supply-orientated system—one in which the state "took everything that the peasants produced"—and unwilling to match the rises in purchase prices with higher retail prices to consumers, the state suffered an increasingly serious budgetary drain as a result of the transactions reflected in Table 8. Other data confirm that by 1983 purchases of all agricultural and sideline products at *chaogou* and *yigou* prices amounted to 52,500 million *yuan* and constituted 53.5 per cent of all extra-market transactions (in 1978 the corresponding figures had been 5,400 million *yuan* and 11.8 per cent).[50] This was a remarkable transformation, even allowing for price inflation in the intervening years. State commercial departments accounted for the bulk (some 87 per cent) of such purchases and grain was by far the most important single item amongst them.

A measure of the cost of changes in procurement policies during the early reform period is given in Table 10, which presents estimates of the value of the benefit received by peasants as a result of increases in farm purchase prices decreed by the state between 1978 and 1983. It is likely that these figures do not take account of the benefits from increased *yigou* sales, in

49. The figure is derived from data in *NYJJZL*, p. 348.
50. *Zhongguo maoyi wujia tongji ziliao, 1952–83*, p. 112.

TABLE 4.10. The Benefit to Peasants of Rises in Farm
Purchase Prices

	Total monetary benefit accruing to peasants (mill. yuan)	As % of total budgetary revenue
1978	1,429	1.27
1979	8,568	8.02
1980	10,425	10.00
1981	14,886	14.65
1982	16,680	15.39
1983	18,514	15.29

Sources:
NYJJZL, p. 103; TJNJ 1990, p. 229.

which case they understate the budgetary burden on the state.[51] Against this background, and with procurement rising sharply again in 1984, one can understand the pressures to deregulate agricultural prices and extend market transactions—factors which contributed to the momentous 1985 decision largely to abandon the 30-year-old state monopoly procurement system for agricultural and sideline products.

The preceding analysis embraces developments only in the early reform period and it is unfortunate that the kind of detailed statistical information contained in Table 8 does not seem to be available for subsequent years. There is no reason to suppose that the trends illustrated there were not maintained until 1984. But from 1985, the looked-for expansion of free markets and establishment of residual contracts with grain and cotton farmers[52] might be expected to have reduced the state's involvement in grain transactions. This does not, however, seem to have been the case. The reluctance of farmers to grow grain, in the face of higher returns available from other crops (let alone from other branches of agriculture or from entirely non-agricultural occupations), combined with difficulties inherent in the new system, compelled the government effectively to re-introduce mandatory quotas. The outcome has been a much more modest growth in market transactions—and a continuing expansion of sales to the state—than might have been predicted from the 1985 policy initiatives.[53]

51. See also Lardy, *Agriculture in China's Modern Economic Development*, pp. 192–9.
52. For a detailed analysis of the policy initiatives of 1985, see Terry Sicular, "Agricultural planning and policy in the post-Mao period" and Robert F. Ash, "The evolution of agricultural policy," both in *The China Quarterly*, No. 116 (1988), pp. 693–702 and pp. 545–51.
53. Claude Aubert, "The agricultural crisis" in Delman *et al.* (eds.), *Remaking Peasant China*, p. 21.

A Brief Digression: The Terms of Trade Between Agriculture and Industry

In order to assess the net welfare benefits to peasants of rises in farm purchase prices, reference should also be made to changes in the prices of goods which they themselves purchased. In short, some consideration needs to be given to the inter-sectoral terms of trade.

It has frequently been argued that a "scissors gap" existed in China during the 1950s, reflecting the under-valuation of agricultural goods relative to industrial products, but that this gap subsequently narrowed. Official price data certainly give strong support to such an interpretation (see Table 11). These data, which reflect the movement only of relative prices, indicate quite unequivocally that the net barter terms of trade moved consistently in

TABLE 4.11. Net Barter Terms of Trade Between Agriculture and Industry, 1952–89

	Index of purchase prices of farm and sideline products (1952 = 100) (P_a)	Index of retail prices of industrial products paid by peasants (1952 = 100) (P_i)	Net barter terms of trade (P_a/P_i)
1952	100.00	100.00	100.00
1957	120.23	102.19	117.65
1962	164.56	115.41	142.59
1965	154.52	107.93	143.17
1970	160.44	102.01	157.28
1975	171.63	99.91	171.78
1978	178.78	100.09	178.62
1979	218.34	100.18	217.95
1980	233.88	101.00	231.56
1981	247.70	102.01	242.82
1982	253.13	103.65	244.22
1983	264.23	104.65	252.49
1984	274.84	107.93	254.65
1985	298.44	111.58	267.47
1986	317.52	114.95	276.22
1987	355.59	120.51	295.07
1988	437.42	138.83	315.08
1989	503.04	164.81	305.22

Source:
Adapted from *TJNJ 1990*, p. 250.

favour of agriculture throughout the entire period from the 1950s until the late 1980s. Further, an index, with 1978 as base year, would show that the improvement in agriculture's terms of trade between 1978 and 1988 was almost identical to that achieved during the previous 26 years—testimony surely to the impact of reform upon the rural sector. Taken at face value, the estimates suggest that in 1978 peasants were able to purchase almost 80 per cent more industrial goods than they could at the beginning of the 1950s; and that just 10 years later, their command over industrial goods had risen by a *further* 80 per cent.

Validity of the kind of exercise illustrated in Table 11 depends, however, on acceptability of the two indices. Whilst the index of farm purchase prices does appear to be meaningful within the desired terms of reference, that of industrial prices facing peasants is more questionable. In particular, it seems that the industrial index reflects the prices of selected consumer items bought by rural inhabitants, but excludes key *producer* goods used in agriculture, such as chemical fertilizers, pesticides and farm machinery. These are goods which were little used in the 1950s, but whose use—especially that of fertilizers—has subsequently grown very rapidly. Without taking into account the purchases of such items, estimates of the net barter terms of trade based on official prices indices may be misleading.

Lack of detailed information on changing farm input prices over time makes it difficult to investigate this issue. However, circumstantial evidence does exist to throw some light on changes in the intersectoral terms of trade. For example, a comparison of changes in the value of production (GVO) and of material costs of production per unit area for various crops during 1965–81 reveals a fairly consistent relationship.[54] Between 1965 and 1978 changes in GVO were matched—and frequently exceeded—by the corresponding changes (rises) in material costs of production. By contrast, 1978 represents a watershed, for during the next three years, as farm purchase prices rose substantially, increases in GVO generally outstripped rises in material costs.

Such evidence counsels caution in interpreting the figures shown in Table 11 and suggests that the improvement in agriculture's terms of trade vis-à-vis industry shown there is exaggerated. The new evidence does, however, appear to confirm a strong movement in favour of agriculture during the initial stages of rural reform. What is more open to question is whether the "scissors gap" continued to narrow after 1984. Official retail prices of inputs showed a sharply rising trend in the second half of the 1980s and this was frequently exacerbated by black-market activities. References to price increases of 100–300 per cent within a two or three year period are by no means uncommon.[55] On this evidence, it seems likely that the narrowing of

54. The relevant data can be found in *NYJJZL*, pp. 456–73.
55. See Aubert, "The agricultural crisis," p. 22. Also Ash, "The evolution of agricultural policy," p. 548.

the price gap between agriculture and industry, which had been maintained through the early stages of reform, had by the late 1980s been halted or even reversed.

Concluding Remarks

This article seeks to investigate the shifting economic relationship between the peasant and the state in China. It does so by examining the changing nature and level of a number of critical resource flows—real and financial—between the two parties. The focus of the analysis is the "decade of reform" (1979–88), although where possible, these more recent developments are set in the context of trends discernible since the 1950s.

The findings of the paper are clear. The data presented in various tables leave no room for doubt that since 1978 the state's economic involvement in the agricultural sector has declined markedly. Fixed investment through the central budget has fallen in absolute terms and agriculture's share of total expenditure on capital construction has contracted quite dramatically. Inclusion of other forms of agriculture-support funding by the central government does not alter the picture. It is true that the decline in construction investment has been offset by a considerable expansion in spending directed towards short-term ends. But in relative terms, the deteriorating position of the farm sector still emerges strongly.

At the same time that budgetary support for agriculture was falling, assistance afforded to peasants through the extension of production subsidies (including tax remissions) was curtailed. In the late 1970s these were an important avenue of support, especially in the provision of key inputs, such as chemical fertilizers, diesel oil, farm machinery and electricity. During the first half of the 1980s many of them were largely phased out.

Within the central agricultural budget, the re-direction of funds towards operational expenses and forms of production support other than capital construction reflects a reorientation of resources towards smaller-scale and shorter-term uses (the purchase of equipment and of working capital). This trend has been underlined by the increasingly important role played by *credit* as a source of assistance to farmers after 1979. The expansion of farm credit during the 1980s was an impressive phenomenon, the growth of agricultural loans outstripping that of rural deposits, albeit from a much smaller base. But this record owed most to the continued willingness of the People's Bank to channel funds to peasant farmers. Attracted by swifter and higher returns available outside agriculture, the Agricultural Bank— the institution which had a special responsibility for overseeing the needs of the agricultural sector—by contrast performed disappointingly; so too, and for similar reasons, did the rural credit co-operatives, whose rapidly-expanding credit base was increasingly used to fund the expansion of town and village enterprises.

But it is surely not coincidental that the decline in direct and indirect state involvement in agriculture occurred precisely at a time when tax and procurement burdens on farmers were significantly reduced and when private savings were accumulated on a massive scale under the impact of unprecedented growth of peasant incomes. If the post-1978 institutional and economic environment was designed to provide an opportunity to promote agricultural development by encouraging peasants' own initiative, these resources, newly at the disposal of rural households, seemed to provide the wherewithal for the realization of this potential.

In the early 1980s farmers appear to have responded positively to the challenge, and private investment in fixed capital formation, as well as the purchase of working capital, accelerated. The momentum was not, however, maintained. On the contrary, the most striking characteristic of developments in the second half of the 1980s was agricultural *stagnation*. The sources of this disappointing performance are many. So too, by implication, are the reasons for the failure of the shifting economic relationship between peasant and state to become more firmly embedded in a system of farming guided by market demand and geared towards commodity production.

From this point of view, perhaps the most intractable problem has been the inability to resolve the issue of land tenure. The principle of public ownership of land remains a shibboleth and although it has had its fierce advocates, privatization seems to have been effectively ruled out for the time being. Nevertheless, the right to transfer *leasehold* rights of cultivated land, enshrined in a Central Committee directive of 1984,[56] does exist. Such official endorsement should, it would seem, have encouraged a more professional and efficient use of land and given peasants enough confidence to invest in their farms' future. In practice this has not been the case and, despite earlier predictions of a mushrooming leasehold market, such quasi-property transactions have not taken place. The reality is that in the absence of any effective rental market in China, the opportunity cost of holding land has remained very low. The resulting institutional uncertainty has added to peasants' anxieties and made them reluctant to engage in long-run investment.

Meanwhile, the changing roles of peasant and state, given shape by the institutional and economic reforms initiated after 1978, have had a significant impact upon the structure of farming. The pre-eminent role of the state as arbiter of what should be produced has given way to an extension of peasants' own decision-making powers. Their response has been to culti-

---

56. "Zhonggong zhongyang guanyu 1984 nian nongcun gongzuo de tongzhi" ("Circular of the Central Committee of the CCP on rural work in 1984"), *NYNJ 1984*, pp. 1–4.

vate those crops which offer the greatest monetary reward. It is a development which neo-Classical economists would applaud. But it has also been the source of further tension between farmers and government. There is, after all, no guarantee that the structure of land use favoured by peasants in their search for income maximization will be the same as that which satisfies the state's priorities. Whilst increases in farm purchase prices after 1978 raised the profitability of crop farming as a whole, they particularly enhanced the value of economic crops. Thus the 1980s witnessed a major expansion in the cash crop area at the expense of that of basic cereals—and this in the context of an overall decline in the arable area. This was the background against which the government was compelled to intervene in an effort to maintain supplies of basic agricultural items—above all, food grains—for the urban and industrial sectors. For all the euphoria which surrounded the attempted liberalization of agricultural production *and distribution* in 1985, maintenance of government control over the real farm surplus soon re-emerged as a policy imperative.

It would be naive to underestimate the potency of such dilemmas and the difficulty of resolving them. What seems clear, however, is that unless they *are* resolved, an effective balance of economic power between peasant and state—one that meets the productive demands of agricultural development, as well as the welfare needs of peasants, and simultaneously allows a rational division of responsibilities between individual farmer and central government—will not be achieved.

Appendix A: Fiscal and Financial Resource Flows into Agriculture

TABLE A1. State Investment in Agricultural Capital Construction, 1953–89

	Volume of investment (mill. yuan)	As % total state capital construction investment
1953	774	8.6
1954	416	4.2
1955	618	6.2
1956	1,188	7.7
1957	1,187	8.3
1958	2,626	9.8
1959	3,292	9.4
1960	4,515	11.6
1961	1,699	13.3
1962	1,439	20.2
1963	2,261	23.0
1964	2,688	18.7
1965	2,497	13.9
. . . .		
1975	3,840	9.4
1976	4,104	10.9
1977	4,175	10.9
1978	5,334	10.6
1979	5,792	11.1
1980	5,203	9.3
1981	2,921	6.6
1982	3,412	6.1
1983	3,545	6.0
1984	3,712	5.0
1985	3,591	3.3
1986	3,506	3.0
1987	4,211	3.1
1988	4,617	3.0
1989	5,065	3.3

Sources:
1953–84 from *ZGGD*, p. 97. 1985–89 from *TJNJ 1990*, p. 166.

TABLE A2. State Financial Expenditure in Support of Agriculture, 1953–87

	Total state expenditure in support of agriculture	Expenditure in support of agricultural production and various operational expenses	Expenditure on basic capital construction	Circulating capital	Expenditure on science and technology	Other	Financial expenditure for agriculture as % total spending for all purposes
				of which:			
1953	1,184	299	577	41		267	5.4
1954	1,351	398	487	26		440	5.5
1955	1,499	582	571	32		314	5.6
1956	2,699	770	1,363	92		474	8.8
1957	2,350	799	1,093	100		358	7.7
1958	4,386	934	3,026	109		317	10.7
1959	5,823	2,205	2,991	242		385	10.5
1960	9,052	3,373	4,543	501		635	13.8
1961	5,488	3,101	1,235	377		775	15.0
1962	3,823	1,929	867	270		757	12.5
1963	5,560	2,219	1,848	409	81	1,003	16.4
1964	6,716	2,092	2,617	213	100	1,694	16.8
1965	5,498	1,729	2,351	288	105	1,025	11.8
1966	5,439	1,911	2,370	246	128	784	10.0
1967	4,582	1,612	2,208	242	30	490	10.4
1968	3,347	1,289	1,223	282		553	9.3
1969	4,803	1,487	1,792	246		1,278	9.1
1970	4,940	1,591	2,252	279		818	7.6
1971	6,075	1,965	3,327	214	5	564	8.3
1972	6,513	2,510	3,147	256	7	593	8.5
1973	8,517	3,549	3,748	302	8	910	10.5
1974	9,121	3,823	3,697	307	13	1,281	11.5
1975	9,896	4,253	3,556	320	10	1,757	12.1
1976	11,049	4,601	3,991	445	78	1,934	13.7
1977	10,812	5,068	3,598	358	93	1,695	12.8
1978	15,066	7,695	5,114	763	106	1,388	13.6
1979	17,433	9,011	6,241	544	152	1,485	13.7
1980	14,995	8,212	4,859	399	131	1,394	12.4
1981	11,021	7,368	2,415	212	118	908	9.9
1982	12,049	7,988	2,881	207	113	860	10.4
1983	13,287	8,666	3,425	77	181	938	10.3
1984	14,129	9,593	3,363		218	955	9.1
1985	15,362	10,104	3,773		195	1,290	8.3
1986	18,420	12,430	4,387		270	1,333	7.9
1987	19,546	13,416	4,681		228	1,247	6.5

Note:
  All figures in million *yuan*, unless otherwise stated.
Source:
  TJNJ 1990, p. 239.

TABLE A3(i). Deposits and Loans of the People's Bank of China

	Total domestic deposits from all sources	of which:		Total loans for all purposes	of which:	
		Rural deposits	As % total deposits		Agricultural loans	As % total loans
1979	134,004	20,371	15.20	203,963	13,680	6.71
1980	165,864	23,984	14.46	241,430	17,588	7.28
1981	200,558	27,840	13.88	276,467	18,972	6.86
1982	228,714	32,994	14.43	305,227	21,245	6.96
1983	276,159	39,127	14.17	343,105	23,119	8.33
1984	338,613	37,243	11.00	441,957	36,808	8.33
1985	427,303	44,956	10.52	590,551	41,663	7.05
1986	538,187	55,964	10.40	759,040	57,037	7.51
1987	657,205	62,630	9.53	903,235	68,583	7.59
1988	742,562	66,955	9.02	1,055,133	81,421	7.72

Note:
All figures in million *yuan*, unless otherwise stated.
Sources:
1979–82 from *TJNJ 1986*, p. 616, except for data on agricultural loans, which are from SSB, *Zhongguo nongcun tongji nianjian, 1989* (*Chinese Rural Statistical Yearbook, 1989*) (Beijing: Zhongguo tongji chubanshe), p. 294; and *NYJJZL*, p. 321.
1983–88 from *TJNJ 1990*, p. 666.

TABLE A3(ii). Deposits and Loans of the Agricultural Bank

	Total volume of rural deposits	Total volume of rural loans for all purposes	of which:	
			Agricultural loans	As % total
1979	29,800	45,100	10,300	22.84
1980	39,500	67,200	12,200	18.15
1986	122,400	199,700	23,500	11.77
1987	149,700	232,300	31,800	13.69
1988	173,100	262,800	36,500	13.89

Note:
All figures in million *yuan*, unless otherwise stated.
Source:
NYNJ 1989, p. 113.

TABLE A3(iii). Deposits and Loans of Rural Credit Co-operatives

	Total volume of deposits	of which:		Total volume of loans	of which:	
		Private savings deposits of rural h.h.s	As % total deposits		Agricultural loans	As % total loans
1979	21,590	7,840	36.31	4,830	3,450	71.43
1980	27,230	11,700	42.97	5,270	3,600	68.31
1985	72,490	56,480	77.91	39,990	23,560	58.91
1986	96,230	76,610	79.61	56,850	30,260	53.23
1987	122,520	100,570	82.02	77,130	41,200	53.42
1988	139,760	113,920	81.51	89,470	45,090	50.40

Note:
  All figures in million *yuan*, unless otherwise stated.
Source:
NYNJ 1989, p. 113.

Appendix B: Tax and Procurement Flows out of Agriculture

TABLE B1. The Agricultural Tax, 1953–89

	Tax levy (mill. yuan)	As % of all taxes	As % of total state revenue
1953	2,751	22.99	12.3
1954	3,313	25.06	12.6
1955	3,072	24.10	11.3
1956	2,965	21.05	10.3
1957	2,967	19.16	9.6
1958	3,259	17.39	8.4
1959	3,301	16.13	6.8
1960	2,804	13.27	4.9
1961	2,166	13.64	6.1
1962	2,283	14.09	7.3
1963	2,400	14.61	7.0
1964	2,589	14.23	6.5
1965	2,578	12.62	5.4
1966	2,955	13.31	5.3
1967	2,895	14.72	6.9
1968	3,002	15.67	8.3
1969	2,956	12.56	5.6
1970	3,198	11.37	4.8
1971	3,086	9.87	4.1
1972	2,837	8.95	3.7
1973	3,052	8.75	3.8
1974	3,006	8.34	3.8
1975	2,945	7.31	3.6
1976	2,914	7.14	3.8
1977	2,933	6.26	3.4
1978	2,840	5.47	2.5
1979	2,951	5.49	2.7
1980	2,767	4.84	2.6
1981	2,835	4.50	2.6
1982	2,938	4.20	2.6
1983	3,296	4.25	2.6
1984	3,484	3.68	2.3
1985	4,205	2.06	2.3
1986	4,452	2.13	2.0
1987	5,181	2.42	2.2
1988	7,369	3.08	2.8
1989	8,320	3.05	2.9

Source:
TJNJ 1990, pp. 229 and 233.

TABLE B2. Grain Production and Procurement, 1952–87

	Total output of grain	Gross grain procurement	As % total output	Net grain procurement	As % total output	Therefore grain re-sales to peasants
1952	163.92	33.27	20.3	28.19	17.2	5.08
1957	195.05	48.04	24.6	33.87	17.4	14.17
1962	160.00	38.15	23.8	25.72	16.1	12.43
1965	194.53	48.69	25.0	33.60	17.3	15.09
1970	239.96	54.44	22.7	42.02	17.5	12.42
1975	284.52	60.86	21.4	43.95	15.4	16.91
1976	286.31	58.25	20.3	40.72	14.2	17.53
1977	282.73	56.62	20.0	37.56	13.3	19.06
1978	304.77	61.74	20.3	42.71	14.0	19.03
1979	332.12	71.99	21.7	51.70	15.6	20.29
1980	320.56	73.00	22.8	47.97	15.0	25.03
1981	325.02	78.51	24.2	48.78	15.0	29.73
1982	354.50	91.86	25.9	59.11	16.7	32.75
1983	387.28	119.86	30.9	85.27	22.0	34.59
1984	407.31	141.69	34.8	94.61	23.2	47.08
1985	379.11	115.64	30.5	58.32	15.4	57.32
1986	391.51	134.60	34.4	100.11	25.6	34.49
1987	404.73	141.15	34.9	109.93	27.2	31.22

Note:
All figures in million tonnes of unhusked grain.
Source:
TJNJ 1988, p. 699.

The Soldier and the State in China: The Political Work System in the People's Liberation Army*

David Shambaugh

The military is a key actor in the political life of many nations. Across the developing and socialist worlds, the armed forces have served as far more than guarantors of national security as they sustain civilian elites in power or often seize it themselves. In China there has been a long tradition of military rule during much of the modern era—one need think only of Li Hongzhang and the Beiyang Army, the Republic's first president General Yuan Shikai, the warlords of the 1920s, or Generalissimo Chiang Kai-shek and the *Guominjun* (the twin sibling of the ruling Guomindang). In post-1949 China former and active-duty military officers (as well as the military as an institution) have been central actors in the political life of the nation, effectively administering the country from 1949–52 and 1967–73. However, this article is not so much about the militarization of politics in China as about the politicization of the military.

Professionalism and politicization are not necessarily mutually exclusive in any army, including the Chinese. Western armies—often considered ideals of apolitical professionalism—have certainly been indoctrinated with the political ideologies of liberal democracy and anti-communism. In the Chinese People's Liberation Army (PLA) professionalism and politics have gone hand in hand for more than 60 years. The PLA has been politicized from its inception. Unlike the western experience, though, this po-liticization has meant administrative control by a single political party (the CCP) and the intensive propagation of that party's political line and values within the military ranks. This chapter examines the politicization of the PLA over the period from 1927 to 1991.

Since the PLA forcefully suppressed the pro-democracy demonstrations in Beijing in June 1989 political work in the military has been dramatically increased. Official statements of the Communist Party and state leadership

* In addition to the members of *The China Quarterly* workshop on "The Individual and the State," the author is particularly indebted to Alastair I. Johnston for his comments on an earlier draft. I also wish to thank the administrative and library staff at the Institute of International Relations of National Cheng-chi University, Taipei, as well as the Chinese Academy of Social Sciences in Beijing for helping to facilitate parts of the research project. Research on Taiwan was supported by the Committee on Scientific and Scholarly Communi-cation with the United States, Academia Sinica, Republic of China, under the IUP–CSSC Language and Research Fellowship Program; research in China was supported by The British Academy/ESRC China Exchange Scheme with the Chinese Academy of Social Sciences.

indicate that they consider the demonstrations of April–June 1989 to have been a "life and death struggle" for the sustenance of Communist Party rule and the People's Republic itself.[1] The PLA was used to sustain Party rule and guarantee the republic.[2] Yet, the hesitancy to employ force displayed by some units and their commanders caused great alarm among Party leaders, and raised afresh the role of civil–military relations in the succession to the post-Deng Xiaoping era. For those leaders engaged in this succession struggle, the execution of Romanian leader Nicolai Ceausescu in December 1989—particularly the role the Romanian military played in his overthrow—deepened concern about PLA loyalty. To ensure continued Party control of the PLA, intensive campaigns have been carried out within the Chinese military since Tiananmen.[3] The PLA's political work system (*zhengzhi gongzuo xitong*) (PWS) has been the central conduit for this indoctrination and continues to be the principal means by which the Party attempts to "control the gun."

Examining the political work system in the PLA also offers the opportunity to reconsider one of the long-standing debates in the field of civil–military relations in communist systems, namely do communist militaries embody the corporate autonomy prevalent in western armed forces or do they constitute a fundamentally different model based on their organic relationship with the communist party/state? What does the Chinese case tell us about this issue?

Theoretical and Historical Considerations

Analysis of the relationship between the soldier and the state in contemporary China requires consideration of the "soldier" in a collective sense. As is amply demonstrated in the other contributions to this volume, it is possible to interview individuals among other social and occupational strata

1. See, for example, Deng Xiaoping's speech to martial law troops on 9 June: "Deng Xiaoping tongzhi zai jiejian shoudu jieyan budui jun yishang ganbu shide jianghua," in Zhonggong zhongyang xuanchuanbu (ed.), *Xuanchuan dongtai: 1989 xuanbianben* (Beijing: Renmin ribao chubanshe, 1991), pp. 109–15.

2. One could view the 4 June PLA intervention as "professional" in that the army acted at the behest of the highest organs of state and the military (the State Council and Central Military Commission), and—as the Chinese authorities have argued—the survival of the Chinese state was at stake. What could be more professional than to ensure national security as directed by the commander-in-chief and other members of the CMC? An alternative interpretation would have it that the Party/state and military were controlled by individuals who constituted a factional grouping, and the PLA intervened in order to sustain this group—rather than the institutions—in power.

3. The political campaigns in the PLA have been paralleled by efforts to increase the stature of the PLA in civilian society via the "national defence education movement" (*guofang jiaoyu yundong*). Similar to the "Learn from the PLA" campaign of 1964, this movement propagates martial values in society, patriotism, reminiscences of past wars, and military readiness.

and collect data on cohorts of Chinese workers, peasants, youth, cadres or intellectuals (often revealing temporal and spatial variation), yet access to individual soldiers is severely restricted for national security and other reasons (and such access has been further curtailed since Tiananmen, particularly by a series of regulations enacted in early 1991 to restrict foreigners' interaction with the PLA).

There also exist non-methodological reasons for considering the soldier collectively. Unlike these other groups, the military occupies a special place in society. Its self-identity is often described as a "corporate" one because of the military's *esprit de corps* and occupational cohesiveness, a cohesion not necessarily shared by these other groups. Moreover, by its very nature, the military has a different relationship with the state—as it stands as the ultimate guarantor of the civilian state and the nation itself.

When discussing the subject of the soldier and the state in China a useful point of departure is the taxonomy set forth in Samuel H. Huntington's classic work on the subject.[4] Writing four decades ago, he posited an ideal-type theory of civil–military relations. For Huntington, the ideal relationship of the modern military to the civilian state was one where "the military profession exists to serve the state."[5] Throughout his study Huntington therefore argued the case of military separateness from the civilian, political state. A professional military is, by his definition, to be politically neutral and subject to civilian control. Praetorian intervention into the political arena is considered anathema in the western ideal type.[6] Huntington's argument hinged on the unique specialized knowledge and technical expertise of the military professional; the military's monopoly of lethal force; the bureaucratic organization and hierarchical structure of authority relations within the military; the derivative corporate identity of the military; the military's clientalistic relationship with the civilian state and autonomous role in civil society; and particularly the socialization of the professional officer corps (referred to as "the military mind"). Thus, in Huntington's schema, the relationship of soldier and state is embodied in the professional officer corps.[7]

Huntington's book stimulated a whole generation of civil–military studies, some of which sought to apply his thesis in other national contexts. However, with very few exceptions, Huntington's conceptualization has

4. Samuel Huntington, *The Soldier and the State: The Theory and Politics of Civil–Military Relations* (Cambridge, Mass: Harvard University Press, 1957).

5. *Ibid*. p. 72.

6. In a subsequent work Huntington amended his ideal type to take account of the upsurge of coups d'etat in the decolonized, developing world. See Samuel Huntington, *Political Order in Changing Societies* (New Haven: Yale University Press, 1968), ch. 4.

7. "The skill of the officer is the management of violence; his responsibility is the military security of his client, society . . . His behavior in relation to society is guided by an awareness that his skill can only be utilized for purposes approved by society through its political agent, the state." Huntington, *The Soldier and the State*, pp. 15–16.

intriguingly *not* been extended to the field of Chinese military studies.[8] Part of the reason for this is the fact that most western PLA-watchers assumed that the political commissar system inherited from the Soviet Red Army created a system of Party penetration of the military that invalidated the Huntingtonian ideal of military corporatism.

The general non-fit of the China case into the Huntingtonian framework is therefore generally attributed to the PLA's revolutionary history and the continued post-revolutionary infiltration of the military by the Chinese Communist Party. The notion of a dichotomized soldier–state relationship based on an autonomous military does not empirically reflect the PLA's past in which political power grew out of the barrel of a gun. An essential symbiosis existed between revolutionary soldiers and Party members in pursuit of state power. The politicization of the military and militarization of the Party at this early stage of development were mutually reinforcing. As a result, "control" of the military by the Party was not then a pressing issue despite the creation of the political commissar system. As will be argued in this study, over time control of army by Party became more salient as the revolutionary symbiosis faded, the PLA increasingly assumed a more professional and corporate identity, and the Party elite had to rely on brute force to sustain itself in power.

During the course of the revolutionary struggle and anti-Japanese war the communist forces developed an extensive and intricate political commissar system designed to infuse troops with revolutionary and nationalistic fervour, conduct propaganda work among peasants, and ensure Party control over the military. This system drew on the experience of the Soviet Red Army as well as an indigenous tradition developed in the Nationalist Army (*Guominjun*).[9] The latter was clearly evident in the training of officers at the Whampoa Military Academy, where communist commissars were also trained until the breakup of the first united front in 1927.

An independent political work system in the communist forces developed from the time of the 1 August 1927 Nanchang Uprising (which gave birth to the latter-day PLA), when a General Political Department was set up under the Revolutionary Committee of the rebel forces that had seized Nanchang. Soon after Nanchang the communist forces underwent reorgani-

8. For two state-of-the-field surveys of CMS see Jonathan D. Pollack, "The study of Chinese military politics: Toward a framework for analysis," in Catherine M. Kelleher (ed.), *Political–Military Systems: Comparative Perspectives* (Beverly Hills: Sage Publications, 1974), pp. 239–69; and Harlan W. Jencks, "Watching China's military: A personal view," *Problems of Communism* (May–June 1986), pp. 71–8. One notable attempt to place Huntington's thesis in the Chinese context is Paul H. B. Godwin's "Professionalism and politics in the Chinese armed forces," in Dale R. Herspring and Ivan Volgyes (eds.), *Civil–Military Relations in Communist Systems* (Boulder: Westview Press, 1978), pp. 219–40.

9. For thorough accounts of these influences and development of the political work system in the Chinese communist forces before 1949 see Jiang Siyi (ed.), *Zhongguo renmin jiefangjun zhengzhi gongzuoshi* (Beijing: Jiefangjun zhengzhi xueyuan chubanshe, 1984); and Xu Kai, "Zhongguo renmin jiefangjun zongzhengzhibu yan'ge," *Junshi lishi*, No. 3 (1990), pp. 50–2.

zation (*zhengbian*), and "Party representatives" (*dang daibiao*) were assigned to the three branches of the Workers and Peasants Red Army; Mao Zedong became the Party representative of the Fourth Front Army.[10] The famous Gutian conference of December 1929 was a pivotal event for institutionalizing the PWS in the communist forces. Mao's speech to that meeting set the tone of army–Party and army–mass relations for the remainder of the revolutionary struggle. It was in this speech that Mao criticized the "purely military viewpoint" and made the case for a politicized military, arguing that "the Party shall always control the gun." The Gutian conference institutionalized the political commissar system (*zhengzhi weiyuan zhidu*), a system further refined in Order No. 6 (February 1931) of the Revolutionary Military Commission and the February 1932 "Provisional regulations for political work of the Chinese Workers and Peasants Red Army" (which created a General Political Department).[11] In the Jingganshan base area, the Fourth Front Army established Party branches at the squad, platoon, company, and regiment levels, as well as establishing the Military Committee as a separate organ within the Party leadership.

This system remained intact during the Long March but underwent further development once the communist forces reached Yan'an. In August 1937 a Political Department was created in the Eighth Route Army, and in October of the same year the CCP Central Committee decided to re-establish a General Political Department under a Central Military Commission.[12] Despite Guominjun demands to subordinate the communist political commissars to their own, dual command systems were sustained during the second united front. Also, the Chinese People's Anti-Japanese Military-Political Academy was established at Yan'an, training 17,740 officers between 1936 and 1939.[13] In October 1945 a General Political Department (*zong zhengzhi bu*) (GPD) was formally established as one of the central headquarters under the reorganized and newly amalgamated People's Liberation Army.[14] From 1945–49 Liu Shaoqi served as director of the reconstituted GPD.[15] The decision on "Perfecting the Party committee system," taken at the Seventh National Congress of the CCP in Yan'an in 1945, restrengthened the Party committee system (as opposed to the political commissar system) in the PLA, which had evidently been abolished earlier due to "Wang Ming's 'left opportunist' line."[16] Thereafter, the Party com-

10. Pu Xingzu *et al.*, *Dangdai Zhongguo zhengzhi zhidu* (Shanghai renmin chubanshe, 1990), pp. 327–8.
11. See respectively, Xu Kai, "Zhongguo renmin jiefangjun zongzhengzhibu yan'ge," p. 50; and "Dangdai Zhongguo" congshu bianji weiyuanhui (ed.), *Dangdai Zhongguo jundui de junshi gongzuo* (Vol. 2) (Beijing: Zhongguo shehuikexueyuan chubanshe, 1989), p. 21.
12. *Dangdai Zhongguo junshi gongzuo, ibid.*
13. As cited in Cheng Hsiao-shih, *Party–Military Relations in the PRC and Taiwan: Paradoxes of Control* (Boulder: Westview Press, 1990), p. 30.
14. *Ibid.*
15. Xu Kai, "Zhongguo renmin jiefangjun zongzhengzhibu yan'ge," pp. 50–51.
16. See Chi Haotian, "Strive to raise the leadership level of the Party committees, and ensure the Party's absolute leadership over the army," *Qiushi*, No. 2 (16 January 1990), pp. 2–

mittee system not only became a key organ of political work in the army, but also a locus of *military* decision-making as well. Unit commanders would make joint battlefield decisions with their Party counterparts and political commissars.

The historical interconnection of the revolutionary military and the CCP in China (and the organizational penetration of the former by the latter) have thus been critically important factors in defining civil–military relations in the post-1949 period. Indeed, the first generation of China's post-1949 politicians were pre-1949 soldiers. The politicization of the PLA during the revolutionary struggle fostered an organizational structure and uniquely socialized military—particularly officer corps—that in the post-revolutionary environment set the PLA apart in corporate terms from the militaries of industrialized or other developing states.

The China case has hence been used by comparativists to create a separate analytical category for the "revolutionary soldier" as distinct from the professional and praetorian soldier.[17] The *professional soldier*, arising out of the Prussian experience, was thought of in Huntingtonian terms and referred to the 20th-century militaries of the United States, Western European nations, Japan, and former British dominions. The *praetorian soldier* (which took its name from the Roman guard) referred to the post-colonial, developing nations of the post-war era in which the military usurped civilian rule either by exercising a veto power in arbitrating between civilian factions, or through seizing power and establishing alternative rule. The coup d'etat is the venue of the modern praetorian. The *revolutionary soldier*, by contrast, is a product of the national liberation movement. In such an environment, an essential symbiosis exists between soldier and political revolutionary in pursuit of state power.

It is therefore the politicization of the military that lies at the core of the relationship between soldier and state in China, and with which this article is principally concerned. What follows is therefore an exploration into the *hyphen* in civil–military relations in China. My essential argument, more generally, is that in the 60 years of its existence the PLA's identity has been inextricably intertwined with the Party/state. Because of its historical origins, a perceived identity of interests, and the organizational devices that facilitate Party penetration of the military, the soldier has come to the rescue of the Chinese state (or more precisely certain leaders and factions within the Party/state) more than once—including during the Tiananmen demonstrations. But these were not praetorian interventions. The PLA intervened precisely because of its *symbiotic* relationship with the Party/state, rather than as a function of Bonapartist tendencies.

10, in *Foreign Broadcast Information Service Daily Report—China* (hereafter FBIS—CHI), 8 March 1990, p. 39.

17. The following discussion draws upon the tripartite division in the writings of Amos Perlmutter. See, in particular, his *The Military and Politics in Modern Times* (New Haven: Yale University Press, 1977).

Thus, just as the Communist Party undergirds the state apparatus in contemporary China (thus giving rise to a Party/state amalgam[18]), so too does it penetrate the military. Huntington's professional/political dichotomy thus proves to be a false one in the Chinese case as the CCP and PLA are intertwined and have sustained each other's power for more than 60 years. In addition, the PLA has long pursued multiple missions in the Chinese economy, polity and society considered legitimate by civilians and soldiers alike. This is not to say that professional values and ethics *qua* Huntington have not taken root in the PLA, as indeed they have, particularly during the 1950s and 1980s. But it is to recognize that politicization and military professionalization are not mutually exclusive—as the Israeli, Vietnamese, North Korean, Libyan, Iranian, Iraqi and Peruvian cases further demonstrate.

The assumption of corporateness prevalent in many studies of the PLA and civil–military relations in China is therefore somewhat misguided. My view of civil–military relations in China shares a great deal in common with William Odom's objection to the corporatist approach when applied to the Soviet military.[19] In 1978 Odom offered an alternative interpretation based on the interpenetration of the military and Party/state. Interlocking elites, high Party membership within the military, the political commissar system, military administration of major public works and regions of the nation, the militarization of symbols in society, and sustained indoctrination were all examples Odom cited in the Soviet case that apply to China as well.

This is not necessarily a unique argument in the field of Chinese military studies. In fact, some observers have cited the organic Party–military connection as evidence that the Chinese military shared the essential characteristics of its Soviet, rather than western, counterpart.[20] While this assumption has underlain some analysis of civil–military relations in China, it was usually explained at the elite level by estimating the percentage of military representatives on the CCP Central Committee or Politburo in order to advance the "interlocking directorate" thesis (see Figure 1).

The PLA as Political Actor

Military leaders have played monumental roles in Chinese elite politics since the early 1950s. The PLA has been a key actor in "civilian" policy making. As Perlmutter and LeoGrande put it in a more general context:

18. See Tang Tsou, *The Cultural Revolution and Post-Mao Reforms* (Chicago: University of Chicago Press, 1986).

19. William Odom, "The Party-military connection: A critique," in Herspring and Volges (eds.), *Civil–Military Relations in Communist Systems*, ch. 3.

20. One of the most persuasive studies to advance this argument is Monte R. Bullard, *China's Political-Military Evolution* (Boulder: Westview Press, 1985).

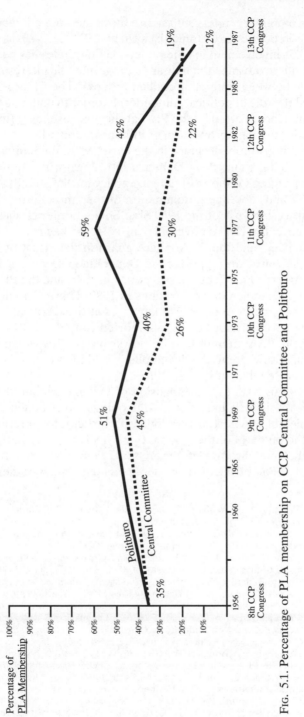

FIG. 5.1. Percentage of PLA membership on CCP Central Committee and Politburo

"To speak of military 'intervention' is a misnomer; the military is a normal participant in politics in Communist systems."[21]

The PLA's involvement in elite policy-making circles has been an important way both to advance the military's programmatic interests and play an arbiter role between competing civilian groups.[22] The Chinese military has also played the role of political contender. In order to understand the strong political influence exerted by the PLA at the elite level over time, one need only consider the high proportion of military cadres who administered the General Administrative Regions in the early 1950s; the military dimension of the Gao Gang affair; Peng Dehuai's showdown with Mao at Lushan in 1959; Luo Ruiqing's critique of defence policy in 1965; the PLA's intervention in 1967 and subsequent domination of the "three-in-one" revolutionary committees; the use of the 1969 Sino-Soviet border clashes to enhance PLA influence; Lin Biao's power play in 1971; the key role of Ye Jianying, Wang Dongxing, and the PLA palace guard in the arrest of the Gang of Four; Xu Shiyou's role in protecting Deng Xiaoping during 1976–77 and then helping to propel Deng back to power in 1978; and the PLA's suppression of the Tiananmen demonstrations in 1989. There is no doubt that the military (or elements of it) played key roles at these critical junctures, but in no case—save perhaps Lin Biao's aborted coup d'etat (if that is what it was)—did the PLA attempt to seize power per se. Praetorian intervention so prevalent elsewhere in the developing world has not manifested itself in the People's Republic of China. Why?

This brings us back to the dimension of Odom's critique that is particularly applicable in the Chinese case—the political work system (PWS) in the PLA. While not underestimating the importance of the interlocking directorate at the pinnacle of the system, the PWS is how the Party principally controls the gun throughout the system. Few have explored this core mechanism of Party control in any depth, and most such studies are dated.[23]

---

21. Amos Perlmutter and William M. LeoGrande, "The Party in uniform," *The American Political Science Review*, Vol. 76 (December 1982), p. 781.

22. For an excellent analysis of these roles, and the nature of military participation in domestic politics more generally, see Harry Harding, "The role of the military in Chinese politics," in Victor C. Falkenheim (ed.), *Citizens and Groups in Contemporary China* (Ann Arbor: Center for Chinese Studies, University of Michigan, 1987), pp. 213–306.

23. In addition to Bullard, *China's Political–Military Evolution*, see John Gittings, *The Role of the Chinese Army* (London: Oxford University Press, 1967), especially pp. 99–118; and Ying Mao Kau *et al.*, *The Political Work System of the Chinese Communist System: Analysis and Documents* (Providence: Brown University East Asia Language and Research Center, 1971); Ellis Joffe, *Party and Army: Professionalism and Political Control in the Chinese Officer Corps, 1949–1964* (Cambridge, Mass.: Harvard University Press, 1965); Jane Price, *Cadres, Commanders and Commissars* (Boulder: Westview Press, 1976). Probably the best, and most recent, study of the PLA political work system is Cheng Hsiao-shih, *Party and Military Relations in the PRC and Taiwan*. Cheng advances the thesis (shared by this observer) that it is not the political commissar system but rather the Party committee system that is really the key organ of political control. For more on the Party committee system in the PLA, and a broader study of civil–military relations, see Jonathan D. Pollack, "Structure and process in

Political penetration of the Chinese armed forces is usually more assumed than explicated. One must begin by examining the parent organ of the political commissar system—the PLA General Political Department under the Central Military Commission.

The History of Political Work in the PLA

The political work system in the PLA built upon the structure set up prior to 1949. The locus of political work in the military since 1949, as before, centres on the General Political Department. The GPD is one of the three PLA general "headquarters" (*zong silingbu*) directly subordinate to the CCP Central Military Commission, the other two being the General Staff Department (*zong canmou bu*) and the General (Logistics) Department (*zong houqin bu*). When the communists came to power in 1949 the organizational structure within the People's Liberation Army forces was not divided into these three general headquarters. This was done during a reorganization of the Chinese High Command in late October 1949,[24] although the GPD did not assume its full status until April 1950.[25] The General Political Department began its post-liberation evolution from this time. Initially, it was divided into five sub-departments: the organization, propaganda, security, culture and youth departments.[26] A liaison department was added in mid-1951 to handle POWs from the Korean War and to conduct propaganda among enemy troops.[27]

The history of the GPD since 1949 has generally paralleled that of civil–military relations more generally.[28] The GPD's directors and its organizational status have reflected both the national politics of the time and the proclivities of the minister of defence and other senior military elites. Since 1949 the GPD has had eight directors: Luo Ronghuan (April 1950–December 1956 and January 1961–December 1963), Tan Zheng (December 1956–September 1959), Xiao Hua (September 1964–August 1967), Li Desheng (April 1970–December 1973), Zhang Chunqiao (January 1975–October 1976), Wei Guoqing (August 1977–September 1982), Yu Qiuli

the Chinese military system," in David M. Lampton and Kenneth G. Lieberthal (eds.), *Bureaucratic Structure and Policy Process in China* (Berkeley: University of California Press, forthcoming).

24. Junshikexueyan junshi lishi yanjiubu, *Zhongguo renmin jiefangjun lishi zidian* (Beijing: Junshi kexue chubanshe, 1990), p. 78.

25. *Ibid.*; *Dangdai Zhongguo jundui de junshi gongzuo*, pp. 22–3; and Xu Kai, "Zhongguo renmin jiefangjun zongzhengzhibu yan'ge, p. 51.

26. *Zhongguo renmin jiefangjun lishi zidian*, p. 22.

27. Interview with Li Yunzhi, deputy secretary-general of the PLA General Political Department, 21 June 1991, Beijing.

28. Much of the historical data in this section draws upon the very informative volume, Guofang daxue dangshi dangjian zhenggong jiaoyanshi, *Zhongguo renmin jiefagjun zhengzhi gongzuoshi (shehuizhuyi shiqi)* (Guofang daxue chubanshe, 1989).

(September 1982–November 1987), and Yang Baibing (November 1987–present).[29]

During the Korean War the GPD adopted the Soviet "one man command system" of military commanders, although political commissars were present in all Chinese units. This is common in the PLA during wartime as battlefield decisions are made by the field commanders (*zhihuiyuan*). The commissars' propaganda work during the Korean conflict was aimed not only at enemy troops but also at maintaining morale among weary Chinese forces.[30]

During Peng Dehuai's tenure as Minister of Defence (1954–59), the role of the GPD was enhanced as the "unified command system" was adopted. According to this system, as set out in the 1954 "Regulations Regarding Political Work in the PLA" adopted by the Military Affairs Commission, "unified command under the Party committee system" meant that, in theory, military commanders, political commissars, and Party representatives in the military jointly made decisions.[31] In practice, however, Party cells were slow to be set up below the regiment level.[32] Political work in the armed forces was apparently also an early bone of contention in Sino-Soviet relations, as Soviet experts assigned to the GPD sought to replicate the single command system where commissars were subordinated to commanders, but this was resisted by the Chinese who preferred the unified command system under the leadership of the Party committee.[33] During the early 1950s the GPD was also deeply involved in non-military activities as the PLA constituted the effective government in the General Administrative Regions. For example, the GPD was charged with helping to implement land reform in areas where "localism" was particularly well-entrenched; with disarming remnant KMT forces and "suppressing reactionary bandits" (*zhenya fandong de tufei*); with implementing the "resist America, aid Korea" (*kang-Mei, yuan-Chao*) campaign in China's cities; with enforcing the "three-anti, five-anti" economic campaigns and "remoulding" (*gaizao*) former capitalists and the petty bourgeoisie; and

29. Ma Jibin *et al.*, *Zhongguo gongchangdang zhizheng sishinian* (Beijing: Zhonggong dangshi ziliao chubanshe, 1989), p. 576.

30. On this point see Alexander George, *The Chinese Communist Army in Action* (Stanford: Stanford University Press, 1967). The GPD's activities during the Korean War are also documented in several recent military histories of the war. See, for example, *Dangdai Zhongguo* congshu bianjibu (ed.), *Kang-Mei yuan-Chao zhanzheng* (Beijing: Zhongguo shehuikexueyuan chubanshe, 1990); Junshikexueyuan junshi lishi yanjiubu (ed.), *Kang-Mei yuan-Chao zhanshi* (Beijing: Junshikexueyuan chubanshe, 1988); Chai Chengwen and Zhao Yongtian, *Kang-Mei yuan-Chao jishi* (Beijing: Zhonggong dangshi ziliao, 1987); Junshikexueyuan junshi lishi yanjiubu, *Zhongguo renmin zhiyuanjun kang-Mei yuan-Chao zhanshi* (Beijing: Junshikexueyuan chubanshe, 1988); Xu Yan, *Diyici jiaoliang: kang-Mei yuan-Chao zhanzheng de lishi huigu yu fansi* (Beijing: Zhongguo guanbo dianshi chubanshe, 1990).

31. See Chi Haotian, "Strive to raise the leadership level."

32. Cheng Hsiao-shih, *Party–Military Relations in the PRC and Taiwan*, pp. 96–7.

33. Interview with GPD, 21 June 1991.

with setting up Marxist study groups and initiating the "great transformation" (*da zhuanbian*) in ideological education for China's intellectuals.[34] In
short, the GPD became an integral part of, and contributor to, building
China's post-1949 propaganda apparatus.

In 1957–58 the GPD underwent an internal reorganization. The youth
department was combined into the organization department as was the
culture department into the propaganda department. After this reorganization the GPD had nine sub-departments: organization, cadre management,
propaganda, security, liaison, mass work, military procuratorate, military
court and secretariat.[35]

During the last two years of Peng Dehuai's tenure as defence minister
(1957–59), military professionalism was generally in the ascent,[36] but the
radicalization of the domestic political agenda had a definite impact on the
GPD. For example, the GPD was given the task of implementing the 1957
Party rectification campaign inside the military. From 5 to 15 May 1957, the
GPD convened the "All Army Rectification Conference."[37] As the campaign unfolded inside the PLA it apparently passed through three phases.
First, the GPD emphasized correcting inefficient workstyle and thereby
contributing to the new professional ethic taking root under Peng Dehuai.
But as Mao lurched towards the left and instigated the "anti-rightist movement" the rectification movement in the armed forces entered a second, and
more radical, phase. "Social contradictions" were discovered in the ranks
and the GPD was charged with pressing "class struggle" in the PLA. A total
of 5,749 "rightists" were identified in the military.[38] The third phase was
marked by the unfolding of the Great Leap Forward in 1958, in support of
which the GPD was again called upon to mobilize the PLA. GPD cadres
were subsequently "sent down" (*xiafang*) to the countryside to assist in
establishing people's communes, strengthen Marxist study groups among
the peasantry, and generally "unfold the communist wind." In early 1959, as
Mao began to retract somewhat on commune policy following the Wuhan
plenum and the "second Zhengzhou" enlarged Politburo meeting, the
GPD continued to press the radical line that communism was at hand.[39]
Thus, going into the critical Lushan Plenum in July, Mao found political
allies in the General Political Department of the PLA even though the
evidence is clear that the PLA High Command—most notably the minister

34. See *Zhongguo renmin jiefangjun zhengzhi gongzuoshi*, ch. 1.
35. Xu Kai, "Zhongguo renmin jiefangjun zongzhengzhibu yan'ge," p. 51.
36. This was evidence, for example, at the expanded (and extended) Military Commission
meeting of May–July 1958 when the themes of "regularization" (*zhengguihua*) and modernization (*xiandaihua*) of the armed forces were dominant. For a report of this meeting see Sun
Weiben (ed.), *Zhongguo gongchangdang dangwu gongzuo da zidian* (Beijing: Zhongguo
zhanlan chubanshe, 1989), p. 355.
37. *Zhongguo renmin jiefangjun zhengzhi gongzuoshi*, p. 121.
38. Their rightist labels were not removed until the GPD promulgated Order No. 55 of 1978
exonerating a total of 11,039 persecuted individuals. *Ibid*. p. 125.
39. See *ibid*. p. 137.

of defence Peng Dehuai—were none too happy with the Chairman's policy direction.[40]

The appointment of Lin Biao as defence minister following Peng's dismissal in 1959 only accelerated the radicalization of the GPD and the political work system in the PLA. Peng's sacking was accompanied by a clean-up of personnel in the upper echelons of the GPD, including the director Tan Zheng.[41] Luo Ronghuan was initially brought back to head the GPD, but was replaced by Xiao Hua following Luo's death in December 1963 (Xiao Hua did not actually assume the post until September 1964, but as deputy director he was *de facto* director after Luo's death). Under Lin Biao the PLA became strongly politicized, although interestingly during his tenure defence expenditure also rose to new levels (which can probably be explained by the two-front national security threats China faced at this time).

Immediately after his promotion Lin began to cultivate a power base in the GPD, probably assuming that this would be a natural point from which to extend control as the General Staff and General Logistics departments were strongholds of allies of Peng Dehuai. Being the Maoist sycophant that he was, Lin began to extol the Chairman's virtues in the PLA and leave his imprint on GPD political work. Tan Zheng, then director of GPD, initially resisted the shift in ideological education and lost the brief struggle with Lin.[42] Subsequently at an important September 1960 Central Military Commission meeting (orchestrated by Lin Biao) Tan Zheng was criticized for "errors" and labelled a member of Peng Dehuai's "anti-Party clique" inside the PLA.[43] On 20 October Lin Biao convened an "expanded meeting" (*kuangda huiyi*) on political and ideological work in the military. This meeting produced a 23,000-character document that would serve as the basis of political work in the PLA until the start of the Cultural Revolution. It clearly reflected the Chairman's thinking on "revisionism" and "phony communism" (Soviet experts had been withdrawn from China two months earlier and the Sino-Soviet polemics were now breaking into the open), on

40. See Roderick MacFarquhar, *The Origins of the Cultural Revolution 2: The Great Leap Forward, 1958–1960* (New York: Columbia University Press, 1983), especially ch. 10; and David Bachman, *Bureaucracy, Economy, and Leadership in China: The Institutional Origins of the Great Leap Forward* (Cambridge: Cambridge University Press, 1991). Among the Chinese accounts of Lushan, perhaps the most notable is that of Li Rui (Mao's former secretary), *Lushan huiyi shilu* (Beijing Chunqiu chubanshe and Henan Jiaoyu chubanshe, 1989).

41. This process began immediately following Lushan and Peng's rebuke by Mao. In late August an expanded CMC meeting was convened to denounce the "anti-Party crimes" and "bourgeois military line" of the Peng Dehuai clique (this "verdict" was reversed by the Third Plenum of the 11th Central Committee in 1978). See Sun Weiben (ed.), *Zhongguo gongchangdang dangwu gongzuo da zidian*, p. 355; and *Guanyu xin shiqi jundui zhengzhi gongzuo de jueding*, p. 103.

42. *Zhongguo renmin jiefangjun zhengzhi gongzuoshi*, pp. 164–5.

43. *Ibid.*; Xu Kai, "Zhongguo renmin jiefangjun zongzhengzhibu yan'ge," p. 51; and interviews with knowledgeable members of the PLA General Staff Department, 23 May 1991, and GPD, 21 June 1991.

countering foreign imperialism and its domestic agents, and on using the PLA as a model of political radicalism. These themes were central foci of GPD political work in the armed forces until 1966. In fact, the origins of the 1964 "four cleans" and "socialist education" movements can be traced to the "decision on strengthening political and ideological work in the armed forces" produced by the conference.[44] Moreover, one also sees the origins of the 1964 "Learn from the PLA" campaign in this meeting. In brief, under Lin Biao's tenure the General Political Department became further radicalized and increasingly served as an experimental laboratory for Mao's campaigns against "revisionism" that would eventually blossom into the Great Proletarian Cultural Revolution.

On the eve of the Cultural Revolution Lin Biao again convened an "All-Army Political Work Conference." With the "Learn from the PLA" campaign still in full swing, the three-week conference (December 1965–January 1966) endorsed Lin's slogan that would be heard repeatedly in coming months—"give prominence to politics" (tuchu zhengzhi).

The GPD became an early casualty of the Cultural Revolution. The first leading victim in the PLA was Liang Biye, a deputy director of the GPD, who was personally purged by Lin Biao in February 1966 for claiming that politics was interfering with military modernization.[45] The GPD itself and its director Xiao Hua came under increased pressure by Lin Biao and the ultra-radical Cultural Revolution Small Group (CRSG), particularly Jiang Qing. A version of the CRSG was established within the PLA in September 1966. Known as the PLA Cultural Revolution Group (PLACRG), and headed by Xiao Hua, it did its best to insulate the army and GPD from the CRSG, but Xiao Hua soon encountered the wrath of Jiang Qing who wanted to subordinate the PLACRG to the CRSG and thereby manipulate the Cultural Revolution in the army.[46] Xiao Hua was effectively purged at this time (autumn 1966) although he would not be "officially" attacked and purged until August 1967.[47] With Xiao Hua in eclipse, GPD deputy director General Liu Zhijian effectively administered the PLACRG until January 1967.

44. *Ibid.* p. 180. A *neibu* history of the PLA indicates that this conference and the emerging document were under the "pernicious leftist influence" of Lin Biao. The decisions of the conference, including the purge of Tan Zheng, were officially repudiated by the GPD on 24 April 1978. See *Guanyu xin shiqi jundui zhengzhi gongzuo de jueding*, pp. 108–13 for this repudiation. Also see Zhongguo renmin jiefangjun junshikexueyuan (ed.), *Zhongguo renmin jiefangjun dashiji* (Beijing: Junshi kexueyuan chubanshe, 1983), p. 365.

45. See Harvey W. Nelsen, *The Chinese Military System: An Organizational Study of the People's Liberation Army* (Boulder: Westview Press, 1981), pp. 102–3. For more on the GPD during the Cultural Revolution see Glenn Dick, "The General Political Department," in William W. Whitson (ed.), *The Military and Political Power in China in the 1970s* (New York: Praeger, 1972), pp. 176–7; and Cheng Hsiao-shih, *Party–Military Relations in the PRC and Taiwan*, pp. 100–9.

46. Interview at the Central Committee Party History Research Office, 28 May 1991.

47. *Ibid.*

When the Cultural Revolution escalated in 1967 following the "January storm" and pressure for military intervention rose, the PLACRG played a leading role in resisting further military involvement.[48] As the PLA was called upon to "support the left," Lin Biao and Jiang Qing succeeded in having Liu Zhijian purged for obstructing the Cultural Revolution in the military. The PLACRG was then reorganized and placed under the dual control of the Central Military Commission and the CRSG, with Jiang Qing being appointed as "adviser." Marshall Xu Xiangqian was personally appointed by Mao to be the new head of the PLACRG[49]—a post not to be sought under such conditions. The PLACRG managed to survive eight difficult months, including the Wuhan mutiny in July, before being abolished as part of the movement to "drag out the small handful of capitalist roaders in the army" in August 1967. Xiao Hua, who had been out of public view for a year, was "dragged out," charged with building an "independent kingdom" in the GPD, and purged in September. Thereafter the GPD "came to a complete standstill" (tanhuan).[50]

This state of affairs lasted until October 1968 when the CCP Military Commission re-established a political work division (zhenggongzu).[51] In October 1969 the GPD was reconstituted with a general office and a skeleton staff, and on 30 April 1970 veteran commander Li Desheng was appointed to head it. For four years Li oversaw an essentially defunct organization (less than 200 individuals worked in the entire GPD xitong[52]). He and the GPD weathered the abortive coup and death of Lin Biao in September 1971.[53] Li's military credentials (as opposed to political pedigree) enabled him to survive the post-Lin purges in the upper echelons of the PLA (although a good number of GPD personnel were purged as Lin Biao accomplices). As part of the major reshuffle of military region commanders in December 1973, Li was reappointed to serve as commander of the sensitive Shenyang Military Region, which put him in charge of forces opposite the Soviet Union during a very tense time. After a year's interval, he was succeeded as GPD director by Gang of Four member Zhang Chunqiao, who attempted to use his new position to build a power base

48. Nelsen, The Chinese Military System, p. 104. This point is also noted in He Chancai and Gao Wangchun (eds.), Xin Zhongguo dashidian (Beijing: Kexue jixue wenzhai chubanshe, 1990), pp. 80, 82.

49. Interview at Central Committee Party History Research Office, 28 May 1991. There is apparently a misunderstanding in the western literature on this point as it is generally thought that veteran Marshall He Long was appointed to head the PLACRG. This was refuted in interviews by scholars in the Party History Research Office as well as the deputy secretary-general of the GPD, who pointed out that He Long had been imprisoned (rangjin) since October 1966.

50. Xu Kai, "Zhongguo renmin jiefangjun zongzhengzhibu yan'ge," p. 51.

51. Ibid.

52. Ibid.

53. According to the current deputy secretary-general of the GPD, the purges in the PLA after Lin's death were limited in number and generally restricted to high levels. Interview, 21 June 1991.

for the Gang inside the PLA and thereby use the military to pursue the Gang's "leftist" policies.[54] This effort was ultimately unsuccessful as Zhang and the other members of the Gang were arrested by the PLA palace guard detachment 8341 following the death of Mao in September 1976. In fact, during 1975 Deng Xiaoping and Ye Jianying apparently tried to undercut Zhang and the Gang's attempts to use the GPD in their attempt to acquire power.[55]

Wei Guoqing, an ally of Mao's successor Hua Guofeng, replaced Zhang as director of the GPD on 29 August 1977. More important, though, was the second rehabilitation of Deng Xiaoping, who soon assumed control of the military. Under Deng's direction a number of GPD personnel were also rehabilitated, including Xiao Hua. Deng circumscribed Wei Guoqing's power but kept him in the job until 1982 when Wei was purged as a member of the "small Gang of Four."

With Deng in command, reforms to professionalize the PLA ensued during the 1980s. For the GPD, this meant at first a decline in prestige and importance under Yu Qiuli's tutelage. Political work was viewed as a means to garner military support for Deng's reform agenda. This was apparent soon after Deng's rehabilitation as he and Ye Jianying were instrumental in convening the key 1978 All-Army Political Work Conference.[56] Both Deng's and Ye's speeches to this key meeting indicated their intent to build professionalism in the PLA. The "Decision" (*jueyi*) resulting from this meeting repudiated Lin Biao's and Zhang Chunqiao's "leftist" influence on political work in the PLA. It also set in motion a series of "rehabilitations" (*pingfan*) of wrongly-purged military leaders: Tan Zheng and Yang Chengwu were rehabilitated in March 1979, Luo Ruiqing in May 1980, Xiao Hua in July 1980, Peng Dehai and Huang Kecheng in June 1981.[57] Under the "new conditions" spelled out in the decision, political work was now to be based on "military science" (*junshi kexue*)—the new code word for military professionalism. Following the conference the GPD initiated a campaign in the armed forces to criticize the "leftist influence" of Lin Biao and the Gang of Four. The GPD was also subsequently reorganized in 1980 and 1985.

Thus from Deng's rehabilitation in 1978 the GPD began a new and more conservative phase in its organizational history. Although since 1960 the GPD had enjoyed high status among the three PLA General Headquarters, with Deng's return the General Staff Department was strengthened, with a concomitant decline in prestige for the GPD. However, after the outbreak of pro-democracy student demonstrations across China during December

54. *Ibid.*
55. Xu Kai, "Zhongguo renmin jiefangjun zongzhengzhibu yan'ge," p. 51.
56. See *Zhongguo renmin jiefangjun zhengzhi gongzuoshi*, pp. 372–7; and *Guanyu xin shiqi jundui zhengzhi gongzuo de jueding*, pp. 122–7.
57. *Guanyu xin shiqi jundui zhengzhi gongzuo de jueding*, p. 158.

1986–January 1987, Deng began to look differently upon the GPD, as he did upon ideological matters generally. He had become concerned about ideological laxity in the ranks as well as society at large.

As student demonstrations were spreading across China during December 1986–January 1987 an expanded meeting of the Central Military Commission (CMC) met in Beijing and, after three weeks of deliberation, adopted the important and hardline document "Decision of the Central Military Commission Concerning Political Work in the Armed Forces During the New Period."[58] The central thrust of the programmatic document was to increase ideological education in order to combat "newly emergent bourgeois tendencies" in society and the military. Deng, Yang Shangkun and Ye Jianying also believed that this task was important enough to put the GPD under new and more ideologically orthodox leadership. In November 1987 GPD director Yu Qiuli was sacked as a member of the "petroleum faction" and ideological hardliner Yang Baibing placed in control. Yang, the younger step-brother of Yang Shangkun, set about resuscitating the political control organs in the PLA and reinvigorating ideological indoctrination in the ranks.

Yang Baibing subsequently emerged as a key figure in the PLA and Party elite during the late 1980s, particularly after Tiananmen. In addition to director of the GPD, Yang was named secretary-general of the CMC in November 1989, which means he is responsible for running the day-to-day affairs of the CMC.[59] He was also a member of the Secretariat of the CCP Central Committee. Yang joined the Party and communist military forces in 1938 and became a political commissar in Yan'an, serving with the Eighth Route Army during the anti-Japanese and civil wars. From 1949 to 1966 he served in a number of GPD jobs in the Chengdu Military region. From 1966 to 1979, according to the *People's Daily*, he was detained in custody (*yuan ya*),[60] although another source says he was imprisoned for eight years.[61] After his release he was transferred to the Beijing Military Region where he served successively as vice-director of the military region GPD, deputy political commissar and head of the Party committee before being promoted to head the GPD in 1987. Yang is known as a tough bureaucrat and hardline (even xenophobic) ideologue. His rise to prominence in the post-Tiananmen political environment is no accident.

58. The text of the document can be found in Feng Wenbin *et al.* (eds.), *Zhongguo Gongchangdang jianshe quanshu, 1921–1991*, Vol. 7 (Shanxi renmin chubanshe, 1991), pp. 473–82.

59. It is widely rumoured inside the PLA that Yang Baibing will soon succeed Yang Shangkun as first vice-chairman of the Central Military Commission, effectively becoming the most powerful military figure in China. Personal communication, Beijing Military Region officer, 23 June 1991.

60. "Yang Baibing tongzhi jianli," *Renmin ribao*, 10 November 1989, p. 1.

61. Jin Bo, "All PLA commanders-in-chief were political commissars: Enigma of Yang Baibing's experience revealed," *Guangjiaojing*, No. 204 (16 September 1989), in FBIS—CHI, 22 January 1990, pp. 82–4.

During Yang Baibing's tenure as GPD chief, publications on the PWS have proliferated and offer a unique opportunity to examine the inner workings of the PWS and the content of political work among the troops.[62] Since the PLA Political Academy (run by the GPD) was amalgamated into the new National Defence University (*Guofang Daxue*) in 1986, the NDU's journal is another valuable source for tracking political work in the PLA.[63] These works emphasize many of the themes set out in the aforementioned "Decision."[64] Political education between 1987 and 1989 also emphasized studying the Party's economic reform programme and open door policy, correcting the "leftist" errors of the Lin Biao era, and maintaining links with the masses. Another important theme in these materials was the ongoing rectification campaign then taking place in the Party and among Party members in the armed forces.[65] It is largely in this context that these political work handbooks address the ideologues' agenda of combating "spiritual pollution," "bourgeois liberalism" and "peaceful evolution," while building "spiritual civilization" and upholding the "four cardinal principles." As will be seen below, since Tiananmen ideological indoctrination—the like of which has not been seen since the Cultural Revolution—has been significantly stepped up in the PLA. As one officer described it, "Since 4 June we have spent at least half of every work week in political study."[66]

The Organization and Structure of Political Work in the PLA

The political work system in the PLA is carried out in several administrative systems (*xitong*). Of these, the PLA General Political Department is by

---

62. See, for example, Junshikexueyuan jundui zhengzhi gongzuo yanjiusuo (ed.), *Xin shiqi jundui zhengzhi gongzuo yanjiu* (Beijing: Junshi kexue chubanshe, 1987); Junshikexueyuan jundui zhengzhi gongzuo yanjiusuo (ed.), *Jundui zhengzhi gongzuo de gaige* (Beijing: Junshi kexue chubanshe, 1988); Zong zhengzhibu qunzhong gongzuobu he Xian zhengzhi xueyuan xunlianbu (eds.), *Zhongguo renmin jiefangjun qunzhong gongzuoshi* (Beijing: Jiefangjun chubanshe, 1989); Chengdu junchu junshi xueshu yanjiu zhidaoyuanhui, *Xin shiqi jundui jianshe sixiang yanjiu* (Beijing: Jiefangjun chubanshe, 1988); Fei Guang *et al.*, *Jundui zhengzhi gongzuo rencai*; Yue Zhongqiang, *Sixiang zhengzhi gongzuoxue yuanli* (Beijing: Jiefangjun chubanshe, 1989); Tian Shuliang *et al.*, *Zhengzhi gongzuo xin silu* (Beijing: Junshi kexue chubanshe, 1989); Ma Yinbao (ed.), *Jundui zhengzhi jiaoyu gailun* (Xining: Qinghai renmin chubanshe, 1986); Zhongguo renmin jiefangjun hongjun zhengzhibu xuanchuanbu (ed.), *Jundui zhuanyue ganbu shiyong shouce* (Hebei kexue jixu chubanshe, 1987); Chen Xiangdong *et al.*, *Zhengzhi jiguan gongzuo lilun he fangfa* (Beijing: Junshikexueyuan, 1989); Wang Wei and Gao Wanglan, *Dangdai jundui daode* (Chongqing chubanshe, 1987).

63. *Guofang daxue xuebao* is now available for foreign subscription.

64. For a summary of the "Decision" see, "'Quanjun zhengzhi gongzuo huiyi jiyao' zhushi tiaomu," *Jiefangjunbao* (29 May 1990), p. 2 (point 5).

65. See Alastair I. Johnston, "Party rectification in the People's Liberation Army, 1983–1987," *The China Quarterly*, No. 112 (1987), pp. 591–630.

66. Interview with Beijing Military Region Officer, 23 June 1991.

far the largest although, as will be seen below, it is not necessarily the most significant as a mechanism of political control.

After multiple internal reorganizations over the years, from 1991 the GPD was divided into 11 functional departments: the Propaganda Department (*xuanchuan bu*); the Cultural Department (*wenhua bu*); the Mass Work Department (*qunzhong gongzuo bu*); the Liaison Department (*lianxi bu*); the Cadre Administration Department (*ganbu guanli bu*); the Military Court (*junshi fayuan*); the Military Procuratorate (*junshi jianchayuan*); the *zhigongbu*, or units directly subordinate (*zhishu*) to the GPD; the Organization Department (*zuzhi bu*); the General Office (*zong bangongting*); and the Security Bureau (*baowei bu*).[67] The GPD table of organization is depicted in Figure 2. This organizational structure is essentially replicated in GPD organs (*zhengzhi jiguan*) down to the regiment level.

This structure captures the range of activities of the GPD and provides the sense that the GPD is by no means merely a system of political commissars.[68] For example, the Propaganda Department works closely with the CCP Propaganda Department and is responsible for "ideological educa-

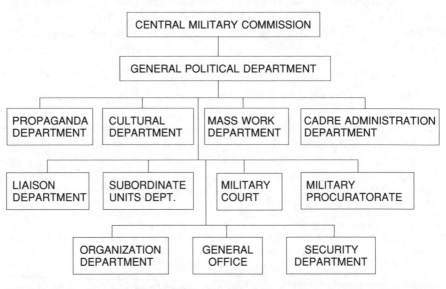

FIG 5.2. Structure of the PLA General Political Department.
Source:
    Xu Kai, "Zhongguo renmin jiefangjun zong zhengzhibu yan'ge," *Junshi lishi*, No. 3 (1990), p. 52; interview with GPD, 21 June 1991.

67. Xu Kai, "Zhongguo renmin jiefangjun zong zhengzhibu yan'ge," p. 52.
68. The following descriptions of functions is based on an interview with the GPD deputy secretary-general, 21 June 1991, and Junshikexueyuan junshi lishi yanjiubu, *Zhongguo dabaike quanshu: Zhongguo renmin jiefangju zhengzhi gongzuo fence* (Beijing: Junshi kexue chubanshe, 1987), pp. 64–9, 72–8, 80–1, 84–98, 122–4.

tion" (*sixiang jiaoyu*) and disseminating the Party line in the PLA as well as "providing guidance" in political content for the sprawling PLA publishing industry, including *Liberation Army Daily* and the PLA publishing house. The Cultural Department oversees all cultural, artistic, musical, sporting and recreation activities in the PLA, and is also responsible for the big-budget PLA film industry (*Ba Yi* Studios). The Mass Work Department deals with establishing links with the civilian masses and conducting pro-PLA propaganda among them. The functions of the Liaison Department are to conduct foreign propaganda during peacetime, and to indoctrinate prisoners of war and otherwise conduct psychological warfare during wartime. The Military Procuratorate and court investigate, prosecute and court martial breaches of discipline in the ranks. The Cadre Administration Department manages all personnel in the GPD, and holds all performance records and dossiers (*dang'an*). The General Office serves as liaison with the Central Military Commission and other concerned institutions. The Organization Department is in charge of "Party building" (*dang jianshe*) and youth work in the PLA. The Security Office conducts counter-intelligence and monitors internal security throughout the GPD, particularly with respect to document dissemination.[69] The *zhigongbu* administers the day-to-day operations of affiliated organs such as the Military Museum, PLA Press, *Liberation Army Daily*, etc., but oversight of the substance of work in these organizations is left to the functional departments noted above.

Thus political work carried out by the GPD encompasses a broad range of activities—much of which has little to do with political indoctrination as it is often conceived of by western analysts. It is also important to understand that the GPD is only one part of a three-tiered organizational system in which political work is conducted in the Chinese armed forces. These three tiers consist of: the GPD political commissar system (*zhengzhi weiyuan zhidu*); the Party committee system (*dangwei lingdao zhidu*); and—since 1978—the CCP Discipline Inspection Committee system (*jilu jiancha zhidu*).[70] They are represented in Figure 3.[71] All three systems are well-entrenched down to the regiment level. At the battalion level and below representatives of all three systems exist, but apparently in a more ad hoc fashion.

69. Document classification and dissemination procedures are set out in the Chinese People's Liberation Army Secrecy Regulations (*Zhongguo renmin jiefangjun baomi tiaoli*). For a brief description of these regulations see *ibid.* pp. 83–4.

70. For a description of the functioning of these systems see Pu Xingzu *et al.*, *Dangdai Zhongguo zhengzhi zhidu*, pp. 323–31; and Deng Yingyi *et al.*, *Jundui dang de jilu jiancha gongzuo gailun* (Beijing: Chang zheng chubanshe, 1988).

71. Both Figure 3 and the following description are based on Xu Kai, "Zhongguo renmin jiefangjun zong zhengzhibu yan'ge"; Pu Xingzu *et al.*, *Dangdai Zhongguo zhengzhi zhidu*, pp. 323–31; Deng Yingyi *et al.*, *Jundui dang de jilu jiancha gongzuo gailun*; Chinese Academy of Social Sciences, *Information China*, Vol. 2 (Oxford: Pergamon Press, 1989), pp. 841–2; Fei Guang *et al.*, *Jundui zhengzhi gongzuo rencai* (Henan renmin chubanshe and Hebei kexue jixu chubanshe, 1986); Bullard, *China's Political-Military Evolution*, pp. 76–83; and Cheng Hsiao-shih, *Party–Military Relations in the PRC and Taiwan*, ch. 3.

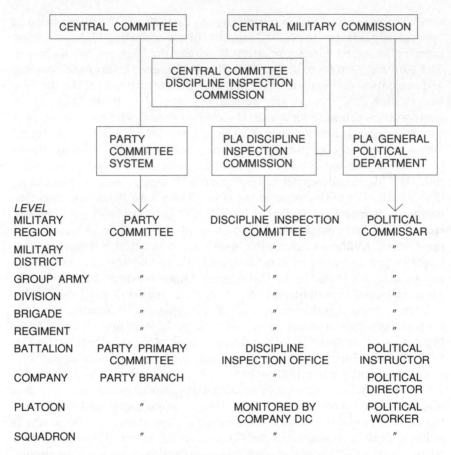

FIG 5.3. Structure of the Political Work System in the PLA
Sources:
  Pu Xingzu *et al.*, *Dangdai Zhongguo zhengzhi zhidu*; Deng Yingyi *et al.*, *Jundui dang de jilu jiancha gongzuo gailun.*

The Political Commissar System

The GPD political commissar at the regimental (*tuan*) level and above is known as the *zhengzhiweiyuan*, or simply *zhengwei*. At the battalion (*ying*) level he is known as the political instructor (*jiaodaoyuan*), at the company (*lian*) level he is called political director (*zhidaoyuan*), and at the platoon and squadron level he is known simply as a political worker (*zhengzhi gongzuoyuan*). It is at the battalion and company levels that the commissar system interacts with the rank and file troops most directly, but it is also at these levels where the *jiaodaoyuan* and *zhidaoyuan*, respectively, are said to be "absolutely" under the command of the Party branch.[72] According to a 1990 source, the commissar at all levels holds equal status to the military commander (*junshi zhibuiyuan*) or senior officer (*shouzhang*), but more importantly both are "directly subordinate" to the leading cadre (*shouzhang*) of the Party committee.[73] Both "must obey" (*bixu fucong*) decisions made by the Party committee, and if the commissar and the commander have disagreements they are to submit (*tijiao*) to the Party committee decision. In principle, during peacetime military decisions are made by the *zhihuiyuan* and political decisions by the *zhengweiyuan*, but in wartime the military commander is said to have precedence over the commissar on the battlefield.[74] The work of the political commissar at all levels, according to this source, is to "transmit the Party's line, policies, orders and decisions." This brief is the same as the Party committee system, but the latter is more importantly an organizational device of Party penetration inside the PLA.

The Party Committee System

The Party committee system is a separate chain-of-command from the political commissar system, although this is rarely distinguished in foreign analyses. It is through this system that *real* Party political control of the PLA is exercised, as the Party committee system (*dangweizhi*) is by far the most powerful of all political work organs in the military. The Party committee system is directly subordinate to the Central Committee of the Communist Party. At the military region (*junchu*), military district (*junfenchu*), and group army (*jituan jun*) levels, Party committees exist in constituent departmental units (*ke dangwei*). A single Party committee (*dangwei*) exists at the division (*shi*), brigade (*lu*), and regimental (*tuan*) levels. At the battalion level there is a "basic level" Party committee (*jiceng dangwei*), companies have Party branches (*dang zhibu*), and Party cells (*xiaozu*) are set up at the lowest levels of platoon (*pai*) and squadron (*ban*). At the military region and district level it is quite common for provincial first Party secretaries to serve simultaneously as chief political commissar, but this is ceremonial. In the intermediate levels, the Party committee heads and political commissars are not the same individual and hence at these key strata a dual-command system exists.[75] Moreover, the Party secretary *cannot* (by regulation) serve as head of the discipline inspection committee

72. See Pu Xingzu *et al.*, *Dangdai Zhongguo zhengzhi zhidu*, p. 329; and Sun Weiben (ed.), *Zhongguo gongchangdang dangwu gongzuo da zidian*, p. 342.

73. Sun Weiben (ed.), *ibid*. p. 328. Also see Zhang Shuitao (ed.), *Dangdai Zhongguo zhengzhi zhidu* (Beijing: Gaodeng jiaoyu chubanshe, 1990), p. 215; and Yun Guang (ed.), *Shehuizhuyi zhengzhixue* (Beijing renmin chubanshe, 1985), pp. 315–28.

74. Sun Weiben (ed.), *ibid*. p. 342.

75. Interview with GPD, 21 June 1991.

(*jijian*), although it is common for the deputy political commissar to head the DIC at these levels.[76] At lower levels, however, the GPD political commissar and the head of the Party branch are often the same person.

The main responsibilities of the Party committee representatives are twofold. On the one hand, they are to watch for signs of "independent kingdoms," military corporateness or general restiveness in the ranks. Party secretaries are the principal vehicle to ensure the subordination and loyalty of the PLA to the CCP, rather than permitting the establishment of an institution with autonomous power. On the other hand, they serve as the transmission belt for propagating the Party line (*fangzhen*), policy (*zhengce*), principles (*yuanze*), orders (*mingling*), and directives (*zhibiao*) throughout the military system.[77]

The Discipline Inspection System

The third leg of the political work system in the PLA is the Discipline Inspection Committee (DIC) system. The DIC system is a sub-system of the Communist Party in the military, but distinct from the Party committee system described above. Its principal function is to monitor the performance of Party members in the military, but it also joins the political commissar and Party committee systems in implementing campaigns.[78] This system was originally established in November 1949 and operated until the Cultural Revolution.[79] It was re-established *within Party committees* at the regimental level and above in September 1978 on the order of the Military Commission,[80] but became a separate system (*xitong*) in January 1980. The first secretary was Gan Weihan, who was replaced by Bo Linxiang in 1985. The DIC secretary reports directly to the CMC Secretary General, currently Yang Baibing.

The main tasks of the DIC from its inception until 1982 were to redress "misjudged cases" (*pingfan yuanjia cuo'an*), and in particular to rehabilitate leading cadres and officers.[81] After its reorganization in the early 1980s, as Alastair Johnston's research has demonstrated, the DIC's principal task was to carry out the Party rectification campaign in the armed forces begun in 1983.[82] As part of this campaign, DIC branch offices were established at the battalion and company levels, although in practice this has by no means

76. Interview with GPD; 21 June 1991.
77. Zhang Shuitao (ed.), *Dangdai Zhongguo zhengzhi zhidu*, pp. 213–14. Also see *Zhongguo dabaike quanshu: Zhongguo renmin jiefangjun zhengzhi gongzuo fence*, pp. 46–9.
78. Deng Yingyi *et al.*, *Jundui dang de jilu jiancha gongzuo gailun*, especially ch. 2.
79. *Zhongguo dabaike quanshu: Zhongguo renmin jiefangjun zhengzhi gongzuo fence*, p. 63.
80. *Ibid.* p. 37. The order was known as *Guanyu tuan yishang geji dangwei chengli jilu jianchayuanhui zhidao*.
81. *Ibid.*, and see fn. 57.
82. Johnston, "Party rectification in the People's Liberation Army, 1983–87." For a daily record of how this rectification campaign unfolded in Party ranks, including in the armed forces, see Xiao Jin, *Zhengdang Dashiji* (Harbin: Heilongjiang renmin chubanshe, 1985).

been uniform. Apparently no DIC organs exist at the platoon and squad levels, as they are effectively managed by the company representatives. Special DIC investigation teams (*jianchadui*) were frequently dispatched to all levels.

By their very nature, the discipline inspection committees may conceivably pose a threat to the traditional Party committee system as they are empowered to investigate and ultimately dismiss Party members in the armed forces. The intimidation factor is enough to cause a great deal of consternation among Party committees as they can no longer wield unchecked power. But that is precisely the reason why Deng instituted the DIC system in the first place. One *neibu* source further indicated that the discipline inspection committees also monitor the implementation of Party directives by the GPD political commissar system.[83] Therefore, the DIC, Party committee and political commissar systems should not be considered as parallel and totally separate, but rather as interlocking and reinforcing systems. This is why in Figure 3 they are depicted as having horizontal (*kuai-kuai*) ties as well as vertical (*tiao-tiao*) authority. As the deputy secretary-general of the GPD put it, "The interrelationships of these three systems are extremely close" (*hen miqie de guanxi*).[84] Illustrative of these overlapping ties is Guo Linxiang's concurrent position as DIC secretary and GPD deputy director.

Thus, organizationally, the Communist Party penetrates the military structure from top to bottom. In addition, Party membership in the armed forces is comparatively high relative to civilian organs. This is not so much the case with peasant conscripts as it is in the officer corps, where virtually all officers are Party members.[85] Party membership in the military definitely improves career advancement.

This, then, is the three-tiered structure of the political work system in the PLA. It is via these systems that significantly intensified political work has been carried out in the PLA since June 1989.

Political Work in the PLA since Tiananmen

To comprehend fully the importance of political work in the PLA since the Tiananmen tragedy, it is necessary to consider not only the events sur-

83. *Zhongguo dabaike quanshu: Zhongguo renmin jiefangjun zhengzhi gongzuo fence*, p. 63.
84. GPD interview, 21 June 1991.
85. *Ibid*. GPD deputy secretary-general Li Yunzhi was reluctant to give an absolute figure of Party membership in the PLA, but indicated that it was between 50–60%—the vast majority of which was constituted by the officer corps. If one assumes that the PLA currently stands at approximately 2.5 million (following the 1986–89 demobilization of one million service personnel), then CCP membership in the PLA today falls in the 1.2–1.5 million range (*not* including those in the People's Armed Police and paramilitary organs). This still constitutes a small fraction of the now 50 million-strong CCP.

rounding 4 June 1989, but also the climate in the military in the period leading up to 1989.

For the PLA, the story of the 1980s was one of streamlining aimed at constructing a more modern fighting force capable of dealing with a number of *external* contingencies.[86] Directed by Deng Xiaoping, Yang Shangkun, Zhang Aiping, Yang Dezhi, Qin Jiwei, and other senior military figures, the PLA was to be made lean and mean. The 11 military regions were amalgamated into seven, and 31 units at and above the army corps level and 4,054 units at or above the division or regiment levels were abolished.[87] More than one million soldiers were demobilized between 1986 and 1989, including considerable numbers of high-ranking officers who were forced to retire. Particular attention was paid to upgrading command, control, and communications (C^3I) in both battlefield and peacetime environments. Interservice combined force operations were practised, and special forces were developed to contend with a variety of combat contingencies. Ranks were officially restored in October 1988 to add a sense of professionalism and improve the command structure.[88] Military training took on a much more professional cast, as the entire system of military academies and colleges was reorganized to improve officer training.[89] Weapons procurement during the 1980s (both indigenous and foreign purchases) enabled the PLA to upgrade its defensive capabilities considerably, but did little to close the gap between more modern militaries. Despite the conscription system, recruitment into the PLA became a problem during this period. As opportunities to make money in the private sector increased, joining the military was no longer seen as the avenue of upward mobility it once was. According to one general, "Up until 10 years ago the PLA could conscript anyone it wanted; it no longer has that power."[90] There is consequently resentment in the ranks among skilled, conscripted personnel. Says one university graduate computer programmer conscripted to do war-gaming for the PLA, "Of course I feel resentment because I could be making much more money in the private sector, doing more interesting programming, and living a better life on more than the 400 *yuan* per month I make as a captain."[91]

86. For a fuller exposition of these trends see Ellis Joffee, *The Chinese Army After Mao* (Cambridge, Mass.: Harvard University Press, 1987); and Alastair I. Johnston, "Changing army–Party relations in China, 1979–84," *Asian Survey* (October 1984), pp. 1012–1039. As Joffee's and Johnston's analyses cover the early Deng era, for discussion of the developments in the PLA in the late 1980s see Yu Yulin, "The PLA's political role since 1987: Continuity and change," in King-yuh Chang, *Mainland China after the Thirteenth Party Congress* (Boulder: Westview Press, 1990), pp. 114–37; and June Teufel Dreyer, "The PLA after the Thirteenth Party Congress," *ibid*. pp. 99–113.

87. Commentator, "Have better troops and weapons, reinforce our Great Wall," *Jiefangjunbao*, 28 September 1989, in FBIS—CHI, 25 October 1989, p. 36.

88. See *Chinese People's Liberation Army and People's Armed Police Rank and Insignia: A Reference Aid* (Washington, D.C.: Defense Intelligence Agency DDB–2680–338–89, 1989).

89. See Lonnie Henley, "Officer education in the PLA," *Problems of Communism* (May–June 1987), pp. 55–71.

90. Interview with Beijing Military Region General, 9 May 1990.

91. Personal communication, Beijing, 10 May 1990.

All these developments in the military during the 1980s serve as the backdrop to Deng's decision to employ the military for internal security in Beijing in 1989. The point is that the PLA had, during the 1980s, been led (and trained) to believe that they should disengage from the political arena and prepare themselves to fight external enemies. When called upon by Deng and the Central Military Commission to enforce martial law, clear Tiananmen Square and reclaim Beijing, the PLA's new professional ethic was fundamentally challenged. As PLA specialist Harlan Jencks has argued, the officer corps may have a distaste for domestic disorder but do not perceive the suppression of disorder as their proper professional task.[92]

The fact remains, however, that the PLA both obeyed and defied orders. Those that disobeyed orders are, needless to say, a deep source of concern to the Party elite that now sees the military as their ultimate guarantor for staying in power. In the wake of Tiananmen numerous reports of rank insubordination circulated inside and outside China. A 22 June 1989 *Liberation Army Daily* editorial chastised those who "assumed an ambiguous attitude and wavered" during the suppression of "counter-revolutionary rioters." General Yang Baibing, in a speech to the All-Army Political Work Conference in December 1989, reported a total of 110 officers who "breached discipline in a serious way" and 1,400 soldiers who "shed their weapons and ran away."[93] This number included General Xu Qinxian, commander of the Beijing-based 38th Army Corps, who was one of the 21 senior officers who were court martialled for insubordination. To underline the problem of insubordination in the PLA in the wake of Tiananmen, PLA Chief of Staff Chi Haotian and other senior officers constantly stress the need to obey orders and observe discipline.[94] Faced with a PLA of questionable loyalty, since Tiananmen the CCP leadership has undertaken an unprecedented campaign of ideological indoctrination in the ranks aimed at ensuring "absolute Party control" over the gun.

Process and content of political work in the PLA since Tiananmen

Political work in the PLA since Tiananmen has been conducted via the three-tier system noted above. The political campaigns have addressed five principal themes: discipline in the ranks; ensuring the "absolute control" of

92. Harlan Jencks, "Party authority and military power," *Issues and Studies*, Vol. 26, No. 7 (July 1990), p. 27. Jencks further develops this theme in his "Civil–military relations in China: Tiananmen and after," *Problems of Communism*, Vol. XL (May–June 1991), pp. 14–29.

93. See Willy Wo-lap Lam, "Yang Baibing reveals army defiance in crackdown," *South China Morning Post*, 28 December 1989, in FBIS—CHI, 28 December 1989, pp. 23–4. For further reports see Lo Bing, "'Rebel troops' inside the army of the CCP," *Zhengming*, No. 147 (1 January 1990), p. 10, in FBIS—CHI, 2 January 1990, pp. 22–3.

94. See Ren Yanjun, "At an all-army training class on order and regulations, Liu Huaqing, vice-chairman of the Central Military Commission, delivers a speech, urging serious enforcement of orders and regulations," *Jiefangjunbao*, 11 July 1990, p. 1, FBIS—CHI, 24 July 1990, pp. 18–19.

the Party over the military; combating the "new enemies" of "peaceful evolution" and "bourgeois liberalization"; improving the quality of basic-level political work in the armed forces; and training Lei Feng-type soldiers.

These five themes have been pursued more or less simultaneously, but the process of carrying out the campaigns can be roughly divided into five distinct phases. The first phase covers the period from 4 June to the "All Army Political Work Conference" of December 1989. The second is the work conference itself. The third covers the implementation at the regimental level and above of the work conference's main programmatic document ("Several questions on strengthening and improving the army's political work under the new situation") from the conclusion of the conference until March 1990. The fourth includes the implementation of the document below the regimental level, particularly at the company level, from March to October 1990. The fifth covers the autumn of 1990, a period in which opposition to the political campaigns in the PLA was apparently expressed before the GPD promulgated a comprehensive new set of regulations for political work.

Phase 1: June–December 1989. Immediately after the invasion of Beijing from 4–9 June 1989, martial law troops began a political offensive aimed at interrogating demonstrators and conducting propaganda work among the citizens of the capital. Various civilian units were occupied by martial law forces, particularly the six "major disaster zones" (*zhongzaiqu*): the Chinese Academy of Social Sciences; the Commission and Institute of Economic Reform under the State Council; Beijing University; Beijing Teacher's College; Beijing Aeronautics Institute; and the China Politics and Law University. Countless individuals in these units were arrested and interrogated. Troops entered innumerable other *danwei* for interrogation purposes and to conduct study sessions about the necessity of suppressing the "counter-revolutionary rebellion." A special exhibition of the suppression was set up at the Military Museum (an affiliated organ of the GPD), GPD-propaganda videos were made detailing the "chaos" (*dongluan*), and a variety of materials were published illustrating how the PLA had suffered casualties and humiliation to save the Party and state from extinction. As one *Liberation Army Daily* article put it, "Our cadres and soldiers came under attack from all sides. They were insulted, scolded, and beaten up. They had never experienced this in the past."[95] Even after conquering the capital, martial law troops were randomly attacked. During the summer 170 cases of attacks on troops were reported, more than one a day.[96]

95. See, for example, Zang Wenqing, "Continue to do ideological, political work well while carrying out the task of enforcing martial law," *Jiefangjunbao*, 7 September 1989, in FBIS—CHI, 22 September 1989, p. 29.

96. Guan Yecheng, "The martial law enforcement troops are attacked every day," *Zhengming*, 1 October 1989, in FBIS—CHI, 3 October 1989, pp. 36–7.

After order was restored the PLA moved quickly to investigate and court-martial recalcitrant troops, as noted above. The DIC spearheaded the investigations, and the GPD's military procuratorate and court prosecuted and tried the cases. By mid-September half the "leadership groups at or above the divisional level" had been investigated.[97] This investigation discovered that 92 per cent of these units had "good or relatively good Party style and discipline." Those in breach of discipline, including seven "high-ranking cadres," were dealt with "sternly" by the DIC and GPD.[98] In November the DIC of the CMC held an enlarged plenary meeting which was attended by all members of the reconstituted CMC. In his speech to the session Guo Linxiang, secretary of the CMC DIC, stressed the need for strict PLA adherence to all Party directives.[99]

The importance of Party control of the military emerged as a principal theme during the autumn of 1989. A National Day editorial in the Liberation Army Daily sounded the call that would be heard repeatedly over the coming months: the Party's "absolute leadership" (dang de juedui lingdao) over the army.[100] Why? Because "the counter-revolutionary rebellion in Beijing gave us a strong lesson in blood and helped us understand that, as a strong pillar for the people's democratic dictatorship, this army has an unshirkable duty to suppress resolutely the hostile forces and reactionaries who attempt to subvert the Party's leadership and state power under certain special circumstances, such as a large-scale counter-revolutionary rebellion breaking out at home."[101] Moreover, the editorial stated that the PLA "is an armed group for carrying out the Party's political tasks," and stressed the need to "maintain a high degree of political and ideological uniformity with the Party central leadership." To this end, the editorial also signalled that the Party committee system in the PLA should be strengthened "so that the guns will always be firmly held by people who are loyal to the Party." Not a word was mentioned about defending the nation against external enemies, military modernization, or other "professional" pursuits. The message was clear: the PLA was to be a political army in the service of those who controlled the Party. The editorial made clear a redefined internal role for the PLA. Maintaining the "absolute leadership" of the Party was cited by the CMC chairman Jiang Zemin and the first vice-chairman Yang Shangkun at the enlarged CMC meeting following the CCP Fifth Plenum in

97. Luo Yuwen, "The army investigates high-ranking and middle-ranking leadership groups," Renmin ribao, 16 September 1989, in FBIS—CHI, 21 September 1989, p. 36.

98. No precise figures for court martials have been released, but the GPD indicated that they were extremely few (jixiao de). Interview, 21 June 1991.

99. Xinhua Domestic Services, 15 November 1989, in FBIS—CHI, 16 November 1989, pp. 29–30.

100. Commentator. "Uphold the Party's absolute leadership, ensure that our army is always politically up to standard," Jiefangjunbao, 1 October 1989, in FBIS—CHI, 18 October 1989, pp. 36–9.

101. Ibid. p. 37.

November as "... *the* most important task in army building"[102] (emphasis added).

An interesting sub-theme of the Party's "absolute leadership" campaign also emerged in the wake of a November CMC meeting. Apparently a faction had existed in the CCP that would really have pleased Samuel Huntington. According to the *Liberation Army Daily*, "some people" had argued the case for the "depoliticization" of the army and the separation of the army from Party and state, and sought to create an army based on the western model that did not "meddle in politics."[103] "Some people" included Su Shaozhi "and his ilk." Su, revisionist Marxist theoretician and former director of the Institute of Marxism–Leninism–Mao Zedong Thought at the Academy of Social Sciences, had been a key adviser to deposed Party chief Zhao Ziyang. The article did not name him, but it insinuated that Zhao—the principal advocate of separating Party and state (*dangzheng fenkai*)—was the ostensible target of criticism. Zhao served as first vice-chairman of the CMC from 1987 until his downfall in 1989. The article concluded, "The advocacy of Su Shaozhi and his ilk to separate the army from the Party is only a component part of their plot to overthrow the Communist Party leadership in favour of the multi-party system."[104]

Another key issue of political work in the armed forces during the first phase of the post-Tiananmen indoctrination campaigns was that of the new enemies "peaceful evolution" and "bourgeois liberalization." The Tiananmen demonstrations themselves were said to be manifestations of the infiltration of these new enemies into China. "Peaceful evolution" is seen as the attempt of the "international monopolist class," notably the United States, to defeat socialism worldwide without firing a shot. As China's leaders watched in horror as one East European communist regime after another fell during the autumn of 1989, the peaceful evolution campaign in China intensified.[105] In the PLA it was waged in the pages of the *Liberation Army Daily* and through the GPD and Party committee systems. Numerous documents were circulated for study throughout these systems. These documents claimed that international monopoly capitalism was wag-

102. Commentator, "Take political strengthening as the most important task," *Jiefangjunbao*, 27 November 1989, in FBIS—CHI, 22 December 1989, p. 14. For more on the CMC meeting and the preceding Fifth Plenum see David Shambaugh, "The fourth and fifth plenary sessions of the 13th CCP Central Committee," *The China Quarterly*, No. 120 (1989), pp. 852–62.

103. See Lin Jiangong, "Refuting the advocacy of separating the army from the Party," *Jiefangjunbao*, 21 November 1989, in FBIS—CHI 22 December 1989, p. 7.

104. The GPD deputy secretary-general denied that Zhao himself had advocated this separation, but said a number of his advisers had. Interview, 21 June 1991.

105. For more on this campaign see David Shambaugh, *Beautiful Imperialist: China Perceives America, 1972–90* (Princeton: Princeton University Press, 1991), ch. 6. Among the many articles on peaceful evolution in the Chinese press see the three-part series in *Ban Yue Tan* in October 1989, carried in FBIS—CHI, 5 January 1990, pp. 17–21.

ing a "smokeless war" inside the ranks of the PLA.[106] The struggle against peaceful evolution was said to be a protracted one that would last indefinitely.

The campaign against bourgeois liberalization in the PLA had actually begun in 1987, but accelerated in the wake of Tiananmen. Stress was placed on "purifying the cultural environment in the barracks." In order to accomplish this lofty task the GPD undertook to clean up pornography (*seqing*) and "unhealthy materials" in the ranks. In Beijing, the "Coordination Centre for Military Colleges and Schools" convened a series of anti-bourgeois liberalization forums.[107] In other locales, the GPD dispatched work teams to PLA publishing houses, libraries and barracks.[108] The work teams discovered that particularly "Guangzhou, Nanjing, Jinan, and coastal areas in which naval forces are placed have a relatively large number of unhealthy media in circulation . . . packed with descriptions of erotic behaviour, sexual acts, murder, violence, and feudal superstitions. . . ."[109] Such materials were to be confiscated, but how should those who possessed them be dealt with? "Concerning those fighters who really expose themselves to reading matter which is obscene and erotic in nature, or have such material in their possession, we should take the stand of giving them positive education and help them wake up. On the basis of ideological work done sufficiently well, we must *arouse* them to part with this reading matter"[110] (emphasis added).

The final element of the first-phase ideological campaigns in the PLA was to improve the quality of grass-roots (*jiceng*) level political commissars and unfold yet another campaign to emulate model soldier Lei Feng. GPD chief Yang Baibing took the lead in launching these interrelated campaigns. In late September he convened a report meeting (*huibao huiyi*) to implement further the 1986 CMC "Outline for grass-roots building of the army."[111] The principal tasks of basic-level work were to institute the anti-peaceful evolution and anti-bourgeois liberalization campaigns.[112] In addition, a new effort to train Lei Feng-type soldiers and cadres was launched, and 300,000

106. See, for example, He Yingquan, " 'The Wolf Has Come' and 'Where is the Wolf?'—Calling for proper alertness to the presence of the enemy," *Jiefangjunbao*, 8 October 1989, in FBIS—CHI, 31 October 1989, p. 28.
107. See Yuan Jun, "Military colleges and schools must become powerful positions for adherence to the four cardinal principles and opposition to bourgeois liberalization," *Jiefangjunbao*, 19 October 1989, in FBIS—CHI, 7 November 1989, pp. 24–5.
108. Chen Xianyi, "Initial achievements made in cleansing the culture environment in army barracks," *Jiefangjunbao*, 28 October 1989, in FBIS—CHI, 17 November 1989, pp. 31–2.
109. *Ibid.* p. 32.
110. *Ibid.*
111. Yang Baibing, "Basing ourselves on the grass-roots level, performing meritorious deeds, and making contributions to building a modernized, regularized, and revolutionized army," *Jiefangjunbao*, 30 September 1989, in FBIS—CHI, 25 October 1989, pp. 37–40.
112. See Commentator, "Fulfill the demands of being politically qualified down to grass-roots units," *Jiefangjunbao*, 23 October 1989, in FBIS—CHI, 9 November 1989, pp. 35–6.

"deluxe copies" of the late model soldier's diaries were printed and distributed by the GPD.[113]

Phase 2: The All-Army Political Work Conference. Six months after Tiananmen, with a siege mentality still gripping the Chinese leadership, the CMC convened the All-Army Political Work Conference from 11–17 December 1989. Yang Baibing presided and 183 "responsible persons" of concerned GPD units and other organizations attended. The conference was attended by the "responsible comrades" of the GPD, the DIC and "directors of the political departments of all major units of the army." The conference linked the demonstrations in China and Eastern Europe, attributing both to the plot of the international monopolist forces to overthrow socialism. The situation in Eastern Europe during the preceding months, particularly Romania where—as the conference met—the Romanian army was fighting Ceausescu's paramilitary police, fuelled the hardline Chinese leadership's paranoia about the loyalty of the PLA. Hence the need to convene the conference. As Yang Baibing told the conference in his opening speech, "This disturbance [the counter-revolutionary rebellion] and the recent developing trend and rapid changes in Eastern Europe have raised many weighty problems (*zhongda wenti*) worth pondering (*sikao*) for our political work. . . ."[114]

The major highlight of the conference was the promulgation of the document "Several questions on strengthening and improving the army's political work under the new situation" (*Guanyu xin xingshixia jiaqiang he gaijin jundui zhengzhi gongzuo de ruogan wenti*). The document and an important "summary" (*jiyao*) were transmitted throughout the army for intensive study. Yang Baibing's speech to the conference was another key item circulated by the GPD for study. Five months later, as study of these materials continued, the GPD also released an annotated summary of the *jiyao*.[115]

The conference document was divided into 10 principal sections, all of which dealt with intensifying political work in the armed forces. Judging from the *jiyao*,[116] the document claimed that the "complex climate at home and abroad" makes it necessary "that gun barrels are wielded by truly politically trustworthy people." The document also declared that under conditions of a "reactionary international tendency" the greatest security

113. See Xinhua Domestic Service, 8 December 1989, in FBIS—CHI, 12 January 1989, pp. 35–6; and Xinhua Domestic Service, 9 December 1989, in FBIS—CHI, 21 December 1989, pp. 30–31.
114. Editorial Department of the *Liberation Army Daily* (ed.), *Jiaqiang renmin jundui de zhengzhi jianshe: quanjun zhengzhi gongzuohuiyi jiyao he youguan lunwen, zhushi tiaomu* (Beijing: Changzheng chubanshe, 1990), p. 25.
115. The *jiyao*, Yang's speech, and the annotated summary can be found in *ibid*. The document itself has not been released publicly, but was transmitted to all Party organs by the CCP Central Committee as Central Document (*zhongfa*) no. 4 of 1990.
116. *Ibid*. pp. 3–23.

threat to China now came in the form of "peaceful evolution" (*heping yanbian*)—an enemy not to be taken lightly. All units should remain on vigilant guard against "infiltration" by these new enemies. Not only must current soldiers improve their political awareness, but new recruits must primarily be evaluated on political orientation, particularly their attitudes toward the "counter-revolutionary turmoil." Since the "reactionary class forces abroad" were linking up with "anti-socialist elements at home to overturn the socialist system," the document stated that the CCP's "absolute leadership" must be strengthened and protected by the armed forces at all times. To accomplish this the document instructed troops to accelerate their study of Marxism–Leninism in order to understand the difficult situation facing the republic, Party, and army. Since the "struggle against peaceful evolution and bourgeois liberalization" was said to be protracted and would be waged in all spheres of society, the document concluded that it was the duty of the PLA and GPD to guard against infiltration not only inside the military, but in the Party and society as well.

Phase 3: Initial implementation. From the close of the All-Army Political Work Conference until March 1990 the GPD began to implement the conference recommendations as expressed in the document "On several questions" and the "summary." This phase covered implementation down to the regiment level. While the GPD circulated these documents to units at all levels, emphasis prior to March 1990 was placed on upper-level units and officers. After March 1990, as will be seen in the next phase, the emphasis shifted to the ordinary soldier.

The documents were transmitted and implemented largely via the GPD political commissar system, although central aims of the campaign were to strengthen the DIC and Party committee systems within the military. To help implement the campaign Yang Shangkun and Yang Baibing promoted Yu Yongbo, former GPD director in the Nanjing Military Region, as one of the five deputy directors of the General Political Department. Yu, a noted conservative ideologue, served together with Yang Shangkun in the Guangzhou Military Region in the late 1970s and was a close ally of brother Yang Baibing in the late 1980s. Yu was immediately placed in charge of instituting the "Lei Feng" dimension of the campaign.[117]

The study of these documents and implementation of their contents began in the uppermost echelons of the PLA. The Headquarters of General Staff convened a study class for 60 GSD Party committee secretaries from headquarters and the division, army and group army levels.[118] The Chief of

117. Willy Wo-lap Lam, "Yang Shangkun ally receives political post," *Hong Kong Standard*, 4 January 1990, pp. 1–2.

118. He Jiangbo and Chen Daiping, "Concentrating attention—sidelights on the first study class of the CCP Committee Secretaries of the PLA General Staff units," *Renmin ribao*, 30 December 1989, in FBIS—CHI, 9 January 1990, pp. 19–20.

Staff Chi Haotian made a key speech on strengthening the Party committee system.[119] The Deputy Chief of Staff Xu Xin also contributed an article on deepening the ideological levels and political reliability of GSD headquarters personnel.[120] The General Logistics Department convened Marxism study classes and laid stress on obeying the directives of Party committees.[121] For the GPD's part, Yang Baibing briefed political commissars at the regiment level and above immediately following the work conference. In February 1990 the GPD released a circular on promoting Marxist philosophy.[122] The circular called on commissars at the regimental level and above to convene short-term "rotational training classes" and Party committees to organize "central study groups." These groups were told to pay particular attention to dialectical and historical materialism.[123]

A particular target of this phase of the campaign was the forces in the Beijing Military Region command, as their political loyalty was deemed most critical as well as most questionable. Yang Baibing personally convened several meetings of personnel to invoke the need for unquestioned loyalty to central Party directives.[124] The Second Artillery, which commands the PLA's nuclear forces, was also singled out for special attention, as the leadership apparently feared politically unreliable soldiers having their fingers on the nuclear button.[125]

During this phase a total of 233 classes to study Marxist theory were convened, which were attended by 15,000 regimental and higher-ranking cadres.[126] Theoretical study was carried out in three principal forms: short-term rotational study classes, study groups within Party committees, and individual study.[127] The National Defence University was charged by the GPD with organizing the first type for army corps commanders, who in turn were responsible for training regimental cadres. Officers and cadres at and above the regiment level were required to attend one such rotational study class per year, and those in Party committees a minimum of two special study groups per month. Secretaries and deputy

119. Chi Haotian, "Strive to raise the leadership level."

120. Xu Xin, "Make strenuous efforts to enhance political construction of the General Staff Headquarters and ensure that the army will always be up to standard politically," *Jiefangjunbao*, 2 March 1990, in FBIS—CHI, 30 March 1990, pp. 39–41.

121. See Liu Anyuan, "Seriously implement the 'summary' of the all-army meeting on political work, strengthen and improve political work in logistics departments," *Jiefangjunbao*, 2 March 1990, in FBIS—CHI, 29 March 1990, pp. 35–6.

122. Xinhua Domestic Service, 6 February 1990, in FBIS—CHI, 7 February 1990, pp. 19–20.

123. *Ibid.* p. 19.

124. See Beijing Domestic Service, 23 January 1990, in FBIS—CHI, 26 January 1990, p. 30; Xinhua, 24 February 1990, in FBIS—CHI, 26 February 1990, p. 26; and Xinhua Domestic Service, 24 February 1990, in FBIS—CHI, 1 March 1990, pp. 30–31.

125. See Li Xuge, "Implement the 'summary' closely in light of realities, make sure that our troops manage to withstand the 'three tests'," *Jiefangjunbao*, 8 March 1990, in FBIS—CHI, 30 March 1990, p. 41.

126. Xinhua Domestic Service, 13 July 1990, in FBIS—CHI, 20 July 1990, p. 29.

127. *Ibid.* p. 30.

secretaries of Party committees were ordered to keep records of attendance.[128]

This phase of implementation of the work conference's decisions also centred on the maintenance of the Party's "absolute leadership" and launching the Lei Feng campaign. Since "international enemy forces" were stepping up their war of "peaceful evolution," the "leading comrade of the Central Military Commission" (Jiang Zemin?) opined that "we must make sure that the guns are firmly kept in the hands of the people loyal to the Party."[129] One *Liberation Army Daily* article expanded on this need:

The political tasks assigned by the Party to the army include resisting aggression by a foreign enemy and preventing internal subversion by an enemy. That is to say, as an armed group carrying out the Party's political tasks, the army should play the role of pillar of state power in both the struggle against overt enemies doing evil openly and the struggle against "peaceful evolution" and subversive schemes. In normal circumstances, public security organs and the armed police force are responsible for maintaining law and order, and there is no need to use the army for this purpose. However, when emergencies occur and the police force is not strong enough to cope with the emergencies, or when the administrative and legal means become ineffective in settling the problems, the Party central leadership, the State Council and the Central Military Commission may decide to use the army to impose martial law and suppress the hostile elements who stage a counter-revolutionary rebellion, thus, controlling the situation and restoring law and order. This is also a function the army should perform. This is determined by the army's position in state power and by the army's nature and is in line with the sacred mission for the army as prescribed by the constitution. As a matter of fact, it is a common practice in all countries of the world to use the army to quell domestic turmoil.[130]

Hardly a more convincing statement could be made about how the Chinese soldier was clearly to be the guardian of Party and state power. To this end, numerous articles pointed to the need to increase the Party's penetration of the armed forces by strengthening the Party committee system.[131]

The GPD also began to press the resurrected "Learn from Lei Feng" campaign with vigour in the first quarter of 1990. Leading military figures contributed articles to the campaign.[132] In case the campaign was falling on

128. Commentator, "Hard and fast measures are necessary for theoretical study among cadres," *Jiefangjunbao*, 27 June 1990, in FBIS—CHI, 18 July 1990, p. 23.

129. Luo Yi, "The gun should be put firmly in the hands of people loyal to the Party," *Jiefangjunbao*, 13 February 1990, in FBIS—CHI, 2 March 1990, p. 24.

130. Wang Chenghan, "Uphold the Party's absolute leadership over the army with great firmness," *Jiefangjunbao*, 18 December 1989, in FBIS—CHI, 15 February 1990, p. 38.

131. See Chi Haotian, "Strive to raise the leadership level"; Gao Aisu, "When meeting with leading comrades of troops in Shanxi, Jiang Zemin stresses absolute Party leadership over the army," *Jiefangjunbao*, 27 January 1990, in FBIS—CHI, 13 February 1990, p. 14; Bai Xuan, "Unwaveringly uphold the Party's leadership of the army," *Jiefangjunbao*, 19 December 1990, in FBIS—CHI, 2 February 1990, pp. 17–19; and Wan Lixing, "The organs which control the army of the CCP," *Dangdai*, No. 7 (6 January 1990), in FBIS—CHI, 9 January 1990, pp. 20–2.

132. See for example, Chi Haotian, "Learn from and carry forward the Lei Feng spirit, strengthen the building of the people's army," *Renmin ribao*, 2 March 1990, in FBIS—CHI, 22

deaf ears (as it most certainly was) the GPD felt the need to issue a special circular in March instructing "all military units seriously to study and implement" the Lei Feng campaign.[133]

Amidst this dramatically-increased political work in the PLA can be detected a subtle counter-current of dissent from army professionals. The All-Army Political Work Conference had barely closed when the defence minister Qin Jiwei, a close Deng ally and military technocrat, published an article in the *Liberation Army Daily* that merely paid lip-service to political work, calling instead for the upgrading of "national defence."[134] This is an appropriate theme for a defence minister, but hardly in the politicized climate of late 1989. A small number of articles continued this theme over the next few months and echoed the professionalism theme, usually in the guise of the "national defence education movement."[135]

Phase 4: Reaching the rank and file. Since the first phase of implementing the work conference's directives concentrated on units above the regimental level and in the three PLA Headquarters, the second phase—which ran until the end of 1990—targeted lower-level units. Thus, beginning in March 1990, the GPD began to focus on the battalion, company, platoon, and squadron levels—the so-called basic (*jiceng*) level. As the director of the Commission of Science, Technology and Industry for National Defence, Ding Henggao, observed: "Leaders at the regimental level and above, particularly top leaders at the army level, play a decisive role in army building and in ensuring that the armed forces will remain politically qualified forever. But when the higher levels are politically qualified, this does not mean that the entire armed forces are also politically qualified ... we should not lose sight of the lower levels."[136] Building Party branches at the company level was the principal focus of this phase of the movement,[137] a

March 1990, pp. 27–30; Li Desheng, "Learning from Lei Feng's spirit is the need of the times," *Jiefangjunbao*, 8 January 1990, in FBIS—CHI, 26 January 1990, pp. 33–4.

133. "PLA general political department issues circular, urging all military units to study and implement the spirit of central leaders' inscriptions and carry out activities of learning from Lei Feng in a deep-going and down-to-earth manner," *Jiefangjunbao*, 6 March 1990, in FBIS—CHI, 29 March 1990, pp. 32–3.

134. See Fan Hao and Qin Hua, "Qin Jiwei contributes article to first issue of *Guofang*, stressing need to strengthen national defence education and promote modernization of national defence," *Jiefangjunbao*, 30 December 1990, in FBIS—CHI, 6 February 1990, p. 10.

135. See Gu Boliang, "Document issued a few days ago by PLA General Staff Headquarters outlines guidelines and tasks for military training in 1990," *Jiefangjunbao*, 9 January 1990, in FBIS—CHI, 30 January 1990, p. 18; Li Jinyou, "Correct understanding of the professional value of servicemen," *Jiefangjunbao*, 8 February 1990, in FBIS—CHI, 2 March 1990, pp. 23–4.

136. Ding Henggao, "Earnestly strengthen and improve ideological and political work; ensure that the armed forces will always remain politically qualified," *Jiefangjunbao*, 3 March 1990, in FBIS—CHI, 30 March 1990, p. 13.

137. For detailed discussions of this process see Organizational Department of the Political Department of the PLA General Staff Department (ed.), *Dangwei jianshe tanyao* (Beijing:

visibly structural effort by the Party to penetrate the military in order to ensure its compliance and loyalty.

The new phase of the campaign was launched with the promulgation of the directive "Programme on strengthening and improving ideological and political education for soldiers" by the GPD in early March 1990.[138] The "programme" instructed political departments at and above the division level to "give guiding opinions on regular ideological education," while those at the brigade and regiment level should possess "decision-making power for conducting education."[139] The programme further instructed Party committee cadres, particularly at the battalion and company level, to ensure that ideological study was included in "routine work schedules."

In June and July select officers from the basic level were brought to Beijing for briefings by Yang Baibing and Chi Haotian.[140] In November a special meeting on building Party branches at the company level and below was convened by the GPD, again with Yang Baibing presiding. In his speech Yang referred to the "Outline for army buildup at the grassroots level."[141] This unreleased document evidently outlined a systematic programme for building Party cells in platoons and squadrons and strengthening Party branches at the company level.[142]

Apparently the memory of nervous recruits fraternizing with demonstrators or abandoning their weapons in the face of angry crowds of Beijing residents during May and June 1989 had convinced the PLA leadership that ideological conformity and discipline must be instilled in every single soldier. No doubt the Romanian precedent further reinforced this conviction. Having already tackled the senior officer corps, the campaign now shifted to relations between officers and soldiers,[143] and enlisted men themselves.

Changzheng chubanshe, 1990; and Organizational Department of the Political Department of the PLA General Staff Department (ed.), *Xin shiqi dang zhibu shuji "liu hui" gaiyao* (Beijing: Changzheng chubanshe, 1991).

138. See "PLA General Political Department promulgates 'programme on strengthening and improving ideological and political education for soldiers'," *Jiefangjunbao*, 12 March 1990, in FBIS—CHI, 11 April 1990, pp. 31–3.

139. *Ibid*. p. 32.

140. See Gao Aisu, "At discussion with comrades attending enlarged meeting of Beijing military regional Party committee, Yang Baibing urges leaders at all levels to work harder and do an even better job in army-building," *Jiefangjunbao*, 22 June 1990, in FBIS—CHI, 9 July 1990, pp. 36–8; Xinhua Domestic Service, 31 July 1990, in FBIS—CHI, 1 August 1990, p. 24.

141. Xinhua Domestic Service, 21 November 1990, in FBIS—CHI, 27 November 1990, pp. 39–40.

142. *Ibid.*; and Commentator, "Adhere to the principle of 'building Party branches at the company level'—on strengthening grass-roots Party branch-building." *Jiefangjunbao*, 8 November 1990, in FBIS—CHI, 27 November 1990, pp. 40–41.

143. PLA General Political Department and Nanjing Military Region Political Department's Joint Investigation Group, "Display Wang Keqin's spirit of fraternal love and mutual help; preserve and develop good relations between officers and men," *Jiefangjunbao*, 25 July 1990, in FBIS—CHI, 22 August 1990, pp. 22–8.

Another key source of concern was incoming recruits. Recruitment training was now to include as much ideological as physical training.[144] Psychological warfare against "peaceful evolution" and other "hostile forces" was consequently revived as part of training curricula.[145] "Psy-war" was deemed the best defence against an enemy that sought to "win victories without fighting a battle by launching a war without gunpowder smoke."[146]

From early April to mid-May 1990 the GPD's *Liberation Army Daily* ran on the front page a 10-part series of articles (the aforementioned annotated summary) meant as instruction material for cadres carrying out the third phase of the post-Tiananmen indoctrination campaign, as well as representing a comprehensive policy statement on PLA policy in the "new period." The series reiterated many themes articulated in the *jiyao*. The first segment concentrated on combating peaceful evolution and bourgeois liberalization, particularly in the barracks.[147] The second instalment changed tack somewhat to try and relate the politicization drive to military modernization, although the connection was indeed tenuous.[148] Part three was a rendition of the "absolute leadership" theme that took "international antagonistic forces and a small handful of people at home" to task for advocating the separation of Party and army and the de-politicization of the PLA. This opined, for example, that ". . . [The] true nature of those erroneous concepts lies precisely in their attempt to make the army shed the Party's leadership and to remove the roadblocks for them to topple the socialist system."[149] Part four turned attention back to bourgeois liberalization and warned: "Since our army does not live in a vacuum, the many germs of bourgeois liberalization are bound to corrode our organisms and pollute the ideas of cadres and fighters."[150] Part five was a defence of communism. Taking note of the various problems in society, this commentary held that, "Some people think that in the initial stage of socialism, it is unrealistic to advocate communist ideology. . . . We hold that in the initial stage of socialism, advocating communist ideology and morality is not only tenable in theory but also feasible in practice."[151] Part six centred on moral educa-

144. See, for example, Xinhua Domestic Service, 18 May 1990, in FBIS—CHI, 21 May 1990, pp. 40–1; Commentator, "Unwaveringly put moral education in first place," *Jiefangjunbao*, 27 July 1990, in FBIS—CHI, 16 August 1990, pp. 29–30; Zhou Chuantong, "The requirement of being politically qualified should be carried out to the letter," *Jiefangjunbao*, 20 September 1990, in FBIS—CHI, 11 October 1990, pp. 26–7.

145. Zhou Min and Ru Bo, "First all-army forum on theory concerning psychological warfare against hostile forces," *Jiefangjunbao*, 12 July 1990, in FBIS—CHI, 2 August 1990, p. 23–4.

146. *Ibid.* p. 23.

147. "Ba baozheng zhengzhishang yongyuan hege zuowei yixiang genben renwu; yitan jiaqiang wojun zhengzhi jianshe," *Jiefangjunbao*, 10 April 1990, p. 1.

148. "Xuyu buke fangsong 'shengmingxian'," *Jiefangjunbao*, 13 April 1990, pp. 1, 4.

149. "Yongyuan ba wojun zhiyu dang de juidui lingdao zhixia," *Jiefangjunbao*, 18 April 1990, pp. 1, 4.

150. "Shanghao zhengzhi jiaoyu de zhuke," *Jiefangjunbao*, 22 April 1990, pp. 1, 3.

151. "Jianchi gaojun de sixiang, daode fazhan," *Jiefangjunbao*, 27 April 1990, pp. 1, 4.

tion.[152] Part seven criticized nepotism and corruption in the ranks and society at large.[153] Part eight centred on army–mass relations.[154] Part nine was a discussion of dialectics and Marxist theory.[155] The final instalment in the series was a wide-ranging defence of the army's internal role and the necessity for adhering to Party directives.[156]

Phase 5: From the autumn "adverse current" to new regulations. As China headed into the autumn of 1990 a modest reformist resurgence was in evidence in the Chinese leadership.[157] This was mostly true in the civilian sphere, but also in the military as professionalist themes began to be re-emphasized. Tensions in the military apparently surfaced around the 1 August army day reception in the Great Hall of the People, and centred around Yang Baibing. According to a usually reliable Hong Kong journalist, Yang tried to prevent several senior retired generals, with whom he was not on good terms, from attending the festivities. In the end they came and later complained bitterly to the Party general secretary and CMC chairman Jiang Zemin about the over-concentration of military power in the hands of the "two Yangs."[158] Several of this group had, in the famous 17 May 1989 letter to Deng Xiaoping and the CMC, expressed their reservations about using PLA troops to suppress the Tiananmen demonstrations—notably Qin Jiwei, Yang Dezhi, Ye Fei, Xiao Ke, Zhang Aiping and Chen Zaidao—and had watched warily as the Yang brothers dominated the CMC at the Fifth Plenum. Not having access to the retired Deng Xiaoping they took their case straight to Jiang Zemin. When news of this meeting reached Yang Shangkun he reportedly labelled it an "August counter-current."[159] The opposition to Yang Baibing is said to reach quite far down into the officer corps, who blame him and the GPD for being "seriously divorced from reality."[160] Yang is also widely rumoured to have run into personal trouble in late 1990 for having maintained a mistress in Wuhan who successfully blackmailed him into moving her to Beijing and maintaining her in luxury.[161]

152. "Jianchi decai jianbei, zhuzhong zhengzhi biaojun," *Jiefangjunbao*, 12 May 1990, pp. 1, 4.

153. "Renzhen zhuahao fanfushi douzheng," *Jiefangjunbao*, 19 May 1990, p. 1.

154. "Baozheng he fazhan lianghao de nei-wai guanxi," *Jiefangjunbao*, 22 May 1990, p. 1.

155. "Shiyong biandengfa, tigao xiaolu," *Jiefangjunbao*, 24 May 1990, pp. 1, 4.

156. "Zai jiaqiang de qiantixia gaijin zai duancheng de jichushang chuangxin," *Jiefangjunbao*, 28 May 1990, p. 1.

157. For further discussion of the changed political climate see David Shambaugh, "China in 1990: The year of damage control," *Asian Survey* (January 1991), pp. 101–114.

158. Lo Bing, "A heavy storm in the high army hierarchy," *Zhengming*, No. 155 (1 September 1990), in FBIS—CHI, 6 September 1990, pp. 39–40.

159. *Ibid.* p. 40; also see Luo Bing, "Defence minister has courageously defeated generals of the Yang family," *Kaifang*, No. 44 (15 August 1990), in FBIS—CHI, 23 August 1990, pp. 35–7.

160. Qi Da, "Young military officers boycott Yang Baibing," *Dangdai*, 20 October 1990, in FBIS—CHI, 25 October 1990, pp. 30–2. On this point see also Jencks, "Civil–military relations in China," especially pp. 24–7.

161. Personal communications with sources in Beijing, summer 1991.

Thus more than a year after Tiananmen reports of deep splits in the military continued to surface. Not only was Tiananmen at issue, but the Yang Baibing-directed political work campaigns of the post-Tiananmen period offended the professional ethic that had taken root in the officer corps prior to Tiananmen.[162] The concentration of power in the hands of the Yang brothers was particularly troubling for several senior commanders. Yang Shangkun possesses tremendous power as president of the republic and the ranking military official on the CMC, while younger brother Baibing holds key staff positions (with control over personnel dossiers and job placement) on both the Central Committee Secretariat and Central Military Commission, as well as the GPD. It is clear that Yang Baibing has tried to use his institutional power, and the aforementioned campaigns, to exert control over the PLA Party structure from top to bottom.

The autumn adverse current perhaps shows that ideological force-feeding may have had the opposite effect on the officer corps from what was intended. Most political campaigns in China are used by those running them to weed out opposition. In this case there were reports of sweeping purges.[163] There is no doubt that Yang's campaigns touched everyone in the PLA. A remarkable summary of political work in the PLA during the previous year published in the *People's Daily* on 3 October 1990 revealed that every cadre in every PLA Party committee at or above the regiment level had been investigated for his political stand; GPD-dispatched investigative teams had spent seven months evaluating leadership groups at or above the army corps level; "offices at or above the divisional level have dispatched 24,000 cadres, in 5,500 work units, to the grassroots, and 2,300 office cadres to company units to work as soldiers"; the three general headquarters trained 1,600 "tutors" schooled in Marxist philosophy to supervise ideological study in PLA Party committees; and "15,000 leading cadres and essential theoretical cadres at the regimental level" had participated in a total of 233 course terms of theoretical study taught by 10,000 cadres from the divisional and regimental level.[164]

As 1990 came to a close, politicization of the PLA political indoctrination of the PLA intensified. In a speech to a work conference convened by the General Staff Department in December, for example, Yang Baibing again stressed the "absolute leadership of the Party" theme.[165] CMC Chairman and CCP General Secretary Jiang Zemin, as well as Yang Shangkun, also

162. This is apparently not only the case among elements of the retired High Command, but particularly among younger officers. Interviews with officers in the Beijing Military Region, 26 May and 23 June 1991.
163. See, for example, Nan Xun, "Massive military purges after 4 June incident," *Ming Bao*, 22 October 1990, in FBIS—CHI, 22 October 1990, p. 29.
164. Li Chenghua and Xu Rujin, "Xin de xingshi—xin de bufa," *Renmin ribao*, 3 October 1990, p. 1; also translated in FBIS—CHI, 18 October 1990, pp. 39–42.
165. See "Baozheng dang dui jundui de juedui lingdao: Yang Baibing tan quanjun jicha gongzuo de genben renwu," *Jiefangjunbao*, 1 December 1990.

addressed the meeting. Both gave their stamp of approval to Yang Baibing's hardline approach.[166]

It was also in December 1990 that the Central Military Commission promulgated an important new set of regulations to govern political work in the PLA (*Zhongguo renmin jiefangjun zhengzhi gongzuo tiaoli*).[167] These regulations remain highly classified and have not been released publicly.[168] Reports in the *Liberation Army Daily* indicate that they reiterate themes set down in the documents emanating from the December 1989 PLA political work conference, and in fact grew out of that meeting. Most notable in these new regulations is Party building in the PLA. Not only is the "absolute leadership of the Party" emphasized repeatedly,[169] but a special emphasis is put on establishment of Party branches below the regimental level as a means of ensuring the former.[170] Countering "peaceful evolution" and "bourgeois liberalism" are also key themes in the regulations.

These regulations are further testimony of the nervousness that the CCP leadership feels about the PLA rank and file should a repeat of 1989 occur. The paranoid and defensive tone of Party pronouncements that link internal and external subversion are indicative of the siege mentality that grips the Zhongnanhai.[171] Should the PLA be called upon again to quell domestic disorder (should the People's Armed Police fail to do the job) the Party seeks to ensure that action will be swift and sure.

The abortive August 1991 coup d'etat and collapse of Communist Party rule in the Soviet Union only emboldened the Chinese leadership's siege mentality and served to intensify the crackdown evident since June 1989. A series of inner-Party documents (particularly *Zhongfa* no. 4) informed Party cadres of the "historical retrogression" (Deng Xiaoping's terminology) that had transpired in the Soviet Union, and warned of the need for heightened vigilance against "peaceful evolution." Naturally, the Chinese leadership was quick to grasp the military implications of the events in Moscow. Immediately after the collapse of the coup, Yang Baibing (in his capacity as secretary general of the CMC and GPD chief) convened an

---

166. See "Quanjun keke yueyue zuohao junshi gongzuo: Jiang Zemin zai zongcan gongzuo huiyi shang yaoqui," *Jiefangjunbao*, 5 December 1990; and "Zhichi zhandou lige zhun, shixian junshi shang guoying," *Jiefangjunbao*, 5 December 1990.

167. See "New rules on PLA control," *South China Morning Post*, 2 January 1991.

168. They are classified "secret, carefully protect" and are disseminated by the GPD in a pocket-size edition to all officers.

169. Of the many articles in the *Liberation Army Daily* on this aspect see in particular "Zhichi dang dui jundui juedui lingdao shi wojun de genben yuanze," *Jiefangjunbao*, 17 April 1991.

170. See, for example, "Baozheng jiceng dang zhibu zuzhi jianquan," *Jiefangjunbao*, 2 February 1991; "Renzhen xuexi he guanche luoshi 'zhenggong tiaojian'," *Jiefangjunbao*, 23 February 1991; and Luo Wangwen, "Quan jun geji dangwei fahui hexin lingdao zuoyong," *Renmin ribao*, 24 June 1991, p. 1.

171. Among the numerous leadership speeches, documents and declarations on this score see Yang Baibing, "Dang de juedui lingdao shi women de jian jun zhihunli jun zhiben," *Renmin ribao*, 24 June 1991, p. 5.

emergency "all-army political work conference."[172] The meeting dealt with the pressing need to heighten ideological work in the armed forces and strictly obey Party orders. Yang told delegates: "The army's political work is faced with more severe tests under the new situation."[173] CMC Chairman and CCP General Secretary Jiang Zemin, CMC first vice-chairman and president Yang Shangkun, and CMC member Liu Huaqing all attended the emergency meeting. Following the meeting Jiang Zemin gave a hardline speech, carried in the *People's Daily*, in which he too warned of the "new situation" confronting China's communists and the PLA. Jiang stressed that army-building is "urgently required by the objective situation. We must never waver in insisting that the Party exercises absolute leadership over the army. The army must obey the command of the Party Central Committee and the Central Military Commission in all its actions. . . ."[174] This is how the Chinese leadership initially responded to the climactic events in the Soviet Union. That is, they concluded—as they had ever since 1989—that a loyal military is the key to their political and personal survival.

Conclusion

Probably not since the days of Lin Biao, if then, has the PLA been subjected to such intense politicization as in the post-Tiananmen period. The explicit goal of these campaigns—for the military to be an armed political tool of the Party—and the manner in which they have been carried out revalidates the political control thesis that has existed on and off in the field of Chinese military studies over the years. We have seen clearly that the Party not only seeks strict control over the gun, but it has three principal organizational devices for doing so: the GPD political commissar system; the PLA Party committee system; and the PLA discipline inspection committee system. It is because of these mechanisms, as well as the 60-year development of the PLA, that I conclude the soldier and the state in China have a generically different relationship from western, or even other communist, militaries.

From one perspective, it could be argued that the two are locked into a symbiotic relationship in which they sustain each other. From another, the structures and processes of control outlined in this study suggest that Party *control* of the military remains a more viable paradigm for understanding the relationship (particularly from 1959–78 and since 1987). If the relationship was more symbiotic, the Party would not go to such great lengths to try and assert its control over the PLA.

172. See "Yang Baibing on importance of ideological work for army facing 'severe tests'," *Summary of World Broadcasts—Far East*, FE/1177, B2/1.
173. *Ibid.*
174. "Jiang Zemin urges army to conscientiously implement Mao Zedong's military thought," *Renmin ribao*, 11 September 1991, *ibid.* B2/2.

Alternatively, perhaps the proper explanation is that the relationship of soldier and state in China has evolved over time from one of symbiosis to control. Shared means and ends brought the CCP and PLA to power through revolutionary warfare. This shared identity of interests sustained the political–military symbiosis through the 1950s, but with the purge of Peng Dehaui and ascent of Lin Biao the shared vision began to diverge as fractured politics in the civilian sphere began to impinge on the post-revolutionary professional mission of the military (it has been shown repeatedly in this article how the GPD has been a radicalized institution in the military, frequently subject to manipulation by Party elites). As the revolutionary thermidor further set in during the late-Mao era the symbiotic identity wore increasingly thin. In its stead corporate professionalism began to take root in the PLA under Deng, but in the late-Deng era nascent military autonomy became a potential threat to Party rule—not because of Bonapartism but because CCP political power needed to rely on the PLA gun for its literal sustenance. In addition to the propaganda system and assertive nationalism, the only remaining weapon in the CCP's arsenal is the coercive apparatus. Political power once again grows out of the barrel of a gun.

This analysis leaves me convinced that the Chinese Communist Party is not going to go down without a fight, and the PLA will be called upon to do the fighting should civil disobedience erupt again. The relatively peaceful collapse of communist rule in the Soviet Union and Eastern Europe will not be repeated in the People's Republic. The bloodshed in Beijing, Chengdu, and Lhasa during 1989 may, sadly, only foreshadow future events.

Postscript

Republication of this chapter warrants reconsideration of its central arguments and evidence. The passage of nearly four years also necessitates some updating. Civil–military relations in China have continued to evolve through the mid-1990s, particularly as a central element in the run-up to the post-Deng Xiaoping succession, but have tended to follow the general patterns outlined previously in this chapter.

The evidence of the last few years bolsters, I believe, my central argument that the PLA and Communist Party elite are interlocking symbiotic entities. Those analysts who argue that the PLA are a professional military wishing to disengage from the political arena are losing currency. This does not mean, however, that the PLA cannot be *at the same time* a political and a professional military. Many years of history, as well as the situation in the PLA in the mid-1990s, suggests that these are not mutually exclusive roles for the PLA. The PLA is currently embarked upon an unprecedented drive for modernization and upgrading, but evidence convincingly suggests that this has not come at the expense of its politicization or political role in the affairs of state.

The military is seen by many as playing the key kingmaker role in the succession, and Jiang Zemin—Deng's anointed successor—has expended extraordinary effort to cultivate support among the armed forces. Hardly a month passes without Jiang visiting one or more military garrisons or institutions, and he has personally (in his capacity as chairman of the Central Military Commission) promoted and removed senior generals from the High Command. Further evidence of the PLA's influence in elite politics came at the pivotal 14th Party Congress when the number of PLA representatives on the Central Committee dramatically increased (to 22 per cent), reversing a 15-year decline. Military representation on the prestigious Politburo also rose, with Admiral Liu Huaqing being inducted on to the ruling Standing Committee.

Without doubt the most dramatic and surprising change in Party–Army relations, since the original publication of this chapter, transpired in the wake of the 14th Congress when powerful CMC secretary and GPD chief Yang Baibing was abruptly removed from these positions (although he was simultaneously promoted to the Politburo, a position he occupies only in name). Yang's elder half-brother Yang Shangkun was also subsequently forced to retire from the CMC (where he held the rank of first vice-chairman) and the Presidency of the People's Republic of China. As detailed earlier in this chapter the Yangs had played vitally central roles in orchestrating the Tiananmen massacre (Yang Shangkun) and the post-Tiananmen cleansing of the ranks of the PLA (Yang Baibing).

Their abrupt removal took all observers by surprise, and was apparently due to Yang Baibing's premature plotting for the post-Deng era. It was widely reported in the Hong Kong press that the younger Yang had convened several meetings of senior military brass in September 1992, on the eve of the 14th Congress, to ensure that the PLA fell under their control upon Deng Xiaoping's death and that the blame for the Tiananmen massacre would be placed on Deng (which, of course, would be partially correct, but would ignore Yang Shangkun's own instrumental role). Yang Baibing's intensive indoctrination campaign aimed at ensuring the "absolute loyalty" of the Army to the Party, as outlined previously in this chapter, had not gone down particularly well in the ranks and among professionalist-oriented officers. Nor had it apparently been particularly well-received among retired elders Xu Xiangqian, Ye Fei, Chen Zaidao, Yang Dezhi, Zhang Aiping, and others. Many of this group of elders had signed the famous 11 May 1989 letter to Deng and the CMC arguing against the use of the PLA to suppress the Tiananmen demonstrations, and had been openly discontented with what they perceived to be a power play by the Yangs to grab power after Deng's passing. Apparently on the eve of the 14th Congress this group plus Generals Liu Huaqing and Zhang Zhen visited Deng at his private residence to report on Yang Baibing's manoeuvring and to demand his ouster. Deng acquiesced and the Yangs were summarily removed from the Central Military Commission—although (to this day) no public announcement was made of the reasons and no internal campaign against the Yangs has been implemented. Yang Baibing appeared at the Congress and is even recorded in the *Liberation Army Daily* as giving a speech a week later, but he disappeared from public life thereafter.

Following the dismissal of the Yangs the next task was to purge the remnants of the extensive "Yang family village" (*Yang jia cun*). Yu Yongbo was appointed to replace Yang Baibing as head of the GPD, but more importantly Deng Xiaoping's personal military secretary (*mishu*), Wang Ruilin, was appointed as deputy chief of the GPD. General Wang was charged by Deng with overseeing the removal of Yang cronies throughout the PLA. This was no small undertaking, as the Yangs (Yang Baibing in particular) had filled the upper echelons of the GPD, and to a lesser extent the General Staff Department, Military Region, and Group Army commands, with his clients. To root out the extensive Yang network General Wang Ruilin engineered a three-phase campaign over a year and a half to progressively weed out loyalists. The first phase lasted from the autumn of 1992 through the spring of 1993 and focused on Yang Baibing's clients in GPD headquarters in Beijing and other central-level institutions. Numerous promotions that Yang had ordered in September 1992 were also reversed in this initial stage. The second phase lasted from the spring through the autumn of 1993 and concentrated on the GPD structure at the Military Region and Group Army levels. The final phase ran into mid-1994 and was concentrated more particularly on Yang Shangkun loyalists in the General Staff and Group Army commands. In 1994 and 1995 the housecleaning was made complete with almost wholesale replacements of officers at the Group Army level and above. This was accomplished through a combination of promotions of younger officers, retirement of older officers, transfers, and purges.

For his part, Yang Shangkun miraculously managed largely to disassociate himself from the purge and machinations of his younger brother. Yang's own individual stature in the Party, Army, and State structure, not to mention his life-long closeness to paramount leader Deng Xiaoping, all helped him to weather the storm. Even before their removal from official PLA positions, Yang Shangkun had managed to distance himself from his half-brother, depsite the fact that the latter did his best to hang his image on his elder brother's coat-tails. Despite retirement, Yang Shangkun continues to play a leading role as a Party elder, but has been careful to remain away from appearances and activities with the military.

The intense politicization of the PLA to ensure loyalty to the Communist Party has, however, outlasted the removal of the Yangs. This is undoubtedly related to the tenuousness of the Deng succession and the need for

PLA support for the Communist Party as an institution and Jiang Zemin's need to build up his PLA power-base in particular. But the continuance of the campaign does also point up the symbiotic relationship outlined earlier in this chapter.

The implications of this symbiosis and efforts to inculcate "absolute loyalty" to the CCP reaffirm, to my mind, the conclusions reached five years ago (outlined in the concluding section above) when this article was first written. The People's Liberation Army is essential to the continued sustenance of Communist Party rule and the existence of the People's Republic itself. Rule by the CCP over the PRC is not likely to implode as in the former Soviet Union and among former East European Communist party-states. The Communist Party in China will not go down without a fight, and the Army will be called upon to defend the party-state. Only time and circumstance will tell whether the PLA will heed the Party's orders, but past interventions by the PLA at the CCP's behest suggest that orders will be obeyed. There may, as in June 1989, be some units that disobey, even defect; this too can be expected in a crisis atmosphere. It must also be noted that the PLA's deepened involvement in commerce has had a deleterious effect on military professionalism and readiness, but I would submit that this involvement provides further incentives for the PLA to prop up the Party and system that provide these commercial benefits. There would probably be substantial pressures in a post-communist China to "professionalize" and depoliticize the armed forces—to make it a national army instead of the Party's army.

Thus there exist substantial incentives as well as coercive reasons for PLA compliance with Party directives. Also, the command and control structure in the PLA has been considerably strengthened and recentralized since 1989. Military Region commanders no longer have authority to move troops in their regions, as these are now all controlled directly by the CMC and General Staff Department in Beijing. The former distinction in command and control between main and regional force units has been changed in an attempt to ensure that regional commanders do not disobey the Centre and become rebel "warlords". One thing is certain: the soldier and the state remain wedded in China and the armed forces will continue to play their century-long role of close involvement in the political life of the nation.

The Intellectual and the State:
Social Dynamics of Intellectual Autonomy during the Post-Mao Era

Michel Bonnin and Yves Chevrier

The relationship between the Chinese intellectual and the communist state experienced some significant changes during the 1980s, although some of the basic patterns established since the 1930s and 1940s were not altered. This contrast is in line with the overall impact of Deng Xiaoping's limited reforms, which gave more room, and more weight, to society vis-à-vis the state, while the basic structures of the latter were left untouched. Social change was the new element which allowed the intellectuals to enjoy more autonomy in organizing their associations and in articulating new ideas. The intellectual with an autonomous base in a more autonomous society emerged from the prevalent pattern of technocratic intellectuals operating within the state framework, a state whose totalitarian scope had deprived them of any social base.

Limited and conditional, this new autonomy was far from political freedom and was only accepted by the regime as long as it did not mix with politics. The rise of new social forces, however, would inevitably have political implications: both indirectly, by shifting the overall balance of the regime, and directly, by leading some social actors to speak publicly reflecting their new role in society. More than any other interest groups created or reinforced by the reforms, the intellectuals were actively involved. Through their numerous new associations and economic ventures they were involved in the overall process of social change as much as any other group. But in addition they were responsible for introducing new attitudes and new ideas conducive to political change.

In the latter respect, as advocates of society's interests, their role was matched only by that of the students. And when some sections of the power elite or among the new class of private entrepreneurs wanted to express new political ideals, they turned to the intellectuals, whose role was therefore central in the attempts at shaping a new relationship between state and society that highlighted the reform decade, especially during its second half.

Did the new definitions and the underlying social and political trends amount to the emergence of an autonomous civil society? The idea was clearly present. Yet its actual implementation met not only with strong resistance within the Party but also with caution arising from the enduring traditions in the intellectuals' own political culture and political vision. This prevented any clear-cut conversion of the accepted social autonomy into a controversial and conflictual political autonomy from crystallizing before 1988–89.

These dynamics have been described mostly from the vantage point of ideas or of politics. Our goal is somewhat different. We are not going to analyse the role of the Chinese intellectuals and their relationship to the state in the context of intellectual or political history, but rather in terms of how they joined the mainstream of post-Mao social change, and how their initiatives helped to shape it. We shall accordingly focus the analysis on how they established themselves in their small groups, institutes, publishing houses and other business or research ventures, in the new sphere of economic and social initiative allowed by the reforms.[1] But before we do this, the basic patterns governing the relationship of the intellectuals to the communist state until the end of the Maoist era have to be recalled, in order to clarify the scope of the post-Mao evolution, and because the new associative setting, and above all, the salons, that were so characteristic of the changes in the 1980s, have their roots in the social dynamics of Mao's regime during the 1970s.

Intellectuals in the Social Dynamics of Communism in Pre-Reform China

The relationship of the Chinese intellectuals to the communist state cannot be described in fixed terms, or from the sole vantage points of Mao's ideas and politics. The 1970s saw a clear erosion of the system of integration and control of the intellectuals reflecting a general trend for the totalitarian features of the regime. But the intellectuals had been involved in its overall social dynamics from the earliest stage of Maoism (i.e. the Yan'an years in the 1940s), as Mao strove to develop for them a unique function in the activist framework of the mass line and rectification process. Yet the instrumentalization of the intellectuals was somewhat counterbalanced by the more traditional practice of patronage and advice in the context of ideological feuds and factional splits in the bureaucratic establishment. This gave to some of the intellectuals more social room and (indirect) political influence than the regime would allow on the surface, even before the erosion of Mao's last years. Thus, in order to assess a complex relationship resulting in seeming paradoxical situations, it is necessary to look at the

1. Our information was mainly gathered from personal interviews with participants contacted mostly outside China after Tiananmen. In some cases, interviewees are deliberately not identified. We do not claim, of course, that the contents of the interviews and the actual social position of the interviewees are representative of the Chinese intelligentsia in general in the 1980s. As is made clear in the article, the decade saw a continuum of change, and we are dealing only with the more marked developments at one end of the spectrum. These developments became clearer at the end of the decade. We believe the sample is representative within these limits.

interactions of these several factors over time. The following will sum up some of the main points.

Mao's instrumentalization and rectification of the intellectuals

Like all other groups in pre-communist Chinese society, intellectuals were absorbed into the totalitarian state through various means of social organization and control. As a result, they lost the autonomous social base they had been able to build in urban civil society during the first half of the 20th century. By serving the communist state, however, they did not regain the privileged status enjoyed by Confucian (that is, state) scholars in traditional China. Being neither part of the working class nor the revolutionary vanguard as such, their fate was to merge within the new socialist order: a ruthless process during the 1950s that became even more ruthless during the 1960s and 1970s, when Mao's policies endeavoured to transform and even suppress the new technocratic elite by which the CCP had tried to replace the "experts," writers and artists inherited from the old regime.

Thus intellectuals had a special place in the Chinese brand of communist totalitarianism. However, Mao's negative reasons for singling them out were compounded by positive reasons, which granted them a unique function in the social dynamics of communism in pre-reform China. This function, and the resulting ambiguity in the intellectuals' status, can be described as the Yan'an predicament. In the non-modern social setting of the liberated areas established by the CCP during the 1940s in some of China's most isolated and archaic rural areas, rallied urban intellectuals appeared as a bridge to the modern world, and to the modern civil society that was missing in revolutionary China. The Party had to check and transform that modernity, because it was doubly foreign—bourgeois and Westernized. But it could also use it, in order to introduce more dynamics into the dialogue of the Party with the (then peasant) masses.

Mao's social dialectics did offset, but not suppress, his anti-intellectual bias. On the intellectual's side, a counterpart was found in the willingness of many rallied writers and artists to submit to the transformation and criticism imposed by the Party, provided they could reform and criticize the state from within. To the anti-intellectual and simply unequal side of the deal, a minority of intellectuals responded with utter dissent.

This polarity in the intellectuals' reaction to state policies has been underlined by Merle Goldman.[2] It stemmed from the literati's tradition of submitting to state power, while advising and criticizing it, in the name of moral values, and from the parallel Confucian tradition (found both in Mencius and Xunzi) of setting principles above the Prince, thus following an orthodoxy that legitimized criticism and dissent while barring political

2. Merle Goldman, *Literary Dissent in Communist China* (Cambridge, Mass.: Harvard University Press, 1967).

pluralism. The individualistic evolution in the neo-Confucian political culture did not suppress the ambiguity, which was also built into the late imperial public sphere (*gong shi*). Yet, as shown by Mary Rankin, the public sphere remained a non-political arena centred on the management of local affairs until the very last decades of the Qing dynasty (see footnote 12). Scholars could participate in national politics, but along the lines of the bureaucratic structures, both formal and informal: see the patronage–advice pattern discussed in the following section. As explained by Goldman, Benjamin Schwartz, Vera Schwarcz and others,[3] these traditional patterns became modern constraints and the source of much tension when national and revolutionary imperatives reinforced the necessity of collective action and values (Schwarcz's *Jiuguo* concerns) at the expense of liberal-individualistic (*Aufklärung*) preoccupations. As a result, modern Chinese intellectuals since the turn of the century have been drawn by the attraction of the state, and tended to identify political action with action within the state, thereby reducing the margin for political opposition to individual withdrawal from politics or to heroic dissent with no hope of finding support in society at large.

The rise of the Communist Party to state power and ideological hegemony led intellectuals into a trap. The new state singled them out as specialized carriers of ideological and social initiative, but also as harsh enemies kept out of the proletarian fold and ruthlessly suppressed when they were called to perform their "historical" task of advising the Party in political terms. The new power was trying to construct the intellectuals as go-betweens, but the result was that many "establishment intellectuals" (see footnote 14), like many Party and state cadres, were scared out of the political process, so that the intellectuals were isolated in the midst of the socialist community. Although they were supposed to bring social energies to the socialist transformation of China, their historical task, as well as their actual status, was to work for the state and to increase its power.[4]

Advice under patronage

Next to this pattern of instrumentalization and rectification, which resulted in recurrent cycles of relaxation (*fang*) and repression (*shou*), another feature emerges by which the intellectuals occupied a special place in the

3. Vera Schwarcz, *The Chinese Enlightenment: Intellectuals and the Legacy of the May Fourth Movement of 1919* (Berkeley: University of California Press, 1986). See also Jacques Andrieu, "Le mouvement des idées" in M. C. Bergère, L. Bianco and J. Domes (eds.), *La Chine au XX° siècle*, Vol. 2 (Paris: Fayard, 1990); Y. Chevrier, "Chine: Fin de règne du lettré? Politique et culture à l'époque de l'occidentalisation," *Extrême-Orient, Extrême-Occident*, Vol. IV (1984).

4. This is one reason why many historians read Mao's China as a resurrection of the Qin system under *Fajia*.

regime's dynamics. Some intellectuals, individually or in groups either institutionalized or informally structured around personal relations (*guanxi*), were drawn into the policy process through patronage exerted by members of the power elite at provincial and national levels. Consulting with scholars was one way for ancient Chinese rulers not only to control the elite (by reducing the power of the feudal aristocracy and organizing a state monopoly on the sanction of scholarship by means of the imperial examination system), but also to establish a bridge between the sphere of government and that of society—a society where the uneducated were the vast majority, with the reputation of being unconcerned with the management of public affairs.

The advisory function of the intellectuals was never institutionalized by the communists as it was in traditional China, and was restricted to a small minority. However the intellectuals were also considered as intermediaries between state power and society, but in a more personal way. And they themselves, as a collective body, regarded the promotion or protection of some among them as providing a functional link with the power elite, a link through which they could express their own demands and, above all, articulate those of the people.

Advice under patronage, as well as personal protection, followed the particularistic structures, and indeed, the power struggles, shaping the dynamics of the bureaucratic establishment. If we notice that *fang–shou* cycles were also linked to conflictual episodes of the life of the Party–state, reflecting difficulties experienced by the power apparatus in managing its own inner conflicts as well as in the management of society and the economy, we may conclude that the need of the divided and embattled power elite to relay its politics via the intellectuals meant for the latter more than a special role. In the general balance of power, it meant that a weaker, conflict-ridden state offered some opportunities for non-state forces to reassert themselves. Deeper difficulties meant wider factional splits and more social fragmentation.

These conditions emerged after the Cultural Revolution shook the foundations of Mao's regime. They have been well documented for rural and urban society.[5] The intellectuals were not unaffected by them, at least marginally. The young educated (*zhiqing*), or elder intellectuals sent to the countryside formed links of personal relation and political persuasion which later led to the establishment of the first salons in the 1980s.[6]

5. William L. Parish and Martin K. Whyte, *Village and Family in Contemporary China* (Chicago: University of Chicago Press, 1978), and *Urban Life in Contemporary China* (1984), have argued the case among many others. See also Claude Aubert, *et al., La Société chinoise après Mao: entre autorité et modernité* (Paris: Fayard, 1986).

6. Interview with WR, 19 November 1990, and Michel Bonnin, "Le Mouvement d'envoi des jeunes instruits à la campagne: Chine, 1968–1980," unpublished Ph.D. dissertation, Paris, École des Hautes Études en Sciences Sociales, 1988, pp. 378–94.

The saga of the salons: initial steps

Our interviews show that a great number of the new intellectual associations and ventures in the 1980s were built around salons, which stemmed from kernels of personal friendships established under these circumstances in the 1970s. As the primary or cellular level of social autonomy, these groups are quasi-impervious to state control and immune from repression, provided the actual power of the state to control society decreases, as was the case after the Cultural Revolution. Overt activities and associations may fall back on these private networks when *shou* is on the rise. On the other hand, however, these minimal cells are a far cry from the Parisian salons where the Philosophes met "le monde" on the eve of the Revolution.

Although the informal groups which appeared on the intellectual scene in the wake of the Cultural Revolution remained private in essence, they carried two significant innovations. First, they were concerned with public affairs. Secondly, they resulted from initiatives taken by the intellectuals themselves, not by the state, even though the factional disintegration of the state and its loss of legitimacy were paramount factors in starting the phenomenon.

The word salon was not used then, except as a pun, when the *zhiqing* reflected on the paradoxical nature of their situation. While Mao's aim was to eradicate all remnants of intellectual power in the cities, the result was to sow the seeds of organizations among the intellectuals in the countryside. The importance of these groups in structuring intellectual resistance to the regime appeared during the democracy movement of 1978–79, which followed the return of the exiles to the cities. Thus *Jintian*, the first non-official literary magazine, was published by a group of young writers sent together to rural exile who had kept links with friends who, like Bei Dao, had been able to stay in Beijing. Their goal was to write in a different manner and to introduce new attitudes. They no longer submitted to state imperatives or values. Rather, they wanted to reflect on their own and be advocates of society versus the state—a state that had lost all prestige and any basis for claim to represent society's interests. Although not revolutionary (political power was not discussed), *Jintian* was suppressed when the movement was repressed, and replaced for a while by an underground bulletin, while the group kept a low profile and refrained from public initiatives.[7]

The example shows that the crisis at the end of the Maoist era provided more leeway for the intellectuals to find a possible autonomy (if not to find an actual echo) in society, thanks to the disorganization of the regime. Yet it also shows that while the initial steps were clearly taken when Mao was still alive, the political context was a decisive factor in shaping the public activities of the salons, after Mao's death allowed the intellectuals to return

7. Several interviews with Bei Dao and Mang Ke (Beijing, 1981; Paris, 1985), and Bonnin, *ibid.* pp. 383–4.

to the cities, by barring them from overtly engaging in politics unless they were protected by members of the power elite, who were playing their own political game.

In order to succeed on the political stage, salons needed patrons. The famous *dazibao* by the Li Yizhe group on socialist democracy and the legal system posted in Canton in 1974 stemmed from an informal study group encouraged by southern and anti-Mao pundits (like Zhao Ziyang and Xu Shiyou) in the context of the *pi Lin pi Kong* campaign. Incidentally, the membership of the group shows that intellectuals could be joined by local officials or Party cadres for discussion of public affairs privately. Such was the case with Guo Hongzhi, who met Li Zhengtian and Wang Xizhe in 1973, well before the group got in touch with the high officials who were to protect them and use them in 1974.[8]

Another famous example is the Study Group on Problems of Chinese Rural Development of the early 1980s, which later split between Chen Yizi's *Tigaisuo* and Du Runsheng's Rural Development Research Centre. The history and legacy of this group, who masterminded the rural reforms, is well known.[9] The "Four Gentlemen" (*si junzi*) who originally comprised the kernel of the group were of the *zhiqing* generation and shared an interest in rural problems. While they were confined to rural exile, they set up a study group whose main conclusions were that China needed drastic reforms. In order to implement their programme, after their return to Beijing they deliberately searched for political backing, using the old method of *guanxi*-building. Thus, they came in touch with Deng Yingtao, Deng Liqun's son, who shared the same ideal and joined the group.

Their success story epitomizes the saga of the successful salons in the 1980s. Proper ways and means had to be found in order to become public and influence the public debate or gain influence in the public sphere. The four *junzi*'s conventional, cautious, and altogether shrewd approach to politics is also representative of a widespread trend of the decade: intellectuals are carriers of a new kind of legitimacy embodied not in the state but in society, to which they are responsible, although they must look to the Party and state in order to exercise this responsibility, with the belief that the power elite is open to counsel and the existing political structure able to change.

The main factor affecting the origins of the salons was the situation of the state. It still constrained their development and the rise of intellectual autonomy during the 1980s, but a new element was then introduced by the reforms, with the changing condition of society, both in itself and relative to

8. On Li Yizhe, see Anita Chan, Stanley Rosen and Jonathan Unger, *On Socialist Democracy and the Chinese Legal System: The Li Yizhe Debates* (Armonk, New York: M. E. Sharpe, 1985).

9. John P. Burns, "China's governance: Political reform in a turbulent environment," *The China Quarterly*, No. 119 (1989), pp. 504–5.

the state. This allowed the intellectuals to take bolder and wider steps in terms of social and economic institutions, if not in terms of political organization.

1978–88: Intellectuals in the Mainstream of Social Change under Political Constraints

To our knowledge, the first salon to claim public existence as a political entity (not under cover of a specialized form of activity such as business or research) was the *minzhu shalong* established in Beida on 4 May 1988 by Fang Lizhi, his wife (Li Shuxian) and others (including several students, like Wang Dan and Liu Gang, who would later become leaders of the Tiananmen movement). Although the salon was set up within the isolated world of a university campus, the step clearly defied the unwritten rule of the 1980s that autonomy could be expressed, and even pressed, through various means but not political ones. The purpose of the *minzhu shalong* was to open a political sphere in an open contest with the existing political order, not to look for convenient niches within that order and for suitable mentors in the power elite.[10]

Fang's initiative showed that the underlying assumption that reforms from within would be feasible with advice from without, allowing the intellectuals to be within the political process while defending their new ideal of loyalty to society's superior interests, was no longer a shared belief. For many intellectuals, the dismissal of Hu Yaobang in January 1987 amounted to a breach of faith, leading some to the conclusion that politics without the state could no longer be eschewed. Until the political lines were drawn, however, the social autonomy of the intellectuals (like that of Chinese society at large) progressed only in the non-political arena.

The general setting: A non-political arena for a new public sphere

Due to the ideological-political standstill declared and maintained from 1978 to 1989 under Deng Xiaoping's aegis, the war waged by the Communist Party against society came to a halt, or failed to gain significant and lasting momentum when it was resumed in 1983 or 1987 (1989–90 will fall into this perspective when viewed with historical hindsight).[11] Exploiting this window of opportunity, a movement towards social autonomy unfolded

10. See, among other sources, *Zhengming*, June 1988, pp. 6–8, and September 1988, pp. 22–5, and Xuan Yan, *Jingdu xuehuo* (Beijing: Nongcun duwu chubanshe, 1989), pp. 37–42.

11. What we call the ideological–political standstill of the 1980s is the basic decision, taken against Hua Guofeng, not to force a political transformation on Chinese society (except in the realm of family planning). The decision was counterbalanced, in Deng's mind, by the assumption that society would not intervene in the realm of the Party, that is in politics. For instance, the anti "bourgeois liberalism" campaign in 1987 was restricted to the Party rank-and-file after some attempts at spreading it to society at large had been made during the first months of 1987.

in the changing framework created by institutional decentralization and the economic reforms. As a result, more autonomous bodies were carved within or out of state structures, and new avenues were opened for employment, careers, business ventures of a semi-official or private nature, that no longer depended directly on Party-state structures.

While individuals of all walks of life were concerned with these developments, intellectuals crystallized best the dynamics of social autonomy. Even when their economic status was undermined by Deng's new economics (in spite of official efforts to mend past breaches, integrate them into the working class and recruit them into the Party), the fact that some intellectuals left the state sector for jobs in the private sector or to start private or collective enterprises, heralded the new trend in a way that was as dramatic, and perhaps even more symbolic, than the return of the old capitalists or the accumulation of new wealth in the countryside.

But there was more. The old custom of officials asking expert advice was considerably extended because of the new objectives set by the Four Modernizations. At the upper level of Party and government leaders, but also at the middle and lower levels in the official structure and in the new realm of semi-official agencies, social scientists were asked to reflect on problems of public policy and decision-making in the fields of economic development, welfare, legal and administrative matters, and even in the political dimension at the time of the Double Hundred Campaign in 1986. Associations were established under official, semi-official or private patronage in order to do so. As the general trend toward "commodification" (*shangpinhua*) also involved the buying and selling of expertise, the political market for intellectual products that was created by the various forms of patronage also functioned as an economic market. Economic and intellectual activities were mixed, and political implications were never very far away, although they were formally excluded.

In addition to Deng's four basic principles, which imposed this rule of avoidance by claiming an absolute monopoly for the Party on politics and ideology, the old patterns of state employment, control and rectification remained unchanged. The vast majority of intellectuals still belonged to state agencies, and few, even among those who set up the new associations, completely broke with them. *Fang–shou* cycles became less stringent, but never stopped, from the Bai Hua affair in 1981 to the campaigns against spiritual pollution in 1983 and bourgeois liberalism in 1987. Critical or

For a general assessment of Deng's policies regarding society and policies, see Y. Chevrier, "Une société infirme: la société chinoise dans la transition modernisatrice" in C. Aubert (ed.), *La société chinoise après Mao: Entre autorité et modernité* (Paris: Fayard, 1986). Stuart Schram gives a detailed analysis of the "ideological standstill" arrived at in the wake of the campaign against "spiritual pollution" in 1984. See Schram, " 'Economics in command?' Ideology and policy since the Third Plenum," *The China Quarterly*, No. 99 (1984), pp. 417–61. The cycles in the implementation of the "standstill" policy are analysed in Richard Baum, "The road to Tiananmen: Chinese politics in the 1980s," prepared for the Cambridge History of China. We thank the author for kindly communicating his manuscript.

unorthodox ideas could be voiced publicly when, and only when, the Party gave the signal. The Double Hundred Campaign in 1986 was a consultative campaign in true Party style, at least from the vantage point of its initiators in the power elite. In spite of the fluctuations introduced by the cycles of political activity, the thaw became more effective with more visible consequences in the mid-1980s.

The most important departure of the post-Mao era from Mao's thought control was that intellectuals were allowed to discuss matters freely among themselves, in seminars, in conferences and even with visitors, although they were not supposed to discuss some sensitive issues publicly. As unofficial politics were barred entirely, the main avenue for intellectual innovation and political action was not yet public debate in an independent political sphere (this central element, and result, of a working civil society was lacking until 1988–89, and failed to prevail in the contest with the state): as shown by the famous think tanks sponsored by Zhao Ziyang, it was still advice under political patronage or debates narrowly confined to academic circles or called and controlled by state authorities.

As a result, autonomy was mainly defined in terms of economic and social freedoms, and constrained within a public sphere where intellectuals could debate around their role as a social power, or indeed, criticize the Party, but could not organize independent political associations. In other words, a sphere of economic and social pluralism emerged between the official sphere of the state and the private sphere of the individual, but no independent political sphere was associated with it. This unbalanced situation was not unlike that of the public sphere during the late imperial period, before the state-building reforms of the last Qing decade opened a political arena and created a civil society in urban coastal areas.[12]

As a result, autonomy within the changing economic and social context was not equivalent to intellectual emancipation. Yet the former definitely supported the latter and contributed to its radicalization, much as had been the case with the politization of local elites after 1895. But even for those who accepted the limits of the evolution in the 1980s, and who were content with expressing their public concerns politically through the established channels of the state or of the Party, belonging to the state or advising it no longer meant that one had to submit to its values or identify its interests to the interests of society: the new concept of legitimacy exemplified by the disenchanted *zhiqing* in the 1970s—the legitimacy of society, to which the intellectuals felt they were primarily responsible—gained ground in the 1980s. Again, this had been the case with the crisis of public values during

12. Under western influence, of course, but with the difference that the politization of the very late imperial public sphere did not curtail its managerial functions, which are not to be found in the post-Mao public sphere. On the pre-modern public sphere and its transformations, see Mary B. Rankin, *Elite Activism and Political Transformation in China, Zhejiang Province, 1865–1911* (Stanford: Stanford University Press, 1986), and "The origins of a Chinese public sphere," *Etudes chinoises*, IX-2 (Autumn 1990).

the final decades of the Qing dynasty, when leading reformers such as Liang Qichao developed the (then) new concepts of legitimacy of the people and of the nation as substitutes to the old ideal of loyalty to the dynasty.

The shaping of China's modern intelligentsia during the last decade of the Qing dynasty anticipated the attitude of most intellectuals in Deng's era in many other aspects. The late Qing reformers had been eager not to enter the formal service of the state,[13] yet they depended on bureaucratic infighting, personal protection and imperial favour, and did not raise the issue of political power until their failure in 1898 led to more radicalization. The 1989 crisis drew the lines as clearly and with a similar sense of drama, although some intellectuals, like Fang Lizhi, had confronted the issue before, in the wake of Hu Yaobang's downfall.

Pending political clarification, that is throughout the decade, ambiguities and shades were more widespread than clear-cut attitudes and formal delineations. On the one hand, the old polarity organized around the supremacy of the state (*fang–shou*, advice–dissent) tended to be superseded by a polarity including society as a major reference endowed with growing weight. But on the other hand, many powerful factors—political constraints, tactical restraint from the intellectuals, their tradition of serving or advising the state, the conveniences of patronage and official employment, together with the open possibility of asserting oneself independently in economic matters and social organizations but only in those—contributed to blur the new image of intellectual autonomy vis-à-vis the state.

Thus the true picture was far from being on the one side the technocratic intellectual serving the state within the framework of the state, while on the other the intellectual with an autonomous base in society served society's interests.[14] The two sides were present, but mostly as a mix. Autonomy as a social process was in a state of transition, a work in progress that can best be described as a continuum.[15]

The continuum of autonomy

Keeping in mind the mixed nature of the process we are looking at, and the fact that not all intellectuals were involved in it, depending on the situation of their organization or the political affiliations of their organizational or personal mentors, we may differentiate three types of organizations at the autonomous end of the continuum.

13. Liang Qichao refused to join Zhang Zhidong's bureaucratic entourage in 1897–98.

14. The status of "establishment intellectuals" has been studied for China in Timothy Cheek and Carol Lee Hamrin (eds.), *China's Establishment Intellectuals* (Armonk, New York: M. E. Sharpe, 1986). See also Merle Goldman, Timothy Cheek and Carol Lee Hamrin, *China's Intellectuals and the State: In Search of a New Relationship* (Cambridge: Cambridge University Press, 1987).

15. Burns, "China's governance," p. 503, describes a "continuum of autonomy" for the "state's intellectual advisers," while we use the concept for social organizations.

First (category 1), non-official, non-governmental associations (described as *minjian, minban* or *zizhi*) are the purest product of Deng's New Deal in that they are institutionally free from any links to the state, thanks to the official recognition of a non-state sector in the economy and to the official opening of a social pluralism.[16]

Secondly (category 2), associations organizationally linked to administrative organs, research bodies, state or (large) collective enterprises, but which do not fall under the direct supervision of political organs, have been a suitable framework for various intellectual-economic ventures, such as research associations or institutes.

Thirdly (category 3), research groups (*yanjiuzu*) or research institutes (*yanjiusuo*) established under central Party organs have revived the advisory function under high bureaucratic patronage, thus enabling some intellectuals with marked political preferences and good personal connections to become influential in the policy process and to express ideas independently of ad hoc Party orthodoxy and institutions.

Minjian associations were on principle not of a political nature. The salons, which were *minjian par excellence*, did not operate as such in the public sphere. They remained groups of friends meeting informally in a private setting until Fang Lizhi's breakthrough in 1988. Their members dealt with "cultural" matters, such as philosophy or literature, which were considered remote enough from actual politics. They were, however, very good channels for the communication and discussion of "new" (often foreign) ideas, that did have political implications in the long run, but seemed esoteric enough to be tolerated. Thus the young professional philosophers and cadres of the Youth League Central Committee interested in western philosophy who gathered at Chen Jiaying's home in the Heishanhu area west of Beijing called themselves the Heishanhu salon and declared themselves *minjian* with no qualms and without attracting much attention, although the philosophical works which were at the centre of their discussions were all unauthorized for official publication (Sartre, Heidegger, Marcuse, etc.).[17] The participation of the scions of high officialdom provided useful protection and, even more crucially, access to *neibu* materials.

---

16. It should be noted, however, that no declared organization was totally free of any institutional link, since each one needed a "tutelage unit" (*guakao danwei*) to be registered. In some cases, however, this tutelage was purely formal, because, firstly, the *minjian* organization was completely independent financially, and, secondly, the leaders of the protecting unit accepted from the beginning to serve only as a "shop sign" (*paizi*). This was the case for our main example of a category I organization, the Beijing Research Institute for Sociology and Economics, whose *guakao danwei* was the Centre for Expertise communication (*Rencai jiaoliu zhongxin*) under the State Commission for Science and Technology; interview of ZL, 28 April 1991, Paris.

17. Each of the first meetings was the occasion for Hu Ping to present a part of the long article he was writing on "Freedom of speech," which was to become one of the most influential expressions of dissident thinking in the 1980s; interviews with ZY, 19 November and 11 December 1990.

Conversely, the informal groups whose members were directly drafted into the high-level policy process (as was the case with the Rural Reform Research Group) were directly in touch with politics because they were integrated into the official structure (albeit, as they saw it, only as a matter of tactical convenience rather than a political engagement to serve the state). Official patronage and institutionalization did not necessarily entail less freedom than private activities when, on the one hand, China's deeply-split high officialdom was debating the content of the reforms and openly reaching towards society via the intellectuals in the process, and, on the other hand, non-official activities had carefully to avoid the political dimension.

Category 2 was most convenient in that it allowed official bodies to exploit the opportunities for privatization offered by the new public sphere. Thus the famous Steelworks of the Capital in Beijing (*Shougang*) set up a research centre when it became an autonomized company (*gongsi*). In view of the fact that the company director was secretary of the Party committee in the former enterprise, and considering the additional dependency of managers in the state sector on various bureaucratic networks, the amount of actual autonomy achieved by the centre is questionable. However it would seem that its members were able to conduct their activities without outside interference.[18]

Looser state controls and quasi private autonomy were also the reasons why many academic bodies created research associations which, in turn, set up their own research groups. For instance, a research group on human rights was created within the Beijing Association for International Comparative Studies on 29 March 1989 with a membership of 20 to 30 scholars and government officials (from the Beijing Academy of Social Sciences, from Beida and various central government departments, as well as several lawyers). The Association itself is a large gathering of academics, university professors and other intellectuals of the Beijing area, and it set up in parallel to the International Comparative Studies Institute of the Beijing Academy of Social Sciences.[19]

Finally, many of these semi-official appendages of the decentralized and autonomized state structure provided backing for *minjian* newspapers and research institutes. Thus surface organizational autonomy could merge into the second category. Publishing periodicals outside the realm of the Central Committee Propaganda Department was one way to gain autonomy. Like the famous *Shijie jingji daobao* (*World Economic Herald*) sponsored by the Shanghai Academy of Social Sciences, the new media heralding China's modernization and structural reforms were often attached to provincial academies. Although these institutional links did not hinder the activity of the new press as long as *fang* was prevailing, they provided a convenient

18. Interviews with YS, 16 June 1990 and with ZG, 14 January 1991.
19. Interviews in Shanghai, March 1989, and in Paris, December 1990, February 1991.

reason for the local power establishment to intervene in difficult times. Thus during the spring 1989 crisis the editor of the *World Economic Herald* was dismissed by the Shanghai Party committee on 27 April.[20]

The autonomy of the new associations and of the new media depended not only on the general political climate but also on the political fortune of their protectors and sponsors. *Qingnian luntan*, the periodical published in Wuhan by a group of young intellectuals was forced to shut down during the 1987 campaign against bourgeois liberalism. Their autonomy had been directly linked to Hu Yaobang's fate through his son. When sent by his father to Hubei in a work team operating during the *zhengdang* campaign in 1984–85, this son, Hu Deping, had been in touch with the group and had shown sympathy for their ideas and project.[21] Similarly, the Hainan Writers Association offered a useful umbrella to the Changsha-printed *Hainan jishi*, thus allowing Hunanese intellectuals like editor-in-chief Han Shaogong— other editors came from Jiangsu and other provinces—to publish a popular (if more cautious) mainland version of the Hong Kong magazines in spite of the official conservatism prevailing in Hunan, until the impact of Zhao Ziyang's downfall and the freeze from the north reached the south in the autumn of 1989.[22]

It would seem safe to conclude that the institutional setting reflected only one side of the process of autonomy, while informal influences and political circumstances shaped many continuities from one category to another.

One strategy, two tactics

The ideological landscape was hardly less blurred than the organizational setting. Most intellectuals at the end of the spectrum considered here, from Chen Yizi to Fang Lizhi and Wan Runnan, shared the same strategy, expressing the shift of allegiance from state to society discussed above: public initiative had to come from the intellectuals, speaking in the name of society. They were an autonomous power, whose legitimacy was rooted in society, not in the state. But the conversion of state activism (or intellectual activism under state control in order to strengthen it) into social initiative was subject to debates and differences when practical means, or tactics, were discussed.[23]

The attitude which was much more widespread, at least until the breach created by Hu Yaobang's dismissal, was the acceptance of the new deal

20. Burns, "China's governance," p. 506.
21. Interview with CC, 11 December 1990.
22. Two issues published post-Tiananmen, in August and September. The latter was claimed as making up for no. 2 that had not been published; interview with HS, 23 April 1991.
23. We leave aside the interesting problem of the cultural connotation of this transfer in the Chinese tradition, from Legalism (government is meant to increase the power of the state) to Confucianism (government is meant to increase the moral quality of the people).

offered by the state. The intellectuals could organize in an autonomous way, their expert advice was welcome. As Chen Yizi and other leading reformers explained many times, they were willing to participate in the political process within the established Party-state structure, because they believed in the genuine reform of that structure. They thought that their being within, as carriers of new ideas and symbols of new social powers, was a sign of change in the state as significant as the reforms engineered by the state and the possibility given to various social groups to operate in a new public sphere without the official structure.

At the same time, they were not oblivious to the overall rule of the game. The Party remained the sole and ultimate master, and one had to know the limits, as well as the turns in the official line.[24] Thus the small groups of economists and legal experts who were instrumental in publishing such influential periodicals as *Jingji guanli* or *Zhongguo fazhibao* were aware of many taboos. In large newspapers, such as *Yangcheng wanbao* in Canton, investigative teams of journalists considered themselves free to give publicity to corruption scandals and to various abuses of power, but only up to a point, as defined by geography and hierarchy.[25]

While many reformist intellectuals were keeping to the limited social pluralism allowed by the regime, and willing to perform their function of specialized and limited counterweights to state power, some criticized the ambiguous or grey practice of autonomy and wanted the new power of the intellectuals to be clearly expressed. One of the latter was Bao Zunxin, the first editor of the *congshu* (collection) *Zou xiang weilai*. From the outset, Bao raised the cardinal issue of the intellectuals' autonomy by questioning the channels of indirect co-operation with the state. The "cultural front" had to be occupied by the intellectuals in an unambiguous fashion. Bao's idea was that the new social power must assert itself as a power per se. Although the direction of the political transformation of the public sphere was indicated, the project fell short of expressing the central issue of power in an explicit way. Bao was replaced as general editor of the collection by Jin Guantao, who had higher academic prestige. But we may speculate that Bao's impatience with the softer and more cautious tactics of his friends was also behind that decision.[26] Caution and self-restraint prevailed until the deepening crisis of the modernization policy started shaking the faith of the intellectuals in a peaceful process of political change in 1987–88.

24. Burns, "China's governance," p. 505.
25. Interviews in Beijing, November 1985; and Yves Chevrier, "Managers and micropolitics: the factory director responsibility system, 1984–1987," in Ezra Vogel and Deborah Davis (eds.), *Chinese Society on the Eve of Tiananmen: The Impact of Reform* (Cambridge, Mass.: Harvard University Press, 1990), pp. 127–8.
26. Interview with ZY, 19 November 1990, Paris.

Business ventures and the circulation of ideas: Intellectuals and the economics of social autonomy

Patronage and debates around the political implications of autonomy were constantly reminding the intellectuals that the new freedom they were enjoying was limited and conditional. Another reminder was the perennial problem of finances. Institutional links to state agencies had material advantages as well as protection. Viewed from the other side, setting up a research group, publication or collection was one way for impoverished academic organs or provincial printing houses to tap the growing market of intellectual products. The convergence of these demands is shown by the many intellectual-academic ventures which associated private and public interests, using the various forms of organizational decentralization and the plurality of ownership systems legitimized by the reforms.

After 1983–84, many salons became public bodies under the guise of editorial committees (*bianji weiyuanhui*) editing collections of books (*congshu*) in association with provincial publishing houses. Thus, the Heishanhu salon became the editorial board for the series *Wenhua: Zhongguo yu shijie*. The project, managed by Gan Yang, was to translate and publish 470 foreign books, including works by Lacan, Foucault, Sartre and Camus (who were still officially banned). An "official" publisher—*Sanlian shudian*—was contacted, a contract was signed. It was understood that translations and editing would be the sole responsibility of the editorial committee, while the publisher would see to printing and diffusion. The latter's royalties would amount to 5 RMB for 1,000 printed characters.[27]

From this and other examples (such as *Zou xiang weilai*, already referred to, whose project under Jin Guantao was to edit 100 books),[28] it is clear that the intellectuals' demand and need of financial means met that of the publishing houses, which were no longer acting as the watchdogs of censorship but as economic operators seeking to take advantage of a third kind of demand, that of the intellectual public eager to read anything new, foreign or modern. It was nevertheless necessary to cover up. In their official contacts with state authorities, editors and publishers claimed that they were selling academic collections. *Guanxi* were put to good use. Jin Guantao's collection was published by Sichuan Renmin Chubanshe (also the publisher for much Tigaisuo-issued material). The editorial committee's cover was the CASS Research Centre on the Problem of Youth, also attached to the Central Committee of the All-China Youth League, where Jin and his friends found many counterparts who had entered the official structure but were practising autonomy from within. While the networks of influence crossed over institutional lines, some active individuals were involved in several committees (and relevant business ventures). Wang

27. Interview with ZY, 19 November and 26 November 1990, Paris.
28. Interviews with ZY and WR, 19 November 1990 and 11 December 1990, Paris.

Runsheng was one of the main editors of the series *Chuantong yu biange congshu* (published by Guizhou Renmin Chubanshe), but he was also on the editorial boards of six other collections.[29]

It became clear that these committees, thanks to their successful and overlapping activities and because of their surrounding rings of influence, were not without some influence of their own. They could indeed publish their own selections. The *Wenhua* committee refused to publish a book by the vice-president of Renmin Daxue in Beijing, who was considered a leftist.[30] Another measure of the growing influence of the intellectuals via the economic sphere was the rapid expansion of the research institutes created to answer the new demand for expertise. The think tanks established within the regular administrative structure operated according to standard procedures. Thus, the contracts between Tigaisuo and various state agencies (for studies, surveys, opinion polls, etc.) reflected the standardization of these procedures rather than any eagerness to "go to the market."[31] On the other hand, private or semi-private institutes were selling expert advice to government agencies and to firms, that is to the market.

It does not seem, however, that this was actually profitable. The institutes needed financial support from other sources. Some depended on "rich" enterprises, private or public, like the *Shehui fazhan yanjiusuo* created by Wan Runnan's Stone Company[32] or the research centre of *Shougang*. The famous *Beijing shehui jingji kexue yanjiusuo* (Beijing Research Institute for Sociology and Economics) established by Chen Ziming was supported by an array of smaller *gongsi*, among them the *Beifang tushu faxingshe* headed by Chen's wife, as well as by the profitable Chinese University of Public Administration by Mail (*Zhongguo xingzheng hanshou daxue*) created by the Institute in order to tap the growing demand for post-secondary education.

The Institute, whose original name had been *Zhongguo zhengzhi yu xingzheng kexue yanjiusuo* (Chinese Institute for Research in Politics and Public Administration), was remarkably active, thanks to the creativity of its director, Chen Ziming, and vice-director, Wang Juntao, a very articulate and experienced "critical intellectual," famous since his "heroic" participation in the 4 April 1976 Movement. Among other activities, the Institute organized a nation-wide survey on "The political culture of Chinese citizens," published a *Yearbook on Chinese Political Science* (*Zhongguo zhengzhixue nian-jian*) and many other books on political matters, as well as a bimonthly journal called *Research in Politics and Public Administration*. It was also the organizer of numerous conferences and, from 1988,

29. *Ibid.*
30. Interview with ZY, 19 November 1990, Paris.
31. Interviews in Beijing, February 1988.
32. See Wan Runnan's interview in J. P. Béja, M. Bonnin and A. Peyraube, *Le tremblement de terre de Pékin* (Paris: Gallimard, 1991), pp. 527–50.

joined with other groups of categories 2 and 3 in organizing them, which shows that it was gaining recognition in more established circles.[33]

Thanks to its independent financial foundation, the group was able to buy *Jingjixue zhoubao*, an economic weekly, from its original owners, the Chinese Federation of Economic Associations (*Zhongguo jingjixue tuanti lianhehui*), a semi-official sponsor gathering academic research associations. At a cost of 300,000 RMB, *Jingjixue zhoubao* was transferred from category 2 to category 1[34] and became the first truly *minjian* periodical.[35]

The galaxy of intellectual projects and economic enterprises revolving around Chen and Wang, together with the Stone Research Centre, epitomized the rising economic power and social influence of the intellectuals, as well as their ability to relate their public activities to the projects of other non-state partners, namely the entrepreneurs. The convergence was not shaped solely by economic needs or by the pursuit of profit. When private or autonomous state entrepreneurs created research facilities, intellectuals were often the true fathers of the projects. And the entrepreneurs had their own programme for public affairs. Wan Runnan suggested that China's modernization was dependent upon the rise of a new middle class of entrepreneurs supported by a strong legal system: hence the emphasis on these matters in his Social Development Institute.

In a way, the entrepreneurs were acting as the state patrons had done, and the intellectuals were happy with the substitution. The circulation of ideas was connected to the circulation of money and to the rise of incipient social elites; it was no longer exclusively connected to the circulation of power in the established state elite. Was this a sufficient answer to Bao Zunxin's impatience? At the very least, it puts the growing commodification of intellectual activities—a disturbing evolution for many intellectuals working for modest salaries in the state sector, and a moral failure for the conservatives who attacked the liberals after Tiananmen— in the right perspective.[36] Viewed from the general context, the commodification of production and trade, and the parallel deconcentration of state structures, drastically curtailed the state's capacity to control the economy and society. As the intellectuals were drawn more into the economics of the public sphere, they discovered the potential for more au-

33. Interviews with WR and ZY, 19 and 26 November 1991, with ZL, 22 April 1991, Paris; see also Li Da, "Shei shi Tiananmen guangchang zhengzheng de 'hei shou'?" *Zhongguo zhi chun*, No. 80 (January 1990), pp. 7–9 and Jian Jun, "Cong tizhiwai jueqi de di san shili," *Zhongguo zhi chun*, No. 85 (June 1990), pp. 58–61.

34. Interviews with ZG, 14 January 1991 and with ZL, 22 April 1991, Paris.

35. Burns includes the weekly in his list of quasi-governmental media owned by provincial academies, "China's governance," pp. 505–6.

36. The managers in state enterprise under the factory director responsibility system implemented since 1984 have been the targets of similar charges levelled against them by local bureaucrats who were trying to defend their vested interests; see Chevrier, "Managers and micropolitics."

tonomy entailed by the evolution. So did the conservatives, who, in addition to reasserting tough thought controls, were careful to destroy the logistics of intellectual autonomy in the wake of Tiananmen. In October 1989 State Council Order No. 43 (the first state regulation on the registration of social organizations since 1950) banned non-declared social groups (including research units, etc.), and forbade the authorized ones from engaging in profit-making activities.[37]

Breaking tiefanwan: The road to social individualization

The progress of autonomy in the changing social context of the 1980s may be measured from another perspective: that of the individual's professional status as a state employee, which involved much more than economic employment. The cellular organization of the *danwei*, that kept the individual in communal bondage, as well as the state allocation of manpower through *fenpei*, were not deeply altered by the reforms. Here again, the intellectuals developed a cautious and flexible approach to the lasting grip of the ancient state structures. They maximized the advantages of *tiefanwan* by not breaking with their *danwei*, while counting at the same time on the new opportunities in the public sphere, much as the writers had done by getting state wages plus royalties on their sales, but on a greater scale.

Thus the development of individualistic values and attitudes, which were so instrumental in shaping the world outlook of the younger *ziwo* generation, went together with caution and flexibility. Zhang Xianyang, a senior researcher at the Chinese Academy of Social Sciences in Beijing who kept his position while joining the Research Centre of the Steelworks of the Capital, was representative of the strategy favoured by most intellectuals. Few went as far as breaking *tiefanwan* by seeking full-time jobs in the non-state sector, as did Zhou Duo, the director of the research centre created by the Stone Company who left his job in the sociology department at Beida. So did Min Qi, one of the most active researchers in Chen Ziming's research centre. Another example is Gao Yu, the vice-president of the editorial board of *Jingjixue zhoubao*, who used to be a successful journalist in the official media.[38]

While they no longer shared the frugal ideals of the profession at large, upwardly-mobile intellectuals believed that their attitude towards material profit, careers and business was a contribution to the country's overall modernization. The New Intellectuals of the May Fourth era had shared a similar belief while giving legitimacy to the professionalization of China's intellectual elite.

37. *China Daily*, 1 November 1989.
38. Interviews with WR and ZY, 26 November 1990, and with ZL, 22 April 1991, Paris.

The Political Dimension

Towards independent political expression

In sum, the intellectuals' overall response to the continuation of the ancient patterns of dominance was to grow social roots while not directly challenging the state and taking advantage of growing divisions in the power elite. A clarification could come only from a clear-cut confrontation with the hitherto avoided political dimension. While some intellectuals had sought such a clarification at an early stage (we remember Bao Zunxin), further initiatives in this respect were made possible by the deepening political crisis highlighted by Hu Yaobang's dismissal in early 1987. On the eve of Tiananmen, many academic intellectuals working for the state, although bitter about their living standards and the mismanagement of public affairs, were still willing to trade material benefits for political influence according to the standard advisory pattern.[39] But some intellectuals, believing in the rising social influence of their group and following Fang Lizhi's epoch-making step in establishing a public salon, were ready to convert it into a political force.

But even before it led to overt politization and to confrontation, the making of a political sphere was the logical outcome of an evolution that became characteristic of the later 1980s. The building of lateral contacts between intellectuals and other social groups was a crucial element in the making of a civil society out of various trends of social autonomization. Contacts between intellectual groups and entrepreneurs were frequent and tolerated by the authorities. In addition to the links that have been described above, private or state managers, through their professional associations, relied on social scientists, legal experts and lawyers, in order to assert their interests. Thus, Cao Siyuan, one of the leaders of the Stone Research Centre, with Zhou Duo, was influential in drafting the bankruptcy law.[40] Business was clearly trying to influence policy-making by using well-connected intellectuals as intermediaries with the political elite. Some exceptional personalities, such as Wan Runnan, embodied all qualifications: Wan has a university degree, started a bureaucratic career, founded a successful private business, and is connected through his family to Liu Shaoqi and Hu Yaobang's circle. The embattled managers in the state sector were also willing to draft intellectuals and lawyers into their associations, in order to offset bureaucratic abuses.[41]

State authorities, on the other hand, have always been on the alert in order to prevent any horizontal linkage between the intellectual world (*zhishijie*) and the workers. The workers who attempted to build such

39. Interviews in Shanghai, March 1989.
40. See n. 18.
41. Chevrier, "Managers and micropolitics," p. 127.

contacts during the first Beijing Spring in 1978–79 were repressed.[42] One source (whom it is safer not to mention at all) indicates that some intellectuals at least considered the issue as the central problem in the regime's evolution.

Building up society's strengths, short of building an overt political sphere, involved problems of geography and raised the issue of centrality. By this, we mean the emergence of a nation-wide community above particularistic (localist) boundaries, such as the one Tan Sitong and the Changsha reformers tried (but failed) to institutionalize in 1897–98 with the organization of the short-lived Nanxuehui. As already mentioned, northern intellectuals found havens of autonomy and career opportunities in the more open and less tightly-controlled south, especially in Shenzhen and Hainan. Leading intellectuals and leading influences, however, were still located in Beijing, with strong regional centres in Shanghai and the south. From these concentrations of intellectual energy, tours were organized in order to reinforce the geographical linkage in the intellectuals' world. Fang Lizhi's famous series of lectures in whose trail the 1986 student demonstrations erupted was not an isolated occurrence. Talks were often organized by local *xueshenghui*. Thus Wang Runsheng gave several hundred lectures between 1986 and June 1989.[43]

In 1988 the movement toward autonomy accelerated as Zhao Ziyang affiliates also became disenchanted with the government after the clash between Zhao and Li Peng and Deng Xiaoping's support for Li over the management of the economic reforms.[44] Our purpose is not to study this process of political transformation per se. Suffice it to say that the clash between the two wings in the power elite not only forced a political polarization, but also offered a credible political alternative as well as the needed protection.

Regarding their direct constituency, the politically orientated intellectuals at the vanguard of the movement were gaining more support throughout China's technical and non-technical intelligentsia at large, as was shown by the success of Fang Lizhi's petition early in 1989. During the spring crisis, the salons in Beijing became virtual political groups.[45] While vertical links fostered by earlier collaboration and patronage were used in order to open channels of communication with the political leadership, as well as between the latter and the student activists on the Square, horizontal developments were clearly taking the lead. The intellectuals, the students and the workers formed organizations of their own, the intellectuals in Beijing with the Intellectuals' Federation (*Zhishijie lianhehui*), the workers with the Capital

42. Victor Sidane, *Le Printemps de Pékin* (Paris: Gallimard, coll. Archives, 1980).
43. Interview with Wang Runsheng, November 1990, Paris.
44. See the interview with Chen Yizi in Béja, Bonnin and Peyraube, *Le tremblement de terre*, pp. 505–26.
45. Interviews with WR and ZY, 19 and 26 November 1990, and with ZL, 22 April 1991, Paris.

Workers' Autonomous Federation (*Shoudu gongren zizhi lianhehui*). A common meeting on 9 May led to the establishment on 23 May of a Consultative Joint Committee of All Groups in the Capital (*Shoudu gejie xieshang lianxi huiyi*), otherwise called (on tracts) *Shoudu gejie lianhehui*.[46] Taking advantage of the state's obvious weakness and near-paralysis, urban society was organizing as a self-conscious and politically motivated whole at the level of an activist vanguard, as had been the case during the May Fourth period in 1919. The momentum was clearly toward the institutionalization of a civil society, although the politicization of the front line failed to be followed by a lasting mobilization in the rank and file of urban society after the state mustered its strengths and struck the students.

No democratic revolution occurred in China in 1989. At the very least, however, the failure so far of the political transformation of the trend of social autonomy that dominated the 1980s is the one unambiguous fact in the grey continuum we have described. As a result, a discussion of the relationship of civil society to state has become essential to our understanding of the status of the Chinese intellectuals and of their role in the 1990s.

From public sphere to civil society

In Europe and in extra-European polities influenced by the European tradition, the existence of fully-fledged civil societies has endowed individuals, among whom intellectuals have often been foremost, to be within public politics, and even within the liberal state wherever pluralism on the political field is part of the state constitution, while not being of the state. In China, although the political transformation of the late imperial public sphere occurred from the Xinzheng reforms (1901–11) to the establishment of the republic (1912–13), both civil society and the non-state arena for public politics (not to mention a liberal political culture) have remained underdeveloped throughout the 20th century, or at best sporadic and localized developments, such as in Shanghai during the "golden era" of the 1910s to 1920s.[47]

Because of the lack of a sphere of politics expressing social interests independently from state power, the role of China's modern intellectuals has characteristically reflected internal and external influences, while their status was drastically diminished in comparison with the imperial period. The new empire under Mao instrumentalized the functional ambiguity while lowering the intellectual's social position to unprecedented depths. Thanks to the post-Mao reforms, Chinese urban society and the intellectuals have been lifted out of the pit, but the process of autonomization they have experienced has also resulted in the resurrection of past ambiguities.

46. Interview with WR, 19 November 1990.
47. Marie-Claire Bergère, *The Golden Age of the Chinese Bourgeoisie, 1911–1937* (Cambridge: Cambridge University Press, 1989).

As the reforms were not carried deep enough economically and politically to allow for a widespread restructuring of the urban social fabric, especially at the upper end of society and in the power elite, the emergence of the new social institutions across the established Party-state institutional and personal networks kept a low and scattered profile, mostly under bureaucratic umbrellas. In this significant but limited change the intellectuals played their part, an important one, while welcoming the opportunity to escape from the Yan'an predicament as a group. Personally, too, they eagerly responded to the new private, semi-private or semi-official ventures in research, publishing, journalism, etc. In so doing, many, although not all, became mobile, even upwardly mobile individuals, freer of the communal structures that still encompass the majority of wage-earners in urban China. While some were deliberately trying to build new links with the power elite, and even to enter the inner circles of official politics as advisers, most were aware and proud of a new in-built strength, although most would not express it against the state. Utter dissent was limited to a tiny minority. As a rule, and in spite of sharp economic frustrations on the part of those (a vast majority) who still depended entirely on rigid state employment and meagre wages, Chinese intellectuals of the 1980s were happy to be back in the mainstream of society.

It would be misleading to scorn these developments because they fell short of the clear-cut institutionalization of non-official institutions, which political scientists view as the one significant step in the transition from authoritarian and totalitarian regimes to pluralism. Social autonomy and social forces may develop by taking advantage of widening cracks in the official power structure. The state's weaknesses (in terms of decentralized decomposition, factional struggles, and social fragmentation) make social groups stronger. The social autonomy (or social pluralism) permitted by the pluralization and privatization of monistic states that are no longer able or willing to maintain their original monolithism, should not by any means be confused with a fully-fledged civil society endowed with autonomous associations organized independently from the state, such as Solidarnosc in Poland or church associations in East Germany before the fall of the Berlin Wall. Yet, if we deem the former irrelevant on the ground of principles, we deprive ourselves of a powerful tool for understanding the social dynamics of totalitarian systems in general, and for grasping the true meaning of the intellectuals' situation in Deng Xiaoping's China in particular, as well as the roots of that situation in Mao's declining years.

In this light, it would be more sensible to differentiate, under the golden line of independence, between various degrees of autonomy giving more or less weight to social actors versus the state (or, indeed, to the connection of social actors with various dissatisfied segments in the state). Thus the upper level of social autonomy related to opposition politics, the criterion of an illegal underground lifted above ground yet not legally or politically institutionalized, could be epitomized by the French literary scene under Louis XVI as studied by Robert Darnton.[48] A true civil society was established in Britain at the same time. In both cases, many ambitious intellectuals wanted to be part of the power elite (and some succeeded), and political opposition was reinforced by the dynamics of the intellectual elite. But, as reported by the admiring Voltaire, British writers and thinkers could do so *de jure*, because they enjoyed rights, while the Philosophes had to depend on the *de facto* protection of Parisian society (structured around the salons) and on that of individual mentors in the official social, and even political, establishment. Although not always sufficient (or dispensed, as Voltaire found for himself), that protection was enough to foster an active social and political opposition, because state structures were deeply eroded on many fronts.

Clearly on this particular count Deng's China, in spite of the many fault lines activated or reactivated by the reforms in Party and state bureaucracies, is not (yet) France under Louis XVI, or China under the Guangxu emperor, when the ideological challenge of the west and the havens of the Treaty Ports split and alienated the elites while they weakened the state, leading to its collapse in 1911–12. Other factors are missing or deficient. The weight of society is still limited relative to that of the state (including vested bureaucratic interests in the *status quo ante*, as well as the political deadweight of the peasantry). While some intellectuals were ready to capitalize on their growing influence as a group on the eve of Tiananmen, urban China as a whole was not witnessing the forceful rise of a middle class. In social terms, the Tiananmen movement did not crown an economic and social success; quite to the contrary, it followed from the failure, the limits and the distortions of the reforms.[49] A last deficiency is the relative weakness of the ideological alternative compared to the potential of mobilization of the Lumières in 18th-century France, of the church in communist Poland, or of Chinese nationalism (including anti-Manchu racism) at the beginning of the 20th century. A discussion of this particular weakness, including the role of traditions, but also of the narrow materialism associated to the economic reforms, is beyond the scope of the present analysis.

This weakness, together with the absolute ban on political organization in normal times, resulted in the absence of an in-depth political integration of the social coalition arrayed against the state in the cities, besides the common rejection of those who occupied the seats of power. The intellectuals who broke from the within–without patterns of non-political autonomy in the public sphere experienced isolation when urban society did not sustain its initial support of the students. Certainly, the political sphere has been

48. Robert Darnton, *The Literary Underground of the Old Regime* (Cambridge, Mass.: Harvard University Press, 1982).
49. See Marie-Claire Bergère, "Tian'anmen 1989," *Vingtième siècle—Revue d'Histoire* (July–September 1990), p. 5.

maintained, and organized, but in foreign lands, where the isolation of the front line of radically political intellectuals is greater than ever.

Although they acknowledge the long-term necessity of buttressing their movement on a stronger and more mature ("better educated") civil society, the intellectuals-in-politics-but-in-exile have to admit that short-term escape from this unseemly situation depends on political developments within the power apparatus, which they can hardly influence. The paradoxical outcome of their political secession is that their final dependency on this or that faction in the state remains unchanged.

Yet although the tactical necessity and the habit of playing the power game may still linger over their political calculations and political culture, they have shed past ambiguities in terms of overall strategy. They no longer view themselves at once inside and outside the state except in the context of pluralistic politics. While being tempted by a strong leader who could lead China's modernization and reintegrate them into the Chinese polity, Gorbachev's sorry evolution, as well as a growing awareness that a Taiwanese-style neo-authoritarian regime would not solve China's problems, had led them to recognize that the state must be transformed in depth. It has so far managed a bureaucratic process of reforms which carefully avoid any efficient and sustained measures for building a modern administrative apparatus or establishing the rule of law, let alone changing the political system. A transformation of the state appears as much a prerequisite for intellectuals to join the process of modernizing China as the equally popular themes of education and cultural modernity. In other words, the intellectuals in post-Tiananmen exile are willing to produce ideas and to advise powerholders, but in the name of pluralism. Politics are the clarifying element which they are no longer ready to eschew.

In conclusion, the Tiananmen crisis was a significant step in the emergence of a civil society from the bleak landscape of totalitarianism, but only one step. An important factor in the evolution was the transformation of the role of the intellectuals. Already, during the preceding decade, their uneasy function as intermediaries between state and society had been reshaped in direct relation to the overall process of social change which had modified the relationship of the state and society. The political step taken in 1988–89 has made it legitimate to discuss their status and function not only from the vantage point of the state, or of the modicum of social autonomy permitted by the evolution of the state, but also from that of the nascent civil society.

That keeping in mind both perspectives—state and society—should still be necessary in order to assess properly the scope of the evolution is a testimony to the transitory nature of the process we are witnessing, a process that is bound to have many steps beyond the one taken in 1989, not excluding backward ones. Developments conducive to social autonomy within the existing political framework have already resumed after the conservative onslaught that followed the Tiananmen killings abated in 1990 (although thought control and ideological repression are still present). But it will take a fundamental political breakthrough and expenditure of much social and intellectual energy before we can speak with no further qualifications (save the still far-reaching one concerning the shifting but enduring weight of the peasantry) of the civil society as the dominant background of intellectual life in mainland China.

Youth and the State*

Thomas B. Gold

Introduction

The three birth cohorts which have passed through the youth stage of their life course since the founding of the People's Republic of China (PRC) in 1949 have had radically different relations with the Party-state. This has brought serious consequences for the Party-state itself, the Party-state's relation with succeeding youth cohorts and for the integration of Chinese society. Unlike the other chapters in this book, which address the relation between specific social groups and the party/state, this chapter analyses a stage of life which all Chinese adults passed through. They brought different things to the youth stage of the life course, and took different experiences into their subsequent careers as workers, farmers, intellectuals, soldiers, or whatever.

This chapter employs the life course approach of sociology to explore the relations between the Party-state and youth in China. The life course approach provides a coherent way to link the progression of individuals and cohorts through the biological life span, with the socio-cultural context and historical events through which the progression occurs. It delineates the social construction of transitions between stages in a life course and the definitions of the activities characteristic of each stage. Most scholars employing this approach trace cohorts over their entire life course or through particular stages, and/or use major historical events such as the Depression, Holocaust or Vietnam War as a way to show how cohorts adapt and societies reconstitute themselves after such disruptions. For China, the Cultural Revolution (CR) functions as this sort of watershed event, as it influenced not only the life course of Chinese people, including those born after it, but also the very construction of the Chinese life course.[1]

After discussion of youth as a stage in the life course more generally, this article reviews youth as a stage in the Chinese life course traditionally and under communism prior to the CR. It then looks at the different effects of the CR on three youth cohorts, before turning to the changing relation between the Party-state and youth during the post-1978 reform period. It is argued that the Chinese Communist Party (CCP) directly and through the

* I would like to thank Glen Elder, Gail Henderson, Martin King Whyte and Reginald Zelnik for comments on this essay at various stages of its development.

1. See, e.g., Weiqiao Wu and Glen H. Elder, Jr., "The best and worst of times in Chinese lives: When, why and how", paper presented at the annual meeting of the American Sociological Association, Miami Beach, Fla., August, 1993.

state and other Party-led organizations has tried to redefine and closely manage the youth stage, but has done so inconsistently, for a variety of reasons. This has resulted in wide gaps between cohorts and generations,[2] making it extremely difficult to integrate Chinese society, to say nothing of re-establishing the type of control the Party-state enjoyed in the first decade after liberation.[3]

Youth as a Stage in the Life Course[4]

Biologically, youth is an unavoidable period in the development of the individual between childhood and adulthood, but the content of youth as a stage in the life course is determined by other forces.[5] These can be addressed through three sets of questions:

First is a series of temporal questions: when does "youth" as a separate stage begin; how is the transition from childhood to youth made; how long does the stage last; and how is the transition from youth to adulthood made?

Second are substantive questions: what is the primary content of the youth stage; what is it supposed to accomplish for the individual and society as a whole?

Third are more contingent questions: how are the decisions about transition and content made; how does the historical context, including the society's international position, influence the life course; how generalized is the ideal typical life course in a society; how do ascriptive characteristics such as birth place, sex, social background and ethnicity influence life chances; how consistent is the youth stage through cohorts?

At its most basic, youth is a transitional stage in the life course between the freedom of childhood and the responsibilities of adulthood. Some societies do not mark it as a separate stage, as very young people assume the

2. "Cohort" refers to persons born in a given period who age together and have roughly similar experiences. "Generation" refers to genealogical categories such as parents and children. See Irving Rosow, "What is a cohort and why?" *Human Development*, 21(2) (1978), pp. 65–75; and Norman B. Ryder, "The cohort as a concept in the study of social change," *American Sociological Review* (hereafter ASR), 30(6) (December 1965), pp. 843–61.

3. Data come from published primary and secondary materials, as well as interviews conducted in China and abroad since the late 1970s.

4. On the life course approach, see John A. Clausen, *The Life Course* (Englewood Cliffs: Prentice-Hall, 1986); Glen H. Elder, Jr., "Perspectives on the life course," in Glen H. Elder, Jr. (ed.), *Life Course Dynamics* (Ithaca: Cornell University Press, 1985), pp. 23–49; and Karl Ulrich Mayer and Nancy Brandon Tuma, "Life course research and event history analysis: an overview," in Karl Ulrich Mayer and Nancy Brandon Tuma (eds.), *Event History Analysis in Life Course Research* (Madison: University of Wisconsin Press, 1990), pp. 3–20.

5. Glen H. Elder, Jr., "Adolescence in historical perspective," in Joseph Adelson (ed.), *Handbook of Adolescent Psychology* (New York: John Wiley and Sons, 1980), pp. 3–46.

adult roles of work and family without an intervening "youth" period. Where it exists, the common pattern is for youth to be a stage initiated by the onset of puberty (age 13–15) when the individual continues to live with the nuclear family and has not established his or her own household, does not work full time, and is undergoing some sort of training. The terminus might be anywhere between 20 and 30. Youths need not make the transition to both work and family simultaneously.

The major content of the youth stage is to prepare adolescents for the adult roles of work and family, so as to be able to continue and reproduce the society.[6] This involves imparting skills, sorting and allocating to adult roles, socializing youth to the responsibilities and norms of citizenship, learning to deal with others outside the home (peer groups), and adjusting to adult roles, that is, finding jobs and mates.

The life course is socially constructed, and the actual content of socialization, education, citizenship and so on varies widely across and within countries. There is variation also in who takes responsibility for these tasks—the family, societal groups such as the church, or the state. Much of modern history has witnessed struggles among these agents over control of the life course of the people. In much of the world, the trend has been for the state to expand its role in constructing and implementing the life course of its citizens, usurping the prerogatives of family and previously autonomous social groups.

Several variables influence the ability of a society to socialize its youth consistently and uniformly. In a rapidly modernizing society there is an explosion in new social roles, values and norms, making it extremely difficult for the society to reproduce itself and for youth to be thoroughly socialized into any particular set of values. The training received does not necessarily prepare one for the situation one faces upon entering adulthood; resocialization continues throughout the life course. This may result in wildly divergent values and experiences among different birth cohorts, to say nothing of the gap between generations of parents and their children. Inconsistent policies and political power struggles obstruct continuity between cohorts. Differing gender roles exist in all societies, and nations comprising a complex mixture of racial and ethnic groups, regions and classes also have trouble achieving consistent or uniform socialization. In the contemporary world, all societies are incorporated to some degree into the global system, which means that foreign influences exert an impact on the internal system, shaping structures and values. Finally, historical events such as wars, depressions, natural disasters and revolutions also play havoc with the life course and, by extension, the consistency or integration of a society.

Marxist-Leninist systems occupy an extreme position as far as conscious

6. It also performs the latent function of keeping them out of the work force.

construction of the life course goes.[7] In these societies, the party, on its own or through the state (which enjoys virtually no autonomy) or a plethora of party-led organizations, attempts to penetrate all corners of the society. It aims to restructure the prerevolutionary life course in order to harness all social energy to achieve party-determined goals. The party encounters constraints: in addition to the residual strength of tradition and social forces, the party has limited manpower, resources and tools to achieve compliance, and also must confront internal dissension which harms consistent implementation of policies.

Marxist-Leninist parties not surprisingly concentrate much of their effort on young people. The parties see youth as less tainted by the old society, therefore more readily captured by the new regime and able to be persuaded to work for its revolutionary goals. Successfully cultivating young people as revolutionary successors can help prevent the old society from reproducing itself and guarantee a large body of citizens mobilizable for the party's cause.

Youth as a Stage in the Chinese Life Course Prior to Communism

The CCP attempted a thorough reconstruction of the life course of the Chinese people as part of its mission of revolutionary transformation. This involved changing at all levels, from nation to family, the environment in which people lived, the agents and content of socialization, people's definition of self and relation to society, the scope for autonomous decision-making, and the ability to control their own life course. Achieving this restructuring required first and foremost usurping the prerogatives of the family.

The Chinese family traditionally was not only the basic production, consumption and socialization unit, it was also invested with quasi-religious significance through the practice of ancestor worship.[8] The family enjoyed a great deal of scope to manage its own affairs independently of the state. Its members literally belonged to the family whose head determined their life course. Males learned that their primary allegiance was to the family

7. The life course literature, even when addressing the role of the state in structuring the life course, has neglected the special characteristics of Marxist–Leninist regimes. E.g. Karl Ulrich Mayer and Urs Schoepflin, "The State and the life course," in W. Richard Scott and Judith Blake (eds.), *Annual Review of Sociology, 1989*, pp. 187–209.

8. Sources on the traditional family include: Olga Lang, *Chinese Family and Society* (New Haven: Yale University Press, 1946); Lee Shu-ching, "China's traditional family, its characteristics and disintegration," ASR, 18(3) (June 1953), pp. 272–80; Marion Levy, Jr., *The Family Revolution in Modern China* (New York: Atheneum, 1949); Lucian Pye, *The Spirit of Chinese Politics* (Cambridge, Mass.: MIT Press, 1968); Richard H. Solomon, *Mao's Revolution and the Chinese Political Culture* (Berkeley: University of California Press, 1971); and C. K. Yang, *Chinese Communist Society: The Family and the Village* (Cambridge, Mass.: MIT Press, 1965).

and its continuance, and that they had to submit unquestioningly to its authority. The head assigned members to various roles to implement a family strategy to achieve wealth and status. Chinese related to the outside world as members of a family, not as individuals. The family was rigorously age and gender stratified. In the Confucian view, one did not establish oneself until the age of 30.

Youth was a distinct stage of the Chinese life course only in elite families and then only for boys. Wealthy enough to spare their labour power, rich families provided sons with a routine education in the Confucian classics to prepare them for civil service exams and entrance to the most prestigious career, that of a government official. The vast majority of children received little or no schooling and made an early transition from childhood dependence to work, mostly farmwork. In any event, most Chinese worked in a family setting, assigned to tasks as part of a family strategy. At all levels of society the transition to marriage, like that to work, was arranged by the family head. Marriages were tactical moves within family strategies to cement an alliance with other similarly situated families. Marriage was patrilocal and families invested little in training their daughters beyond what was necessary to make a good match for them.

The state, conceived as a larger version of the family, reinforced the family system, and legal codes dealt harshly with unfilial children. An entire family was liable for punishment for crimes committed by a member. There were few alternative roles for young Chinese outside the family. This system was successfully transmitted and reproduced across dynasties, generations and historical events.

Long before the communist victory, however, the Chinese family system and the social structure which underpinned it began changing in the face of war and challenges by new values and norms introduced from abroad. Ba Jin's autobiographical novel, *Family*, chronicles this process in an elite extended family in Chengdu, in China's hinterland province of Sichuan. Schools, congregations, political parties, modern armies and business enterprises offered Chinese youths alternative statuses, sources of information, ways of thinking, focuses of loyalty, financial independence, and channels for activity which had not existed before. Youths were prominent in many of the revolutionary events of the first half of the 20th century, in particular the May Fourth Movement.[9] The nationalist and communist parties had large youth contingencies. Youths in this revolutionary era saw that their actions really could make a difference.

9. See Jon L. Saari, *Legacies of Childhood: Growing up Chinese in a Time of Crisis* (Cambridge, Mass.: Harvard University Press, 1990); and Jeffrey Wasserstrom, *Student Protest in Twentieth-Century China: The View From Shanghai* (Stanford, Calif.: Stanford University Press, 1991).

The 1950s Cohort: Liberation Brand

After assuming national power, the CCP continued to rely on the family to perform key functions, particularly in the rural areas.[10] However, in Leninist fashion, it also set about building a hierarchical system of Party-led organizations, including the state, which dominated most people's lives. Strongest and most pervasive in the urban areas, these organizations assumed many of the family's traditional functions. Much of the family's power shifted to the Party, and the newly "liberated" individual's sphere of autonomy was kept from expanding.

The CCP-state moved forcefully to control the life course of all Chinese, but it naturally had the widest scope with children and youths as it could dominate virtually their entire life trajectory: education, employment and career, residence, marriage, fertility, interpersonal relations and observable life style. The Party not only wielded tremendous power, it also enjoyed great legitimacy, which facilitated compliance. The desire of ambitious parents to have their children succeed in the new system also played a positive role in transmitting new values. The CCP thus officially formulated and implemented a youth stage for the life course of all Chinese.

The *Modern Chinese Dictionary* defined youth (*qingnian*) as "that stage of a person's life from age 15 or 16 to 30 or so." This encompassed people in and out of the school system, married and single, employed and unemployed. Their membership in the same birth cohort meant that, as the lowest common denominator, during the same period they received training to assume responsible roles at the proper, though unspecified time. During the youth stage, Party-led organizations in schools, worksites, recreational associations and neighbourhoods were charged with inculcating the official values in youths and closely monitoring their behaviour and thoughts, testing their suitability as revolutionary successors. The Party's direct control over rural youths was less pervasive than with urban ones, but with collectivization and the imposition of strict controls against outmigration except through military service, the Party effectively gained dominance over the life course of rural youths as well.

Urban members of the cohort born between the late 1940s and the mid-1950s, "the '50s cohort,"[11] the first one raised completely under the Red Flag, received an education emphasizing ideological and moral education as

10. Judith Stacey, *Patriarchy and Socialist Revolution in China* (Berkeley: University of California Press, 1983).

11. The Chinese popularly label cohorts by decades, based on common experience, even if their actual birthdate crosses decadal lines. I wish to thank Pan Wei for clarifying this. The Chinese officially also talk of the first (Long March era), second (received secondary education in the 1940–50s) and third (what is here called the '50s) cohorts (*tidui* commonly translated as "echelon"), using the communist movement as the time line. The '50s cohort is also called "*Jiefang Pai*" ("Liberation brand"), a pun on when they were born, and the name of a Chinese-made truck. There were approximately 140 million people born between 1947 and 1954.

well as standard academic subjects.[12] Core values included such things as collectivism, redness and expertise, glorification of Mao, altruism and unquestioning acceptance of Party leadership. Class counsellors and teachers kept close watch on them. Teachers, themselves subject to tight supervision having grown up in the old society, kept files on every student which would follow them throughout their lives. Hua Linshan relates how entering middle school and knowing he now had a file made him feel very adult.[13]

Pupils carried a handbook of rules and regulations. The teacher wrote a monthly report in it and the student had to hand it back after the parents had read and chopped it with their personal seal. Class counsellors read each student's required diary weekly. Teachers closely monitored students to ensure they dressed neatly, always had a clean handkerchief and clipped fingernails. As the school week lasted five and a half days, students spent a large part of their time under communist-led supervision.

The authorities further laboured to create a peer culture inside and outside school conducive to eliciting the desired behaviour and useful for continued socialization. The Party wanted to reorientate interpersonal relations from friendship to comradeship, introducing a political component into all such ties, with all Chinese putting loyalty to the Party above that to particular individuals.[14] A reported 50 per cent of eligible children joined the Young Pioneers between the ages of 9 and 15, but membership in the Communist Youth League (CYL), which guided the Pioneers, entailed more rigorous criteria. The CYL was more elitist as a result. It was open to youths aged 15 to 25, and was a proving ground for membership of the CCP, which one could join at 18.[15]

As the state took over the school system and socialized private business it monopolized higher education and employment, as well as access to them.[16] However, the criteria for upward mobility shifted erratically be-

12. Theodore H. C. Chen, "Elementary Education in communist China", *The China Quarterly*, No. 10, (1962), pp. 98–122; Charles Price Ridley, Paul H. B. Godwin and Dennis J. Doolin, *The Making of a Model Citizen in Communist China* (Stanford: Hoover Institution Press, 1971).

13. Hua Linshan, *Les Années Rouges (The Red Years)*, (Paris: Editions du Seuil, 1987), p. 27.

14. Ezra Vogel, "From friendship to comradeship: The change in personal relations in communist China," *The China Quarterly*, No. 21 (1965), pp. 46–60.

15. The fierce competition to join the CYL, often with tragic consequences, is discussed in Gao Yuan, *Born Red* (Stanford: Stanford University Press, 1987), pp. 20–21. Anita Chan argues that "league members tended to exhibit stronger traits of authoritarianism than non-members" due to "their watchdog role, the stringent organizational discipline they adhered to in the hierarchical climate of the league, and their need to present themselves to others as role-models of an authoritarian belief-system." (Anita Chan, *Children of Mao* (Seattle: University of Washington Press, 1985), p. 215). On the CYL, see James R. Townsend, "Revolutionizing Chinese youth: a study of *Chung-kuo Ch'ing-nien*," in A. Doak Barnett (ed.), *Chinese Communist Politics in Action* (Seattle: University of Washington Press, 1969), pp. 447–76.

16. Lynn T. White III, *Careers in Shanghai* (Berkeley: University of California Press, 1978); and Martin King Whyte, "The politics of life chances in the People's Republic of China," in Yu-ming Shaw (ed.), *Power and Politics in the PRC* (Boulder: Westview Press, 1985), pp. 244–65.

tween poles of political activism (redness) and academic achievement (expertise) caused by struggles within the Party over the nation's priorities and how best to achieve them: what type of person should be recruited into the elite?

Students became sensitized to which criteria reigned at a particular time, and developed personal mobility strategies combining elements of class background—an ascriptive characteristic—and the achieved characteristics of academic skills and political activism.[17] Students saw political campaigns as tests, opportunities to demonstrate their moral virtue, and therefore useful for upward mobility. For youths from bad class backgrounds (such as capitalists or bourgeois intellectuals) these opportunities were especially important for accumulating political capital and overcoming negative factors.

The Party-state thus imposed its image of Chinese society[18] as well as its definitions of reality, truth and the meaning of life on the nation's young people. The Party-state held hegemonic power over this through its monopoly over the media and access to the outside world and alternative sources of information, especially after the break with the Soviets in 1960. The Chinese communists did not define youth as a time for the individual's autonomous quest for self-identity and meaning as in the West;[19] youth's challenge was to submit to and accept the official definition of these things in the fashion of the selfless, unquestioning soldier Lei Feng.

The spate of memoirs by members of this first cohort, as well as interviews over a number of years, has convinced me of the high degree of success the CCP achieved with this cohort. The Party's legitimacy bolstered by the exemplary behaviour of cadres, the political stability and the improved standard of living, all contributed to this success. Youths generally accepted the Party's definition of reality and its explanations for dissonance between what they were taught and what they experienced.[20] For instance,

17. Middle school life in the first half of the 1960s is well described by Susan Shirk, *Competitive Comrades* (Berkeley: University of California Press, 1983) and from 1960–1980 in Jonathan Unger, *Education Under Mao* (New York: Columbia University Press, 1982). Shirk distinguishes three principles for awarding life chances in any society: a meritocracy, where they depend on achievement; a feodocracy, where they depend on ascription; and a virtuocracy, where they depend on demonstration of virtue (p. 4). The third one characterized China for the period she studied.

18. Anita Chan, "Images of China's social structure: the changing perspectives of Canton students," *World Politics*, XXXIV(3) (April 1982), pp. 295–323.

19. A classic article on the "discovery" of the youth stage in the West is Kenneth Keniston, "Youth: A 'new' stage of life", *The American Scholar*, 39 (Autumn 1970), pp. 631–54.

20. A memoir such as Fulang Lo, *Morning Breeze* (San Francisco: China Books and Periodicals, 1989) reveals a startling lack of self-reflection. Other memoirs covering the '50s cohort, in addition to the previously-noted Gao Yuan, Hua Linshan and Lo Fulang, include: Gordon A. Bennett and Ronald N. Montaperto, *Red Guard* (Garden City: Anchor Books, 1972); Neale Hunter, *Shanghai Journal* (Boston: Beacon Press, 1969); Liang Heng and Judith Shapiro, *Son of the Revolution* (New York: Knopf, 1983); Ken Ling, *The Revenge of Heaven* (New York: G. P. Putnam's, 1972); Ruth Earnshaw Lo and Katherine Kinderman, *In The Eye of the Typhoon* (New York: Harcourt Brace Jovanovich, 1980); Luo Ziping, *A Generation Lost* (New York:

they accepted the explanation that the imperialists and Soviets were responsible for the Three Bad Years, not the CCP. If youths failed to attain goals, they blamed their class background, insufficient virtue or individual cadres. But they did not blame the system itself or its right to determine their life course. The widespread optimism and enthusiasm of the 1950s reinforced much of what they learned in school. This is not to deny a degree of cynicism, especially among those older people who knew something about the rest of the world.[21] But youths apparently submitted to the dictates of the system and its interpretive framework, rather than thinking they could change the system. It was not until the CR, when "the gap between reality and ideal had become too wide to bridge"[22] that the first post-liberation cohort began to ask fundamental questions about the system itself.

The Effect of the Cultural Revolution on the '50s Cohort

The CR had its most direct effect on those Chinese who were in their youth stage at the time, especially urban students, and in particular, the high school graduating classes of 1966–68, known as "*laosanjie*". Closing down the school system (even though most CR activities were built around the school) and the CYL, compounded by the organizational disarray of the Party and state apparatuses, suddenly shattered the confining womb in which the youths had spent their entire lives up to that point. Memoirs and interviews confirm that they initially perceived the CR as another test of their suitability as revolutionary successors. It made sense within the context of the education and political socialization they received. Too young to have participated in the war of liberation or to have proved themselves in the other campaigns since 1949, to them the CR at last offered a chance to plunge into a political battle and demonstrate their commitment to the Party and its cause. Some, especially those of a bad class background, saw

Henry Holt, 1990); David Milton and Nancy Dall Milton, *The Wind Will Not Subside* (New York: Pantheon, 1976); Anchee Min, *Red Azalea* (New York: Pantheon, 1994); Nien Cheng, *Life and Death in Shanghai* (New York: Grove Press, 1986); Wu Ningkun, *A Single Tear* (New York: Atlantic Monthly Press, 1993); Yue Daiyun and Carolyn Wakeman, *To The Storm* (Berkeley: University of California Press, 1985).

21. A clear example is Tung Chi-ping and Humphrey Evans, *The Thought Revolution* (New York: Coward-McCann, Inc., 1966). Tung was born in 1940. In his extremely important 1957 speech, "On the correct handling of contradictions among the people," Mao expressed concern that "quite a number of young people are unable to see the contrast between the old China and the new . . . ," therefore "lively and effective political education" had to be carried on constantly. (Mao Tse-Tung, *Quotations from Chairman Mao Tse-tung* (Peking: Foreign Languages Press, 1966), pp. 289–90). Most of the selections in the "Youth" chapter of the Little Red Book are from the 1950s and reveal an undercurrent of anxiety about their trustworthiness. One motive behind the Cultural Revolution was a desire to recommit youth to the Party's cause.

22. Anita Chan, *Children of Mao* (Seattle: University of Washington Press, 1985), p. 190.

it as a chance to accumulate political capital, useful for their future careers. For others it offered an opportunity to attack officials, teachers or classmates they saw as obstructing their careers, usurping positions they believed their own parents should hold, or responsible for an insult or injury at an earlier time. Some youths saw it as a chance to get out from under stifling control and more or less run amok.[23]

When the CR began, the youths did not think independently; they tried to imagine what the Party, as personified by Chairman Mao, wanted them to do. Accordingly they acted to purify the new system which they were told bad cadres had tried to pervert for their own ends. In big-character posters they aped what they read in the press or what people with inside information about power struggles told them to write. They organized Red Guard groups among classmates to attack authorities and enemies within the revolutionary ranks. When they travelled around during the great link-up and exchange of revolutionary experience they got sidetracked by tourism, but did not criticize the system. Going up to the mountains or down to the countryside (*xiafang*) was also a test of their revolutionary credentials, even though many resisted it and sought ways to remain in the cities.[24]

The experience in the rural and mountainous areas proved catalytic. After years of being told about socialist victories in the countryside, they were shocked at the grinding poverty and primitive standards of living and technology, the peasants' unfamiliarity with socialism, their superstition and hostility to having urban youths descend on their villages. Opportunities for further education looked bleak, and their initial career expectations appeared dashed, but the low cultural level in the countryside afforded even middle school students the chance to employ skills they had learned, making a very early transition to the work stage of the life course. Some became teachers, athletic coaches, performers, accountants, technicians and team leaders.

23. These are, of course, gross generalizations. I personally know several youths of "bad class background" whose parents kept them home during the CR, refusing to let them out, compelling them to study. This paid off in 1977 when the university entrance exams were revived. Others encouraged their children to go along to protect themselves since it seemed to be the thing to do. Luo Ziping joined the Red Guards to avenge her parents but also embarked on a rigorous self-study regimen (Luo Ziping, *A Generation Lost*).

24. Luo Ziping and Fulang Lo present *xiafang* as almost entirely coerced, whereas in the early days many youths did go willingly. On rustication, see: Thomas Bernstein, *Up To The Mountains and Down To The Villages* (New Haven: Yale University Press, 1977); Michel Bonnin, "Le mouvement d'envoi des jeunes instruits à la campagne: Chine, 1968–1980" ("Chinese educated youth: The rustication movement, 1968–1980") (unpublished doctoral dissertation, L'École des Hautes Études en Sciences Sociales, 1988); Weiyang Chao, "Rusticating Chinese educated youth: adaptation processes," in Scott Morgan and Elizabeth Colton (eds.), *People in Upheaval* (New York: Center for Migration Studies, 1987), pp. 159–79; Richard Madsen, *Power and Morality in a Chinese Village* (Berkeley: University of California Press, 1984); Shi Xiaoyan, *Beidahuang* (*The Great Northern Wilderness*) (Beijing: Zhongguo qingnian chubanshe, 1990). The three very popular novellas by A Cheng, "Chess King," "King of Trees" and "King of Children" provide an offbeat view of the rustication experience.

If these experiences did not confront them with the gap between the Party's definition of reality and the really real, then the Lin Biao Affair pushed them over the brink. When Mao's close comrade-in-arms and constitutionally-prescribed successor turned out to have always been an enemy, many youths began to reflect upon their entire education under communism, in particular the sacrifices they had made ostensibly for the sake of the CCP's lofty goals. In the countryside, away from constant Party supervision, urban youths began to discuss these issues and arrive at unorthodox conclusions.

The consequences, all unintended, of the CR on the relation between the first cohort and the Party-state can be summed up as follows:

(1) Youths learned to organize on their own, for their own ends. They initially organized Red Guard groups to support Mao and attack enemies, but the important thing is the skill.

(2) The unrelenting, irreconcilable dissonance between experienced reality and the Party's construction of reality compelled them to think for themselves. As a result, they saw through (*kantoule*) everything. They no longer saw the world in manichaean terms but as complex, with shades of grey and middle characters, as in literary works criticized during the CR. They suffered a crisis of faith (*xinyang weiji*) in Marxism-Leninism-Mao Zedong Thought, the CCP and socialism. But they still retained a very traditional sense of obligation to serve the nation and of patriotism.

(3) Removed from their families and urban networks, they had to fend for themselves. This made them hard-nosed, practical and impatient with slogans. They knew the importance of power, and learned how to fight with fists and cunning to get what they wanted. They learned how the system really operated, and became adept at using, for example, *guanxi* (connections) and *houmen* (the backdoor).

(4) They felt they had been tricked, used as pawns in what was nothing more than a power struggle, and that they had lost the chance for the career, family life and standard of living years of intense anticipatory socialization had led them to expect. They became determined to make up for this loss, to set their own goals, and to gain control over their own life course should the opportunity present itself. This cohort carries its indelible wounds like a battle flag.[25] Its members spearheaded the 1976 Tiananmen Incident and the 1978–79 Democracy Movement, seeking redress for what they had

---

25. The genre of "wound" or "scar" (*shanghen*) literature is its anthem. For selected stories, see Geremie Barme and Bennett Lee, *The Wounded and Other Stories of the Cultural Revolution* (Hong Kong: Joint Publishing Co., 1979). In the late 1980s, this cohort led the search for the roots of Chinese culture in an effort to explain the country's continued failure to modernize and democratize. Some fictional examples of the search can be found in *Spring Bamboo*, Jeanne Tai (trans. and ed.), (New York: Random House, 1989). The most famous work is the 1988 television documentary, *River Elegy* (*He Shang*).

suffered and the introduction of a new system to ensure that CR-type upheavals could not happen again.[26]

(5) From the Party-state's perspective, this cohort had become out of control. They had demonstrated a very dangerous penchant for violence and disrespect for authority. These youths could no longer be mobilized by the Party; on the contrary, they organized themselves.

The '60s Cohort: A Swing Group

The 337 million people born between 1955 and 1969 comprise something of a swing group. The CR hit them at the childhood stage of their life course, allowing most of them to pass their youth stage in a time of relative stability and predictability. They were too young during the high tide of the CR to have been directly affected, although the experience of their parents and older siblings certainly left a mark. Their relation with the Party-state has not been as tumultuous, although it is rife with contradictions. The post-1978 reforms offered them an opportunity to start afresh, but many were too scarred by the decade of chaos to settle down and do so.

The primary education of urban children of the '60s cohort was lopsidedly politicized, leaving a large number of poorly educated, undisciplined youths. (The education of rural children was already marginal.) Childhoods spent in an era of lawlessness and disrespect for authority (as embodied by the 1973 model child, Huang Shuai, who lambasted her teacher for improper thought) had an impact on the cohort, especially in surging rates of previously negligible juvenile delinquency.[27]

By the time they reached high school and college age, the Party-state had calmed the situation, emphasizing academic excellence, so some of them were well-prepared when the college entrance exams were revived in 1977. Many went directly from senior middle school to post-secondary education, where they intermingled with members of the '50s cohort, whose students themselves comprised a frequently combustible mixture of those who entered under CR leftist criteria and those who made it via the exam route. A high percentage still went to the countryside until the late 1970s, but the programme had changed so that they went to the suburbs rather than the remote hinterland, and they knew they would be rotated back to the city in a few years.

26. Andrew J. Nathan, *Chinese Democracy* (Berkeley: University of California Press, 1985). See also Liang Heng and Judith Shapiro, *After the Nightmare* (New York: Knopf, 1986).

27. Liu Xinwu's pathbreaking story, "Class counsellor", describes the type of children raised in the 1970s. At one extreme are unruly delinquents; at the other are mindless slogan-shouters. Teachers faced a difficult challenge imposing order over them and motivating them to study. One of the better feature films on the subject, *Juvenile Delinquents*, made in the mid-1980s, emphasized the social origins of the problem. See also Chihua Wen, *The Red Mirror* (Boulder: Westview Press, 1995).

When the reforms began in 1978, this '60s cohort was still in its youth stage. With the reforms, the Party-state shifted the emphasis of its work from class struggle to the Four Modernizations, stressing the need for stability in order to achieve the material happiness the programme would bring. As part of this drive for stability and order the state promulgated China's first criminal code in 1979 and undertook a mass campaign to educate people about law. It used public trials and numerous executions, many of whose targets were members of the '60s cohort, to get the point across.[28]

In addition to the Public Security Bureau, courts and educational system, the Party turned to the CYL to socialize, control and sort youths as it had prior to the CR. Abolished in 1966, the CYL was not revived until 1978. It turned out to be wholly inadequate to the task entrusted to it. The CYL stresses lofty ideals of sacrifice and collectivism while all the signals from society, and even the Party itself, glorify material consumerism and privatization.[29] Not surprisingly, this glaring contradiction caused confusion among youth. Pan Xiao's 1980 essay "Why is life's road getting narrower and narrower?" forcefully expresses this confusion.[30] Raised to believe in lofty ideals as embodied by Lei Feng and other communist heroes, she could not resolve in her mind the contradiction between the ideals, the reality around her and the near-total lack of idealism on the part of her contemporaries. From the other side, CYL cadres and activists revealed confusion about their roles and how to motivate youth by communist ideals while the Party itself preached consumerism. The Party's evasive answer: the CYL's job is to implement the Party's tasks and embody its teachings.[31]

The Party-state's control over this cohort has been less direct than that over its predecessors during their youth. An implicit pact has taken shape: if its members study and work diligently the Party guarantees improving material living standards and minimal political demands. For many youths, the CYL performs little beyond a social function, holding parties and outings. With family-individual income-earning as the key to an improved standard of living, a career in the Party or state has lost some of its attraction, and CYL membership has accordingly lost much of its appeal as a primary mobility route.

Not only have the ideological appeals fallen on deaf ears, but the economic structural reforms have compelled youths to assume responsibility

28. This reached something of a high point during the 1983–84 Anti-Spiritual Pollution campaign. See Liu Ping, "Dakai shajie houmian" ("Behind the big killings"), *Zhongguo Zhi Chun (China Spring)*, 6 (September 1983), pp. 9–10.

29. This dilemma is well discussed in Stanley Rosen, "Prosperity, privatization, and China's youth," *Problems of Communism*, XXXIV(2) (March–April 1985), pp. 1–28.

30. In Helen F. Siu and Zelda Stern (eds.), *Mao's Harvest* (New York: Oxford University Press, 1986), pp. 4–9. See also Liu Xinwu's story, "Awake, my brother" where a member of the '50s cohort uses official "logic" to reason with his cynical '60s cohort brother.

31. See a collection of revealing articles and responses in John P. Burns and Stanley Rosen (eds.), *Policy Conflicts in Post-Mao China* (Armonk: M. E. Sharpe, 1986), esp. pp. 53–80.

for their own economic well-being, linking reward with effort. In the countryside in particular, the replacement of the commune system with the production responsibility system revived the family as the primary production, consumption and distribution unit. Because the rural family had never completely lost these functions, rural youths adapted quickly to the new environment. As better-educated members of their families, youths spearheaded much of the entrepreneurial outburst of the 1980s, responding to the common slogan, "stimulate the initiative of the individual."[32]

In the urban areas, the economic stagnation which the Party-state confronted at the end of the 1970s compelled it gradually to abandon its former policy of guaranteed job assignments to all urban youths, with the exception of university graduates. With state enterprises bloated, the authorities faced a backlog of millions of unplaceable, often poorly-educated youths. They became "youths waiting for employment" (*daiye qingnian*). With no legitimate way to seek employment, and attracted by the consumer goods that began filling the store shelves, some turned to crime, exacerbating the delinquency problem. The state then encouraged job-waiters to set up collectives and, in a bold departure, legitimized the "individual economy" (*geti jingji*) of actual private business. University graduates continued to be subject to job assignment, but middle school graduates confronted a newly-revived labour market. Those who gained employment in the state sector enjoyed the benefits of a unit (*danwei*)—housing, health care, recreational facilities—as well as the disadvantages—close supervision, dependency on the cadres for coupons for rationed goods, and political pressures.[33] Even in the state sector, the policies of enterprise autonomy, where enterprises became responsible for their own profit and loss, and smashing the iron rice bowl, foisted more accountability on to workers. Employees of collectives rarely enjoyed a comparable benefits package. They lived with their parents and were subject to Party-state supervision in the work unit and neighbourhood. Those who embarked on the private road enjoyed the greatest freedom from Party-state control. Many were former delinquents unwanted by other units.[34] They were eager to avoid supervision and enjoyed the freedom to travel around China, keep their own hours and ignore as best they could the pressures to participate in Party-led group activities. They had to deal with the state constantly in the guise of various bureaus concerned with industry and commerce, taxation, sanitation, police and so on, but the

32. Youths comprise a high proportion of the floating population of rural folk working in the cities.

33. Andrew G. Walder, *Communist Neo-traditionalism: Work and Authority in Chinese Industry* (Berkeley: University of California Press, 1986).

34. A number of films and stories described in a positive light members of this cohort who turned from juvenile delinquents into law-abiding private entrepreneurs. One of the better works is 1990's *Black Snow*; the hero is destroyed by a decadent society.

degree of freedom they enjoyed, especially compared with most urban dwellers, represents a significant social phenomenon.[35]

This cohort holds an ambivalent relation to the Party-state. While its members are not as profoundly disillusioned as the '50s cohort, never having held the same idealism or expectations and not having grown up in the optimistic 1950s, the CR made them cynical about the Party's ideology and the state's competence. They automatically disbelieve what the Party tells them, but have nothing left to fill the vacuum. Some have turned to religion—Christianity in particular, with its western aura; others to western philosophies such as existentialism; some to blind worship of the west. The CCP and CYL recognized their inability to mobilize this cohort in the same way as they could the '50s cohort at a similar stage in its life course trajectory. They tried to adopt new measures to deal with the '60s cohort towards the end of its youth stage, but as the demonstrations of 1985 and 1986–87 demonstrated, many of its elite members had different ideas.[36]

At best, one might argue that the most educated ones who remain in China aspire to careers as technocrats, steering clear of political activism and joining the CYL and Party purely for careerist reasons. The remainder have no illusions. They want to improve their living standards but have little optimism about the system's ability to deliver what they see as an adequate pay-off.[37] The university students, at least, had an extraordinarily idealized vision of the United States, and many positioned themselves to go abroad, giving up on China altogether.[38]

The 1970s Reform Cohort

If the '60s cohort is a swing group, the '70s cohort of 221 million people born between 1970 and 1978 is at the extreme of alienation. The major benefi-

---

35. Thomas B. Gold, "Urban private business and social change," in Deborah Davis and Ezra F. Vogel (eds.), *Chinese Society on the Eve of Tiananmen* (Cambridge, Mass.: Harvard University Press, 1990), pp. 157–78.

36. For an official view for foreign consumption, see You Yuwen, "China's youth today," *China Reconstructs*, XXXII(10) (October 1983), pp. 29–33. A CYL handbook from that time is Huang Zhijian, *Qingnian Tedian yu Gongqingtuan Gongzuo* (*The Special Characteristics of Youth and the Work of the CYL*) (Beijing: Zhongquo qingnian chubanshe, 1983), which acknowledges youth as a time of seeking and questioning. Orville Schell captured the mood of this cohort and the influence of Fang Lizhi, Liu Binyan and Wang Ruowang over it in *Discos and Democracy* (New York: Pantheon, 1988).

37. Tani Barlow and Donald Lowe found members of this cohort "inexperienced and kind of dull," especially when compared to the members of the '50s cohort they taught in Shanghai in the early 1980s. Tani E. Barlow and Donald M. Lowe, *Teaching China's Lost Generation* (San Francisco: China Books and Periodicals, 1987), p. 11. See also Beverley Hooper, *Youth in China* (Ringwood, Australia: Penguin, 1985).

38. *Ibid.* In an epilogue the authors stress the disillusionment a select sample of their students felt when actually in the United States.

ciary of the reform programme's depoliticization of life, increased autonomy from direct Party control, expansion of opportunities and alternatives, opening to the outside world and improved standard of living—all of which came about as a result of the destructiveness of the CR—the '70s cohort ironically has posed the greatest challenge yet to the fundamental legitimacy of the communist regime. It participated in the widespread demonstrations of 1986–87, and spearheaded those of 1989.

The older members of the '70s cohort spent their early childhood during the tail-end of the CR,[39] but developed awareness in the course of the 1976 Tiananmen Incident, overthrow and trial of the Gang of Four, 1978–79 Democracy Movement, and de-Maoification which occurred during their later childhood. As youth, this cohort was taught to equate socialism with nationalism, the Four Modernizations and development of the productive forces, to uphold socialism with Chinese characteristics, to be innovative and ambitious. If the CCP held up Lei Feng as the model for the '50s and '60s cohorts, Chrysler chairman Lee Iacocca's autobiography gained the most currency among the '70s cohort. The CCP told them that getting rich was glorious as it would increase the nation's wealth, stimulate the economy and motivate the idlers to strive harder. Individualism clearly outweighed collectivism. Family and class background lost their determinative influence on life chances; individual achievement in the new "socialist commodity economy" attained prominence.[40] The revival of key schools and vocational schools reintroduced the sort of officially sanctioned inequality which fuelled resentment.

If, as argued above, the Party-state made an implicit pact with the '60s cohort that it could enjoy depoliticized security, the pact with the '70s cohort promised depoliticized wealth and individual freedom. At least, that is how many youths understood it.

In the rural areas in particular, the rapid growth of the non-agricultural sector, including large private enterprises in some cases more closely linked to foreign and Overseas Chinese interests than to the Chinese authorities, continued the trend of autonomy. In the urban areas, especially after 1984, the private economy continued to expand in size and scope, with even university graduates opening consulting firms and computer companies to official acclaim. The state announced that, beginning with those matriculating in 1989, university students would find their own jobs, thus shifting more

39. William Kessen (ed.), *Childhood in China* (New Haven: Yale University Press, 1975) describes this period. Memoirs include: Li Lu, *Moving the Mountain: My Life in China From the Cultural Revolution to Tiananmen Square* (London: Macmillan, 1990) and Shen Tong and Marianne Yen, *Almost a Revolution* (Boston: Houghton Mifflin, 1990).

40. Of course, family background retained importance. For instance, intellectual families encouraged their children to study hard, etc. Gender (the Party encouraged girls to leave the work-force and glorified home making), nepotism and what Walder calls "principled particularism," that is, favouritism to Party members and activists, were also crucial. But increasingly the individual fell back on himself or herself.

responsibility on to their shoulders. The authorities encouraged youths to "bring their talents into full play" (*fahui caineng*), letting them increasingly decide for themselves what their talents were, instead of assigning jobs based in the first instance on the state's needs. In the early 1990s, the authorities encouraged state workers and intellectuals to "go into the sea" (*xiahai*), meaning take up a business career, which intensified this trend.

The opening to the outside world seriously compromised the Party-state's control over the cohort. The Special Economic Zones such as Shenzhen occupied an extreme position, but foreign experts at schools and institutes in all major cities, resident foreign businessmen and technicians in enterprises, tourists traipsing throughout the country, foreign popular culture broadcast, published and performed live, and the excellent chance to study abroad all exerted powerful attraction to youths. In particular the pervasive presence of Chinese from Hong Kong and Taiwan dramatically proved that Chinese people, given a conducive system, were fully capable of modernizing their economy, social system and culture. Unrealistic as it may be, impressionable youths hold up these Chinese societies as well as the United States as standards by which to compare their own lives.[41] This increases the sense of relative deprivation. It has also bred a strong sense of disliking everything Chinese as well as an inferiority complex, two serious problems which the CYL tries to combat, although with little more than cheerleading platitudes.[42] Many works of popular culture clearly reflect this attitude, in particular, fiction by Wang Shuo, such as *The Operators* (*Wanzhu*), and the songs of Cui Jian, such as the cult favourite, "I have nothing to my name" (*Yiwu Suoyou*).[43]

The reform authorities argued that diversity and competition were necessary to stimulate the enthusiasm of workers, students, farmers and intellectuals during the current open-ended "primary stage of socialism." Stanley Rosen has examined numerous limited circulation opinion polls conducted during the 1980s and demonstrated the tremendous diversity of opinions and values, especially among young people.[44] Lack of knowledge about or belief in communism was rampant. The official media conveyed the same

---

41. See my article on "Hong Kong and Taiwan popular culture", *CQ* Dec. 1993, pp. 907–25.

42. Bei Qun, "Women ying youdi guoqingguan" ("The views we should have about the national situation") *Zhongguo qingnian* (*Chinese Youth*) (March 1990), pp. 3–4; and Xiao Lin, "Jizhong liuxing 'yishi' di xishuo" ("Analysis of some kinds of popular 'consciousness'"), *ibid.* pp. 5–6.

43. On Wang Shuo, see Geremie Barme, "Wang Shuo and *Liumang* ('hooligan') culture", *Australian Journal of Chinese Affairs*, 28 (July 1992), pp. 23–64. To Barme, Wang Shuo's *The Operators* illustrates disaffection and lack of interest among the youth of this cohort. See also the story by Liu Yiran, "Rocking Tiananmen", in Geremie Barme and Linda Jaivin (eds.), *New Ghosts, Old Dreams: Chinese Rebel Voices* (New York: Times Books, 1992), pp. 5–21. On Cui Jian, see Andrew F. Jones, *Like a Knife: Ideology and Genre in Contemporary Chinese Popular Music* (Ithaca, NY: Cornell University East Asia Program, 1992).

44. For instance Stanley Rosen, "The impact of reform policies on youth attitudes," in Deborah Davis and Ezra F. Vogel (eds.), *Chinese Society on the Eve of Tiananmen* (Cambridge, Mass.: Harvard University Press, 1990), pp. 283–305.

message, accepting diversity, pluralism, questioning and even the emergence of interest groups as a necessary, if not totally desirable, outcome of structural reform.[45] Such articles reveal the shift to relativism from absolutism, the substitution of economics and technical skills for politics, individualism for collectivism, indulgence and money worship for abstinence and morality, and so on, virtually turning the values of the 1950s on their head. Popular youth culture reflected and fuelled this. Cui Jian's nihilistic, indulgent rock song, "I have nothing to my name" (*Yiwu Suoyou*), achieved cult status as the anthem of the cohort. Oddly enough, although the Party expanded the sphere for individual autonomy, youth still felt helpless to control their own lives. Memoirs and my own interviews from the 1988–89 era revealed this.[46] One of the motives behind the demonstrations of 1989 was to call attention to the corruption of the job assignment process and what youth saw as a stifling of their talents by the authorities.

Many Chinese and foreign observers remarked on the self-centredness and indulgence of this cohort, while not denying its intelligence. By the late 1980s, university students concentrated on preparing for the TOEFL exams to go to the United States, gambling and romance, or "TDK," not the brand of cassette tape, but TOEFL, dancing and kissing. They resented the job assignment system, wanting to control their own careers.[47]

But they had a highly inflated view of their capabilities.[48] They expected fast promotions and good incomes. Young workers seemed to have lost the work ethic, and, like rural and urban private entrepreneurs, scrambled for money (*xiangqiankan*) and consumer goods. The obsession filtered down to school children who began to drop out of school, arguing that "studying is useful but doesn't bring money."[49] Youths interviewed in spring 1991, repeatedly said that the only thing their cohort believed in was "money." With it, you can get anything you want.

The Party-state acknowledged that the times were different, the 1980s were not the same as the 1950s. Youth were not the same and the demands

---

45. E.g. Liu Yuejin, "Shinian gaigezhong jiazhiguan di shige zhuanbian" ("Ten changes in values during a decade of reform"), *Xinhua Wenzhai*, 2 (1989), pp. 13–16 (orig. in *Gongren ribao*); Lu Ren, "Dui qingnian jiazhiguan duoyuanhua qingxiang di fenxi" ("Analysis of the trend of pluralization in the values of youth"), *Shehui*, 1 (1986), pp. 13–15; Gu Jieshan and Zhang Xiang, "Shehui zhuyi chuji jieduan liyi quntilun" ("On interest groups during the primary stage of socialism), *Guangming ribao*, 29 February 1988, p. 3.

46. For instance Michael David Kwan, *Broken Portraits* (San Francisco: China Books and Periodicals, 1989) and Richard Terrill, *Saturday Night in Baoding* (Fayetteville: University of Arkansas Press, 1990).

47. E.g. Jin Xiaoming, "Fenpei: Yige naoren di guaiquan" ("Job assignments: an irritating odd trap"), *Banyuetan*, 21 (10 November 1988), pp. 16–18. This frustration was another major motivation of the 1989 demonstrations.

48. Xiong Sihao, "Expectations at odds with realities," *Beijing Review*, 44 (29 October–4 November 1990), pp. 27–9.

49. E.g. "Rengxia shubao di xiaoshangren" ("Little merchants drop their bookbags"), *Renmin ribao* (overseas edition), 25 February 1989, p. 4.

on them should also not be the same.[50] But that did not translate into efficacious policies. Rosen has argued that peasant youths who used to join the PLA as a route out of the village now join it to learn skills and make connections they can use in their later lives as entrepreneurs.[51] Added to the school dropout rates, the potential consequences for the quality of the military and work force are obvious.

Youths' attitude to official organizations also changed. With the rise of a new non-state mobility channel and the depoliticization of life, membership of the CYL or CCP lost much of its allure. The All-China Youth Federation, the umbrella united front organization targeting youth, began to publicize many of its other 36 constituent members besides the CYL, such as the YMCA and YWCA, and social rather than political activities to win back support. The CCP determines its recruitment targets based on its political line, meaning it desires technically-skilled members, especially university students, but they seem reluctant to join up.[52] In 1988 university students began to initiate their own non-Party-affiliated organizations.[53] This trend gathered momentum during the spring of 1989 when groups throughout society established "autonomous" (zizhi) associations, which even CCP members joined. Members of the '50s cohort, such as Wan Runnan, Chen Ziming, Ren Wanding and others, played an active role, usually behind the scenes. The 1989 movement was a culmination of a decade of continued retrenchment of the Party-state from control of the individual life course along with the individual's active expansion of the sphere for autonomous action.

The events of 1989 elicited a brutal and unimaginative set of policies by the Party-state to stem this tide of autonomy. The hardliners determined that one of Zhao Ziyang's major errors had been laxity on the ideological front which permitted the influx of spiritual pollution and bourgeois liberalization, things to which young people are especially susceptible.[54] To counter this alleged western plot of using peaceful evolution to erode the CCP's authority, the leaders decided to step up ideological education, including trotting out that model of unquestioning obedience, Lei Feng, for yet another round;[55] to require a year's military service for freshmen at

50. Huang Zhijian, Qingnian tedian yu gongqingtuan gongzuo (Special Characteristics of Youth and the Work of CYL) (Beijing: Qingnian chubanshe, 1983).

51. Stanley Rosen, "Value change among post-Mao youth: The evidence from survey data," in Perry Link, Richard Madsen and Paul Pickowicz (eds.), Unofficial China (Boulder: Westview Press, 1989), pp. 193–216.

52. Ibid. p. 213.

53. Shen Tong chronicles the process at Beijing University in Almost A Revolution (Boston: Houghton Mifflin, 1990), pp. 135ff.

54. Throughout 1988 Zhongguo qingnian (Chinese Youth), the CYL's organ, ran a six-part series extolling this cohort's seeking truth from facts (and not falling for slogans), initiative, desire to get rich, diversity of beliefs, new attitude to love, etc.

55. In 1990 I interviewed cadres from the All-China Youth Federation. They staunchly defended the revival of the Lei Feng cult, asking what was wrong with the values he embodied. They did not seem to grasp his irrelevance to the lives of most Chinese youth. They also argued

some elite universities; to purge unsuitable members of the Party; to suspend plans to replace job assignments for university graduates with individual job search; to clamp down on foreign influence and the ability to study abroad; and to tighten the control of the unit over workers.[56] Reports indicate that this is having a minimal effect.[57] On the one hand, CYL and CCP members are loath to implement such unpopular policies, partly out of fear that the verdict of June 4 will be reversed. On the other hand, acceleration of economic reforms, boosted by Deng Xiaoping's "Southern Tour" in early 1992, have provided unprecedented opportunities to go abroad, work in foreign or joint venture companies, and start up one's own enterprise. These choices involve much less direct supervision by Party cadres, and also function as safety-valves for potentially discontented and rebellious youth.

Conclusion

The CCP defined the youth stage as a time for socialization, training and sorting future adults, much as any society does. As a Marxist–Leninist party, it took the responsibility for these tasks upon itself, eliminating competitors, especially the family. Since 1949, the CCP has changed many of the central values it teaches youth, the skills it determines are most valuable to master, and the criteria by which it sorts youths into adult roles. It has altered these because of its perception of the changing needs of China, which is also a function of internal power struggles. Politicians have used youth as a weapon in these battles.

Three birth cohorts have passed through the youth stage since 1949, and their experiences during this stage have varied wildly. This has left them with very different views about the nature of China, socialism, the world and themselves.

that part of their job is to inculcate correct values among youth. See Stanley Rosen, "The effect of post 4-June re-education campaigns on Chinese students", *China Quarterly*, 134 (June 1993), pp. 310–34.

56. For some typical statements soon after the events, see, "CYL's role at universities stressed," *Foreign Broadcast Information Service*, 4 August 1989, pp. 21–2, (orig. *Guangming ribao*), and "Interview with CPC education director," *ibid*, 5 August 1989, pp. 13–15 (orig. *Liaowang*).

57. Rosen, "Value change among Post-Mao youth." A survey conducted at Beijing University in May 1990 by the Graduate Student Association revealed a sense of hopelessness, distrust of the state (especially as regarded forthcoming job assignments), and a desire to go abroad. Published in *Kaifang*, (September 1990), p. 55. According to some foreign observers interviewed in Beijing in May 1991, the year of military service seemed to have had some effect. Not only are the trained students at Beijing University segregated from upper classmen, they avoid contact with them. Authorities at one key university admitted in January 1991 that many of the best students are not taking the entrance exams for the top schools because they do not want to do the year's military training, and they do not want to subject themselves to job assignments that could send them anywhere in the country. They prefer to go to provincial or municipal universities.

Ironically, the cohort that may have benefited the most from all the upheavals is the '50s cohort. The CR steeled and tempered it in a different way from any of the other cohorts, including the one just senior to it. It is the most self-reflective and realistic about China, experienced in surviving and dealing with people of many backgrounds and classes, skilful in organization and in the use of power. Many of its members received a second lease on life after the reforms began, returning to the cities, finding jobs, going to university and finally finishing the tasks of their youth stage in their 30s. They are becoming the Party-state, joining the CCP primarily from utilitarian motives. They are moving into leadership positions at the local levels and important managerial positions at the centre. They comprise a large number of the members of reformist think tanks. They are spearheading bold reflective directions in art.[58] They have few illusions about communism, but do understand power and the need to exercise it. They recognize the need for reform as well as the impossibility of reproducing the system of the 1950s and the bankruptcy of the present system, although they differ on the proper solutions to the current crisis. In addition to dealing with the domestic society, they need to find a way to mobilize and win back the reservoir of talent now abroad and reluctant to return. It will be up to them to channel the talents and energies of the younger cohorts while overcoming those groups' alienation and self-centredness. This includes their own offspring, the products of the single-child policy, the '80s cohort.[59]

58. For example, the avant-garde artists profiled in Andrew Solomon, "Their irony, humor (and art) can save China" (*The New York Times Magazine*, 19 December 1993, pp. 42ff., and *Defunct Capital* (*Feidu*), the erotic best-seller by Jia Pingao, described in Lincoln Kaye, "Reining in erotica", *Far Eastern Economic Review*, 18 November 1993, pp. 40–1.

59. For empirical studies of this cohort, see Ann-ping Chin, *Children of China: Voices From Recent Years* (New York: Knopf, 1988) and Joseph J. Tobin, David Y. H. Wu, and David H. Davidson, *Preschool in Three Cultures: Japan, China and the United States* (New Haven: Yale University Press, 1989).

The Dynamics of Civil Society in Post-Mao China*

Gordon White

Any enquiry into the emergence of "civil society" in post-Mao China is bedevilled both by the ambiguity of the term "civil society" itself and the complexity of the historical processes it is used to describe. This confusion extends far beyond the Chinese case, since the idea of "civil society" has been embraced across a broad spectrum of ideological persuasions and used to analyse a wide variety of countries in what used to be called the First, Second, and Third Worlds. In the United Kingdom, for example, theorists of the right and left have recently argued for the crucial importance of "civil society" as a force to protect social cohesion against the ravages of market forces or provide the organizational basis for an alternative form of democratic governance to the traditional bureaucratic state.[1] In Central and Eastern Europe, it was the experience of political struggle against communist regimes which gave "civil society" the enhanced currency it has enjoyed over the past decade and a half, particularly the experience of Solidarity in Poland.[2] In the developing world, many countries have been undergoing programmes of economic liberalization, which has led to discussion about the interrelationships between (spreading) markets, (retreating) states, and (emerging) civil society and their implications for the "Third Wave" of democratization in the region.[3]

These discussions can help to throw light on the Chinese case. As a communist country undergoing social changes and political stresses, there is a clear resonance with Eastern European experience. As a poor agrarian society undergoing radical economic liberalization and a redefinition of the character and role of the state, there is shared experience with other developing countries. However, analysts have used the term in widely different

* The author would like to thank Jude Howell for her valuable comments on the first draft of this chapter.

1. For a recent example of the latter, see Paul Hirst, *Associative Democracy: New Forms of Economic and Social Governance* (Cambridge: Polity Press, 1994), who argues the case for "associative democracy". For a valuable review of the "civil society argument" by a United States political theorist advocating "critical associationalism", see Michael Walzer, "The civil society argument", in Chantal Mouffe (ed.), *The Dimensions of Radical Democracy* (London: Verso, 1992), pp. 89–107.

2. For a review of the role played by civil society in Eastern Europe and other communist countries in the 1980s, see Robert F. Miller (ed.), *The Development of Civil Society in Communist Systems* (Sydney: Allen and Unwin, 1992).

3. I have discussed the relationship between civil society and democratization in developing countries in my "Civil society, democratization and development (I): Clearing the analytical ground", *Democratization*, Vol. 1, No. 3 (1994), 375–90.

ways and the "civil societies" revealed in concrete empirical studies have also turned out to be hugely diverse. Given the roots of the idea of "civil society" in Western experience, moreover, its utility in explaining processes elsewhere has proven patchy. China's distinctive historical trajectory and social character should prompt caution about the extent to which the concept can help us to understand contemporary processes of socio-political change there.

In spite of the potential dangers of ambiguity and ethnocentrism, however, the idea of "civil society" does contain much which is relevant to the central theme of this book, the relationship between the state and the individual. It leads one to focus on the balance of power between state and society and to investigate the ways in which members of society act both to protect themselves from powerful states and to exert sufficient influence to institutionalize a realm of freedom and civil/political rights. In practical terms, moreover, the paradigm of "civil society" provides a potent political weapon for those struggling to curb the arbitrary powers of an authoritarian state and set a process of political liberalization and democratization in motion.

The Search for "Civil Society"

A serviceable definition of civil society

There has already been a good number of theoretical discussions about the intellectual pedigree and different meanings of "civil society", both in the general literature of social and political theory and in recent scholarship on China by both Western and Chinese scholars.[4] I shall spare the reader yet another one and concentrate rather on two main tasks: first, to distil the main ways in which the term is commonly understood in contemporary debate and, second, to use these meanings to guide an empirical enquiry into socio-political processes in contemporary China.

One can detect two conceptions of "civil society" which are often used interchangeably and contribute to the confusion which surrounds the term: they could be called a sociological and a political conception. The first, *sociological*, conception, which draws on continental European sociology and philosophy, is that of an intermediate associational realm situated between the state on the one side and the building blocks of society on the

---

4. A recent review by Ma Shu-yun, "The Chinese discourse on civil society", *China Quarterly*, No. 137 (March 1994), pp. 180–93, contains references to most of the relevant theoretical discussions as well as providing a useful overview of the views of Chinese intellectuals. Gu Xin, in "A civil society and public sphere in post-Mao China? An overview of Western publications", *China Information*, Vol. 8, No. 3 (Winter 1993–94), pp. 38–52, provides a valuable overview and assessment of the debates over "civil society" and the "public sphere" in Western work on China.

other (individuals, families, and firms), populated by social organizations which are separate from the state, enjoy some degree of autonomy from it, and are formed voluntarily by members of society to protect or extend their interests or values.[5] The second, *political*, conception, which derives from the Anglo-American liberal tradition of political theory, equates civil society with "political society" in the sense of a particular set of institutionalized relationships between state and society based on the principles of citizenship, civil rights, representation, and the rule of law.[6]

A good deal of the analysis of "civil society" in the Chinese context tends to run these two conceptions together by linking the emergence of "civil society" to pressures for (liberal) democratization.[7] While there has been a clear historical relationship between these two processes in Western contexts, there is no need at this stage to superimpose this experience on the Chinese case by identifying civil society only with those organizations which favour or facilitate democratization. One inevitably ends up trawling through different types of social organization and trying to decide which ones are truly "civil", in terms of their political proclivities, as opposed to those which are temporarily or permanently "uncivil", "pre-civil", or "non-civil". In the Chinese context as elsewhere, the sociological universe of "civil society" is very diverse. Rather than adopt a narrower and more restrictive notion of civil society, based for example on Habermas or Rousseau, I prefer to begin the enquiry with a hopefully complementary approach which tries to come to terms with the current diversity of associational life rather than directing attention to just one sector or dimension of it.[8] This approach would also attempt to delink the concept of "civil society" from any specific tradition of political thought, avoiding thereby the "risk of getting involved in an ideological or teleological exercise" which Gu Xin rightly warns about.[9]

Using the sociological approach in the first instance would enable us to

---

5. This usage is perhaps closest to Durkheim's idea of intermediate "secondary groups" (Émile Durkheim, *Professional Ethics and Civic Morals* (London: Routledge, 1992), p. 45) and excludes both firms and families from the scope of "civil society". The exclusion of firms poses problems in the Chinese context, an issue to which I shall return at the end of the paper.

6. Hugh Roberts defines "civil society" in these terms in "Editorial", *IDS Bulletin*, special issue on "Politics in Command?", Vol. 18, No. 4 (1987), pp. 1–6.

7. For an example of this approach, see Martin K. Whyte, "Urban China: A civil society in the making?", in A. L. Rosenbaum (ed.), *State and Society in China: The Consequences of Reform* (Oxford: Westview Press, 1992), pp. 77–102.

8. The use of more theoretically focused approaches can also prove valuable in throwing light on the political dynamics of the reform era: for example, Sullivan's use of a Rousseauian approach (Lawrence R. Sullivan, "The emergence of civil society in China, spring 1989", in Tony Saich (ed.), *The Chinese People's Movement: Perspectives on Spring 1989* (London: M.E. Sharpe, 1990), pp. 126–44) and the debate about the applicability of Habermas's notion of the "public sphere" in the special edition of the magazine *Modern China* Philip Huang (ed.), "'Public sphere'/'civil society' in China?: Paradigmatic issues in Chinese Studies, III", *Modern China*, Vol. 19, No. 2 (April 1993).

9. Gu Xin, "A civil society", p. 52.

paint a broader picture of the social forces which might hinder as well as foster democratization. In work on other developing societies, distinctions have been made between different types or sectors of civil society: for example, between "modern" interest groups such as trade unions or professional associations and "traditional" organizations based on kinship, ethnicity, culture, or religion; between those organizations with explicit political roles and those which are either outside politics or only intermittently involved; between formal organizations and informal social networks based on patrimonial or clientelistic allegiances; between legal or open associations and secret or illegal organizations such as the Freemasons or the Mafia; and between associations which accept the political *status quo* and those which seek to transform it by changing the political regime or redefining the political community (as in the former Yugoslavia).

The relationship between the sociological and political conceptions of civil society then becomes a second-stage enquiry. The extent to which a specific civil society may or may not give rise to some kind of liberal-democratic political order is a fascinating area of investigation in itself and would deal with important political variables such as the formation of a politically influential public opinion, the issue of agreement between social elites on a coherent set of institutions and rules of the political game, the spread of a new political culture of citizenship, and the institutionalization of legal rights. One would expect that different categories of associations would vary in their attitudes to the prospect of democratization, ranging from support to indifference, opposition, and subversion. Any statement to the effect, for example, that a "strong" civil society is conducive to democratization would be meaningless unless one went further to identify the precise political character of a specific civil society. As Bayart has argued in the African context, "The advance of a civil society which does not necessarily contain the democratic ideal does not in itself ensure the democratization of the political system."[10] Conversely, the statement that a "weak" civil society is not conducive to democratization is equally suspect: witness the case of the Soviet Union, where the main thrust towards democratization came from within the party/state apparatus and not from the pressures of civil society. As Rueschemeyer and his colleagues have pointed out, civil society is only one potential component of the political impetus towards democratization. The others, which may be decisive in certain instances, are international pressures and the influence of domestic state-based elites.[11]

I shall mainly be using the sociological approach to civil society in this paper. My main purpose is to focus on changes in the organizational structure of Chinese society: specifically, to investigate the extent to which a new

10. Jean-Francois Bayart, "Civil society in Africa", in Patrick Chabal (ed.), *Political Domination in Africa* (Cambridge: Cambridge University Press, 1986), p. 118.
11. Dietrich Rueschemeyer, Evelyn Huber Stephens and John D. Stephens, *Capitalist Development and Democracy* (Cambridge: Polity Press, 1992).

kind of intermediate stratum of social organizations has in fact emerged and changed the relationship between state and society. As evidence of "civil society", we would be looking for the development of social organizations which demonstrate characteristics of spontaneity, voluntariness, and autonomy in their constitution and activities. To the extent that our enquiry does reveal the existence of this new sociological phenomenon, we can then go on to reflect, albeit somewhat speculatively, about the political implications of this new social realm as a force for democratization.[12]

A methodological caveat. Although we are guided by a notion of "civil society" as an ideal type, we also recognize that any specific organization in the real world may be only a partial reflection of the ideal. Moreover, though the ideal type "civil society" does suppose a separation between it and the state, in the real world the two spheres overlap and interpenetrate to varying degrees.

The dual dynamic of civil society in post-revolutionary China

We are concentrating here on the development of civil society during the era of Chinese "market socialism", which began in 1978. To understand the formation of civil society during this period, it is necessary to set it in the context of the broader dynamics of state–society relations in the post-revolutionary period. From this longer-term perspective one can identify a dual dynamic in the emergence of a civil society. The first is a *political dynamic* which reflects the impact of Marxist-Leninist political institutions on a society and the political tensions and conflicts to which this gives rise. In this context, civil society characteristically takes the form of resistance to state control on the part of organizations with explicitly political agendas. In the context of the former state socialist societies, the classic case of this dynamic was that of Poland, where Solidarity embodied a generalized political opposition to state control and waged a Gramscian "war of position" against it. This civil society impetus takes a variety of forms: an organizational challenge to create new political institutions to replace or

12. This article draws on the findings of a collective research project (also involving Jude Howell and Shang Xiaoyuan) which investigated the market dynamic of civil society through fieldwork in China during 1991–93. It was supported financially by a grant from the UK Economic and Social Research Council with supplementary assistance from the United Nations Research Institute for Social Development and the Ford Foundation. Our thanks are due to these organizations. The research focused primarily on the urban sector and on two types of organizations—official "mass organizations" and new-style "social organizations". Our work on these two types of organization has enabled us to come to a judgement about the analytical value of the civil-society approach and has also led to a preliminary mapping of the broader constellation of associational life in contemporary China, pointing out directions for future research. For an analysis of our research findings by one of the team, see Jude Howell, "Refashioning state–society relations in China", *The European Journal of Development Research*, Vol. 6, No. 1 (June 1994), pp. 197–215, and "The poverty of Civil Society: Insights from China", Discussion Paper No. 240, School of Development Studies, University of East Anglia, Norwich (May 1993).

undermine those of the *ancien régime*; an ideological challenge to the values of the Marxist-Leninist state religion mounted by critical individuals and institutions; and a cultural challenge through the spread of heterodox patterns of social belief and behaviour in opposition to the official system of social morality.

In the Chinese case, one can argue that the *political dynamic* of civil society has been in operation since the beginning of the communist era in 1949. In retrospect, the organized upsurges which occurred during the Hundred Flowers Movement of 1956–57 can be seen partially as the reactions of certain social groups against the imposition of the new system. In its early phases, the Cultural Revolution can also be seen in part as a political mobilization of distinct social forces and interests against the party/state, but operating within the ideological framework and institutional constraints of the Chinese communist system at its "high" phase. The April 5 Movement of 1976 reflected widespread mass antagonism to the political hegemony of the radical left and the destructive political struggles of the previous decade and was based on the partially spontaneous mobilization of popular social networks.[13] The Democracy Movement of 1978–79 exploited the weakened condition of the communist party/state after the traumas of the Cultural Revolution decade and represented the first signs of a political opposition with a radically different programme of political reform comparable to its counterparts in East/Central Europe.

The second dynamic of civil society is a *market dynamic*, analogous to the "Great Transformation" wrought by the spread of market relations in Western societies.[14] In this context, civil society is a consequence of a separation between state and society resulting from the rise of a market economy and the concomitant redistribution of social power away from the state to new strata which are thereby empowered to rein in and restructure the state. In the context of the former state socialist countries of East/Central Europe, the only case of this dynamic was that of Hungary, where the spread of a "second economy" in the 1970s and 1980s led to what Hungarian sociologists called a "second society", an associational sphere which was organized in ways radically different from and increasingly counter to the state.

In the Chinese case, one can argue that this market dynamic has emerged in the post-Mao era as economic reforms have brought about socio-economic changes which have shifted the balance of power between state and society and reduced the capacity of the state to control and manipulate society. To the extent that these changes occur, they create the basis for a

13. For an excellent analysis of the social dynamics of this movement, see Sebastian Heilmann, "The social context of mobilization in China: Factions, work units, and activists during the 1976 April Fifth Movement", *China Information*, Vol. 8, No. 3 (Winter 1993–94), pp. 1–19.

14. The classic analysis of this process is by Karl Polanyi, *The Great Transformation: The Political and Economic Origins of our Time* (Boston: Beacon Press, 1957; 1st pub. 1944).

new sphere of social association which can be characterized as "civil society". This would imply a new relationship between social organizations and the state, moving away from a system of totalistic control to a more pluralistic one in which social organizations become more separate and autonomous, representing the interests of their social constituencies rather than the control imperatives of the state.

The distinct character of the post-1978 reform era is that, for the first time, both dynamics have been in operation. This era has its own complex political dynamic of civil society, the peaks being the student movement of 1986 and the urban mobilizations of 1989.[15] While the post-1979 era has seen oscillations in the degree of political relaxation and control, the period as a whole has been one of relative political relaxation, characterized by a reduction in the degree of politicization of everyday life and the expansion of areas of activity—cultural, economic and technical/professional—which are relatively free of political controls (when compared with the previous era of Maoist "politics in command").[16] At certain periods, particularly during 1988 and early 1989, the political atmosphere was relaxed to an extent which encouraged (and indeed almost promised to legitimate) the emergence of social organizations of the civil-society type.[17] However, these political fluctuations were taking place within a rapidly changing socio-economic context in which the market dynamic of civil society was already well under way. We thus need to think of the development of civil society in the era of economic reform as a complex interplay between these two socio-political dynamics. In the pre-reform era, the party/state ruled through a system of cellular encapsulation of society; in this institutional strait-jacket, it was difficult for a political challenge from society to take organizational form and, if it did, the state retained the political wherewithal to repress it. However, when the logic of the command economy

15. For analyses of the rise of "civil society" in the Democracy Movement of early to mid-1989, see Clemens S. Ostergaard, "Citizens, groups and a nascent civil society in China: Towards an understanding of the 1989 student demonstrations", *China Information*, Vol. 4, No. 2 (Autumn 1989), pp. 28–41, and Thomas B. Gold, "The resurgence of civil society in China", *Journal of Democracy*, Vol. 1, No. 1 (Winter 1990), pp. 18–31. For a sceptical view about the significance of "civil society" in 1989, see Andrew G. Walder, "The political sociology of the Beijing upheaval of 1989", *Problems of Communism*, Vol. 38, No. 5 (July 1989), pp. 309–29.

16. Over the entire post-revolutionary period, the political dynamic of civil society mobilization has an ambiguous relationship with the oscillation between periods of political control (*shou*) and relaxation (*fang*) which has characterized relations between state and society in post-revolutionary China. Some upsurges have come about as a response to prolonged periods of *shou* (the 1976 April Fifth Movement, for example), while others have been stimulated by periods of *fang* (notably during the Hundred Flowers Movement in 1956–57 and the Democracy Movement in 1978–79). The reform era itself has its own oscillations between *shou* and *fang*: for an overview of the dynamics of *shou* and *fang*, see Gold, "The resurgence of civil society in China".

17. For a review of this process, see He Baogang, "The dual roles of semi-civil society in Chinese democracy", Discussion Paper No. 327, Institute of Development Studies, Brighton (August 1993), pp. 4–6.

begins to change and members of society begin to assume control over economic and social resources as a consequence of market reform, the capacity of the state to reimpose control through traditional institutional means begins to weaken.

Thus the political dynamic and the market dynamic of civil society are interactive and reinforcing. In particular, the latter impinges on the former by weakening the ideological authority and organizational reach of the state, thereby reducing its generalized capacity to repress political alternatives. The institutions of market society offer recruits, allies, and resources to the political opposition and provide bolt-holes if they fail. To the extent that the opposition offers political alternatives more conducive to the interests of the new strata arising from an emergent market order, the two sets of forces may ally to organize a political offensive against the state.[18]

The Impact of Economic Reform on State–Society Relations: The Rise of an Intermediate Sphere

Changes in state–society relations: The dual impetus

The social impact of the post-Mao economic reforms has been profound and it intensified in the 1990s as the Chinese economy experienced a prolonged and unprecedented boom. The economy has diversified in both sectoral and institutional terms and, in consequence, Chinese society has become more complex and differentiated. New groups and strata have emerged with their own distinct interests: for instance, "new rich peasant" households in the rural areas, private and "collective" entrepreneurs in both cities and countryside, and more independent members of the "liberal professions". Although the vast proportion of the population have benefited materially from the reforms, some have benefited more than most and there is a widespread consciousness of growing *inequalities* between regions and social strata.[19] Measures to increase the autonomy of public enterprises, the rapid growth of the private and collective sectors, and measures to deregulate markets in labour and capital have resulted in a redistribution of power in society away from party/state institutions to public-sector managers, private/collective entrepreneurs, household enterprises, and individuals able to sell their skills in the emerging labour market.

18. Though there were elements of this alliance during the mobilization of 1989, they were still fairly inchoate. However, the continuing spread of market relations lays the foundations for a repetition of this alliance, in much stronger form, in some future context of political turmoil.

19. A 1994 survey by the State Planning Commission identified fourteen occupational groups found to be "wealthier than others", including speculative shareholders, famous artistes, private businesspeople, lawyers, and "people doing a lot of moonlighting" (reported by *New China News Agency*, Beijing, 8 October 1994).

Reforms in both industry and agriculture—notably the *de facto* privatization of agriculture in the early 1980s and the mounting pressure on state enterprises to adapt to the demands of a market economy—have weakened the key institutions which "encapsulated" the population in the pre-reform era—the "unit" in the cities and the "collective" in the countryside. Moreover, the previous control over population flows enforced through the system of household registration (*hukou*) was breaking down in the 1990s. In consequence, Chinese society has become more fluid and dynamic in both geographical and occupational terms. Urban workers have left their jobs in the public sector to start small businesses; officials and professionals have left their secure but increasingly unrewarding jobs on the government payroll to seek their fortunes in the private or collective sectors (the phenomenon of "plunging into the sea"); peasants from rural hinterlands have left for local towns and cities, creating a growing "floating population" existing within the interstices of urban life; people from poor regions have moved within and between provinces in search of a better life; and young workers have been drawn to foreign-invested enterprises in the Special Economic Zones and other open areas along the coast.

The social changes brought about by economic reform have also led to feelings of insecurity and discontent among more threatened or disadvantaged sections of the population. These have fuelled social unrest and instability, accompanied by a widely perceived decline in standards of public order and morality. In consequence, by the mid-1990s the Chinese state was facing a more volatile and assertive population and increasingly widespread social unrest in both cities and countryside which threatened to reach critical proportions.[20]

As we shall see below, these social changes and pressures have taken on an organizational character as a wide variety of new forms of association have sprouted like bamboos after the rain. To this extent, one can talk of a *societal impetus* towards the emergence of civil society in the form of new types of intermediate association representing the interests and aspirations of evolving social forces and seeking greater autonomy from, and influence over, the party/state. At the same time, however, there has also been a powerful *state impetus* whereby political and governmental institutions have sought to adjust to social change, ameliorate growing tensions between state and society, channel growing pressures for access and participation, and avert the political danger posed by a decline in governability and control.

This state response is many-faceted and involves multifarious

---

20. During 1993 and 1994, warnings about actual and potential social unrest were mounting on all sides. For example, see one account from an official youth journal: Liu Dafu, "The key to unshakeableness for 100 years is unshakeableness for 10 years", *Zhongguo Qingnian* (*Chinese Youth*), No. 1, 1993, excerpts of which are translated in BBC, *Summary of World Broadcasts: Far East* (hereafter *SWB: FE*), No. 1668.

realignments and implicit deals between state institutions/officials and emergent social forces.[21] Two aspects are particularly important for our enquiry: repression and incorporation. Certain organizational expressions of social opposition and unrest, particularly those resulting from the political dynamic of civil society, have been dealt with repressively, most dramatically in the Beijing Massacre on 4 June 1989. As the conversations of CCP leaders published later reveal, they found the political challenge mounted by the demand from students and workers during this movement for voluntary and autonomous organizations free from the controls conventionally exerted on "mass organizations" by the party/state particularly threatening. For example, Li Peng is reported as having said that "If we recognize the 'College Students Autonomous Federation' just because the students insist on it, then we will be most likely to recognize a solidarity trade union if the workers insist on their demands, won't we?" Yao Yilin allegedly added that "Peasants will establish peasants' organizations as well, then China will become another Poland. For this reason, we must never give in."[22] In this particular form, civil society levelled a rapier at the heart of the institutional logic of Marxism-Leninism.

If we focus on the nature of the state response to the market impetus towards civil society, however, efforts at incorporation have been predominant. Implicitly or explicitly, the party/state authorities have been moving towards something resembling a socialist form of state corporatism.[23] The essential elements of corporatism have been defined by Schmitter as follows:

Corporatism can be defined as a system of interest representation in which the constituent units are organised into a limited number of singular, compulsory, non-competitive, hierarchically ordered and functionally differentiated categories, recognised or licensed (if not created) by the state and granted a deliberate monopoly within their respective categories in exchange for observing certain controls on their selection of leaders and articulation of demands and supports.

21. To understand the shifting patterns of accommodation and adjustment between state institutions/officials and social forces/interests, we would need a broader analysis which traces both the dynamics of economic and cultural policy as a whole and the formation of informal networks linking the denizens of state and society along lines of common interest.

22. For an account of these conversations published in the Hong Kong press, see Lin Musen, "A CCP document reaffirms the Tiananmen massacre", *Cheng Ming*, 1 February 1992, in *SWB: FE*, No. 1305. Other, more reformist, CCP leaders such as Wan Li were allegedly more sympathetic to the idea of autonomous student organizations in 1989: for example, see Lo Ping, "Wan Li on the June 4 lesson", *Cheng Ming*, 1 June 1993, pp. 12–13, in *SWB: FE*, No. 1706.

23. For a thoughtful application of the notion of corporatism to contemporary China, see Jonathan Unger and Anita Chan, "China, corporatism and the East Asian Model", conference paper, Contemporary China Centre, Australian National University, Canberra (January 1993). Also see Jude Howell, "Civil society or corporatism? Organisational change in post-Mao China", conference paper, World Congress of the International Political Science Association, Berlin, August 1994.

As we shall see below, the reform era has seen the emergence of a plethora of "social organizations", whose establishment and relationship to state institutions embody the main elements of this corporatist pattern. Many of these, such as professional and academic associations, reflect the impact of a calculated political decision by the Dengist leadership to grant greater autonomy and recognition to professional expertise. Many reflect the process of sectoral differentiation in the economy and the rise of influential new economic forces such as private and "new collective" business. The impetus towards incorporation has been haphazard and gradual. The state's first reaction to the challenge posed by the rise of new economic and occupational interests and the societal impetus towards their taking organizational form was the desire merely to control and regulate. This was particularly apparent in the aftermath of the Tiananmen events when there was a hasty effort to identify, discipline, and monitor social organizations through a system of compulsory registration administered by Departments of Civil Affairs. It was not the case that these organizations had been independent or unregulated before; indeed many if not most had been established under the sponsorship of state institutions at different levels of government and had been subject to sectoral, *ad hoc*, or localized forms of regulation. The post-Tiananmen impetus was to impose a universal, codified, and centralized system of regulation and control, ultimately intended to take legal form. Accordingly, a set of "Regulations Governing Registration and Administration of Social Organizations" was issued in October 1989.[24]

The major motive behind these Regulations was the desire to establish control over a potentially threatening social phenomenon, and in practice the registration process has operated as a powerful mechanism of subordination and exclusion of officially unacceptable forms of social organization. However, a more explicit corporatist motive has gradually emerged which emphasizes the complementarity between social organizations and the state as components of a new system of socio-economic regulation. This idea, first floated by the economist Xue Muqiao in 1988, argued that, in the economic sphere, social organizations could "serve as a bridge between the state and the enterprises" in a new form of "indirect" regulation and direction of the economy which avoided both the previous deficiencies of Stalinist directive planning and the future dangers of anarchic markets.[25] This idea has gained currency during the 1990s, particularly in the industrial sphere, as part of a general movement to "transfer the functions of government organs" (*zhuanbian zhengfu jiguande zhineng*) whereby social organi-

24. A text of these Regulations was published in *Renmin Ribao* (*People's Daily*) on 9 November 1989 and is translated in *SWB: FE*, No. 0621.
25. Xue Muqiao, "Establish and develop non-governmental self-management organizations in various trades", *Renmin Ribao* (*People's Daily*), 10 October 1988, translated in Foreign Broadcast Information Service, *China Report*, No. 88/201.

zations become in effect an intermediate level of economic governance.[26] Movement in this direction (notably the transformation of certain central light-industrial ministries into "general associations") has brought China closer to the pattern of state–business relations characteristic of other East Asian economies, notably Japan and South Korea. Indeed, the Japanese system has been cited as a positive model for emulation by Chinese policy-makers.

The overall result of this dual impetus from both state and society is an intermediary sphere populated by a wide variety of social organizations which have developed along with and as a consequence of the Dengist reforms. These organizations have different types of relations with a party/ state machine which is itself undergoing institutional change in an effort to create a new, stable relationship with a rapidly changing and potentially threatening socio-economic environment. The purpose of the next section is to depict this new pattern of state–society relations using a broad brush.

The "civil society" constellation

In contemporary China it is difficult to find an ideal-type "civil society" organization which fully embodies the principles of voluntary participation, separation from the state, and self-regulation. Though organizations of this kind exist, they do so within the interstices, or outside the realm, of state controls. Within that realm, however, the principle of a fully autonomous and self-regulating social organization has not been formally recognized. While the official regulations for the registration of social organizations do go some way towards granting them an institutionalized status by recognizing them as "legal persons" (*faren*), the registration procedures and preconditions are highly restrictive and their interpretation is still left to administrative discretion. All officially recognized organizations are thus, to a greater or lesser degree, controlled by and dependent on state institutions. Outside that realm, there are organizations which are excluded from official recognition yet live a limbo life of informal activity; there are organizations which, while disapproved of officially, are none the less tolerated or winked at by the authorities; and there are underground organizations subject to repression. Yet each of these categories of social organization embodies, to varying degrees, the associational characteristics of "civil society". This partial and patchy "civil society" is made up of a complex and rapidly changing social constellation with many layers and many different types of relationship with the party/state.

---

26. For a comprehensive report on the changing functions of industrial trade associations prepared by the Industrial Economics Association, see "Fully affirm the important status of industrial trade associations in a socialist market economic system", published in the journal of the Chinese Construction Industry Association, *Jiancunhui Bao* (*Construction Association News*), No. 6, 1993.

If we categorize these layers in terms of the nature of their relationship with the party/state, the range is from "caging", through (various degrees of) incorporation, to (more or less intermittent) toleration and repression. Let us discuss each category in terms of this gradation.

The caged sector: the mass organizations. The old-style "mass organizations" (*qunzhong zuzhi*) of the pre-reform era, namely the All-China Federation of Trade Unions (ACFTU), the Women's Federation (WF), and the Young Communist League (YCL), had been subordinated to the party as the three main "pillars" of its organized base of social control and support. As Leninist "transmission belts", they had virtually no organizational autonomy and any attempt to become more assertive, as in the case of the trade unions in the early and mid-1950s, provoked a backlash from the party.[27] However, the reform era's combination of limited political liberalization and rapid socio-economic change provided opportunities and created pressures for these organizations to claim greater separation and independence from the party/state.

In the case of the trade unions and the Women's Federation, this movement was visible for several years before the Tiananmen events and began to reappear with growing force in the mid-1990s. In a detailed study of the ACFTU and the WF over the entire reform era, the author and his colleagues found that during the 1980s they showed growing signs of a desire to expand their operational autonomy by distancing themselves from the party and attempting to represent their social constituencies more effectively.[28] However, when the CCP leadership reasserted controls over the official mass organizations in the aftermath of the Beijing Massacre, the trade unions struck a Faustian bargain with the party, whereby they sacrificed greater autonomy for greater access to and influence over official policy-making at both national and local levels. By the mid-1990s, however, the accelerated pace of economic reform was already unravelling this compact. The legitimacy and influence of the official trade unions were being undermined, on the one side by the stresses and strains of the economic reform process and its ambiguous impact on their memberships, and on the other side by the increasingly debilitating constraints imposed by their continued dependence on the party. Their dilemma was highlighted by the emergence of alternative organizations—in the form of illegal autonomous unions and workers' groups—which could lay much greater claim to the title of real representatives of their members and thus can be seen as organizational expressions of civil society in the full sense. As a much

27. For an account of the fluctuations in the status of the trade unions in the pre-Cultural Revolution period, see Paul F. Harper, "The party and the unions in Communist China", *China Quarterly*, No. 37 (January–March 1969), pp. 84–119.

28. Gordon White, Jude Howell and Shang Xiaoyuan, *In Search of Civil Society: Market Reform and Social Change in Contemporary China* (Oxford: Oxford University Press, 1996), chs. 4–5.

weaker organization, the WF was effectively brought to heel after Tiananmen, but it too faced a similar dilemma in the 1990s as it found itself ill-equipped to defend women suffering from the effects of market restructuring and witnessed the growth of informal women's groups which challenged its claim to monopoly representation of women's interests.

As for the YCL, it suffered a great loss of political influence and social appeal during the reform era because the party no longer regarded it as the crucial channel of political recruitment. Moreover, since joining the party was no longer the only way for ambitious young people to move up in society, the previous role of the YCL as a pathway to upward mobility was increasingly obsolete. Moreover, official policy encouraged the depoliticization of youth and their involvement in activities—occupational, cultural, and recreational—which they could increasingly obtain on the market and not through the good agencies of the party or the YCL. In a local study of the changing role of mass organizations in a small city in Zhejiang province, we found that the local YCL cadres felt that they had been abandoned by the party; indeed they described themselves as "orphans". Their institutional response was to try to attract young people through cultural and recreational activities, since there was no longer any interest in politics, but they were finding it difficult since these things were available on the market and they lacked the financial resources in any case (which led them to try to piggy-back on the local unions, which had more money).[29] If this case is a straw in the wind, one can hardly expect that the YCL has much of a future.[30]

The situation of these three mass organizations is different in that the trade unions, unlike the Women's Federation and the Young Communist League, has a guaranteed financial basis and an expanding constituency, particularly among workers in the burgeoning new collectives and foreign-invested enterprises who are becoming increasingly aware of the need for union representation and protection. Yet the three organizations are similar in that each has pressing reasons to try to bend the bars of party control and establish themselves as more bona fide mass organizations. They are like birds which would like to escape from a cage and yet find it difficult not merely because the bars of the cage are still strong, but also because they have become accustomed to the advantages of cage life.

The incorporated sector: the new social organizations. A new stratum of officially recognized "social organizations" (*shehui tuanti*) has rapidly

29. For a detailed analysis of this local case-study, see Gordon White, "Prospects for civil society in China: A case-study of Xiaoshan city", *The Australian Journal of Chinese Affairs*, No. 29 (January 1993), pp. 63–87.

30. These judgements about the decline of the YCL are based on research in the urban areas. A more recent case-study of a developed rural county in Guangdong, however, suggests that the YCL still plays a significant role among rural youth, not least because alternative sources of entertainment and recreation are not as plentiful as in the cities.

emerged at both national and local levels during the reform era, including business and trade associations, professional associations, academic societies, and sports, recreational, and cultural clubs. Their numbers had already reached over 1,100 national and 100,000 regional/local ones by the time registration regulations were introduced in October 1989 and, though the rate of growth slowed in the clamp-down after Tiananmen, their numbers began to grow again in the early 1990s. By late 1993 there were over 1,460 registered national social organizations, 19,600 at the provincial level, and over 160,000 at the county level.[31]

As the key element in a potential corporatist sector, these organizations are ambiguous and heterogeneous entities when viewed from a "civil society" perspective. Rather than constituting an associational sphere which embodies the growing power and assertiveness of social forces emerging from radical market reforms, they are an institutional terrain in which the interests and objectives *both* of increasingly influential social forces *and* of still-powerful state institutions are interwoven. As such they constitute a socially ambiguous institutional sphere which "braids" state and society in new and heterogeneous ways.

In spite of much misleading official vocabulary about their being "popular organizations" (*minjian tuanti*), closer inspection reveals a continuum of different mixes between what one might call the state and the societal element of each organization. At one extreme, there are a minority of organizations which are totally controlled by the government (*guanban*), which are essentially extensions of the state machine. At the other extreme is a minority of organizations which are not considered important enough to be worth controlling on a continuing basis (usually recreational, academic, or cultural groups), which can be regarded as real "popular organizations". Most social organizations contained a mixture of both components, roughly called semi-governmental/semi-popular (*banguan banmin*). Overall, as of 1993 at least, when this research was conducted, the state component tended to predominate within this mix.[32]

In practice, the state component implied not only the need for each social organization to obtain formal approval by registering with the appropriate Department of Civil Affairs, but also the requirement to "link up" (*guakao* or *guikou*) with a specific government agency which acted as its "superior department" or official sponsor.[33] Moreover, a social organization might

31. For these statistics, see "New regulations for registering social organizations", *New China News Agency*, Beijing, 31 October 1989, and an interview with officials of the Social Organizations Management Office, Ministry of Civil Affairs, Beijing, in October 1993.

32. For a detailed description and analysis of these new-style "social organizations", see White, Howell and Shang, *In Search of Civil Society*, ch. 2.

33. If a social organization is unable to secure an official organization as sponsor, it is prevented from registering. For example, in the city of Shenyang, the Football Fans Association was unable to get the local Sports Association to sponsor its application for official recognition.

receive all or part of its finances from the state, and one or more of its key leaders might be appointed by the "linked" state agency, which might also require it to carry out certain official "tasks". Conversely, the extent to which an organization was self-financing, chose its own leaders, and organized its own activities according to the wishes and interests of its members were indices of its societal or "popular" character. However, the "popular" dimension of a social organization is reduced because of the official requirement—a central feature of corporatist systems—that only one organization is allowed to represent each social group or economic sector within a given administrative area. So in any locality there will be one Private Enterprises Association, one Individual Businesspeople's Association, one Calligraphy Association, one Lawyers' Association, one Accountants' Association, and so on.

As studies of corporatist systems elsewhere have revealed, they are hard to construct and maintain and this intermediate sphere, which He Baogang calls "semi-civil society", is in flux and ridden with tensions.[34] There is a constant tension between the regulations and the reality of social organizations as the latter acts to make the former obsolescent. For example, the requirement that there should be only one association of its kind in each area is often challenged. One local case in point was the contest for formal recognition by two competing associations of accountants in the northeastern city of Shenyang in 1992. At the national level, there was a similar competition between rival calligraphy associations which had to be solved by negotiation and merger. However, official regulations are applied "flexibly" at local levels, with local governments seeking to increase their freedom of manoeuvre as part of an effort to establish local corporatist systems involving collaboration between government agencies and local socio-economic interests, organized in the associations, to promote local development.

Moreover, the official policy of "transferring government functions" in the mid-1980s has led governments at all levels to think of ways in which former government activities could be transferred to associations as part of a semi-privatization of governance. This role of associational governance has increasingly been built into law. For example, the law on "Protecting Consumers' Rights and Interests", promulgated in October 1993, contained a chapter defining the role of consumers' associations in "supervising commodities and services and protecting consumers' legitimate rights and interests". Similar provisions were made in the law on registered accountants issued at the same time.[35] At the same time, governments faced with severe fiscal constraints are also trying to reduce the burden of supporting social organizations, prompting the latter to make efforts to generate their own

34. He Baogang, "The dual roles", p. 8.
35. For English texts of these laws, which were adopted by a meeting of the National People's Congress Standing Committee on 31 October 1993, see *SWB: FE*, Nos. 0308 and 0309.

finance and become more autonomous as a matter of institutional survival. This involves setting up their own businesses, exploiting any real estate at their disposal, and providing paid services to their members. This in turn is a spur for them to be more sensitive to the needs of their own social constituencies and, because less dependent on the state, less beholden to it. Some social organizations are better at this than others and some of the latter are on the way to becoming desiccated organizational shells, posing a problem for their former state sponsors and their social constituencies alike: the former lack the resources to resuscitate them and the latter lack the right to replace them.

At the same time as the direct role of government gradually recedes, the power of social interests is increasing, a phenomenon particularly visible in the spheres of private business and the professions. The rising role of trade associations is visible, particularly in the localities, in both the urban and rural areas. These can provide tangible benefits to their members in terms of gaining access to state agencies, providing market information and promotional services, making business contacts, preventing "unfair" competition, establishing and monitoring technical standards and business practices, and the like. The rising power of the liberal professions is also visible: for example, lawyers are increasingly moving out of government service to establish their own private partnerships and the number of lawyers is expected to double (to 100,000) by the year 2000. Private medicine and education are also expanding rapidly.[36] Semi-official and private newspapers and journals have also proliferated over recent years, outrunning the capacity of the state to control and regulate them, and journalists have become increasingly vocal in agitating for greater professional freedom and legal protection.[37]

All of these trends may be gradually shifting the balance within social organizations away from the state to the society component and converting them into associations of a more "civil" nature. This operates directly through exerting pressures within the organizations themselves and indirectly through the threat or reality of alternative organizations arising to challenge their monopoly. It is to this "counter-world" of alternative organizations that we turn in the next two sections.

The interstitial "limbo" world of civil society. Particularly during the period leading up to Tiananmen and in the early to mid-1990s, when the pace of economic reform accelerated, there has been a rapid growth of urban associations which have either not achieved formal official recognition or have achieved it through connections with sympathetic agencies or indi-

36. For a report on the expansion of private schools in Beijing, for example, see the report in *New China News Agency*, Beijing, 23 March 1994, in *SWB: FE*, No. 1984.
37. For a report on the demand for legal protection by lawyers in Guangdong province, for example, see *Lian He Bao*, Hong Kong, 10 December 1993, in *SWB: FE*, No. 1872.

viduals. One dramatic example was the growth of "salons" of intellectuals in 1988–89, which provided much of the thought and some of the organizational initiative behind the social mobilization of early 1989. These operated through informal connections and meetings and intermittently through formal public events such as conferences and seminars. In the early 1990s, this form of informal association took a less explicitly political form, and operated through an increasingly dense system of networks of like-minded people (such as journalists, artists, rock musicians, homosexuals, or martial-arts specialists), often focusing on specific locations such as clubs, karaoke parlours, dance-halls, and bars as well as private homes.

One particular area of expansion, for example, was that of women's groups. Some of these have found shelter as "second-level associations" under the formal auspices of an officially recognized social organization (for example, the Women Journalists' Association, the Women Entrepreneurs' Association, or the Women Mayors' Association). Some of these have been encouraged and protected by officials in the official Women's Federation. But the early 1990s have also seen the emergence of informal, unrecognized women's groups without official sponsors, small salons which meet to discuss issues specific to women.[38]

Other "limbo" associations include those in formation, which are intending to seek official recognition, those that are having difficulty obtaining registration, and those that have failed the registration procedure. One example at the national level, observed in 1993, was the Green China Association, a small association devoted to environmental issues; at the local level, the Women Writers' Small Group in Xiaoshan city in Zhejiang province was in existence as of the time of our interview in mid-1991, but had not yet registered because of a fear on the part of the municipal Women's Federation that it would not pass the registration procedures.

On the urban scene, the growth of this interstitial world of semi-formal and informal forms of association was becoming denser in the mid-1990s, fostered by the social space and opportunities opened up by the breakneck pace of economic transformation during this period. Although this sphere is subject to periodic harassment, one can argue that the trend is becoming irreversible. Although much of this organizational activity takes non-political forms, yet (as in the case of cultural organizations before Tiananmen) it can become rapidly politicized in suitable circumstances and could form part of the basis for a repeated organizational upsurge along the lines of 1989. The key role in its expansion is being played by members of the intelligentsia and emergent professional strata, groups whose potential social influence is increasing as they become more integrated with the world

38. For more detail on these groups, see White, Howell and Shang, *In Search of Civil Society*, ch. 5.

of business through their growing propensity to "plunge into the sea" of commerce and industry.[39]

While the above phenomena would be characteristic of cities and larger towns, the rural areas have also seen a proliferation of semi-formal and informal associations throughout the reform era. These include traditional organizations based on kinship or ethnicity; Buddhist and Daoist religious groups based on existing, reconstructed, and new temples and shrines; informal local "cliques" and brotherhoods; and local-place associations (*tongxianghui*), some of which have been transplanted to the cities, where they provide an organizational basis for rural migrants.[40]

Some of these organizations have caused concern to the local authorities: for example, when disputes between single-clan villages have led to armed fights between them;[41] when traditional religious practices have interfered with state policies (such as that of encouraging cremation over burial); or where local "cliques" and brotherhoods have become involved with gambling and other forms of crime. However, it is very common for local authorities, including party officials, either to wink at the resurgence of these pre-revolutionary forms of association, or actively to support and even participate in them. Local officials may use these ties to strengthen their own authority and build up the local economy. For example, party officials in Muslim areas may promote religious revival to gain preferential policies from the state or to encourage potentially lucrative contacts with Islamic countries in the Middle East. Entrepreneurial local officials in coastal provinces with large migrant populations overseas use *tongxianghui* to encourage business contacts and attract capital from overseas Chinese.[42] These pre-revolutionary forms of social association do constitute a growing organizational sphere which embodies the basic characteristics of "civil society". However, as in the case of urban social organizations, the relationships between them and the local state vary a great deal, ranging from mutual suspicion and uneasy co-existence to active co-operation and mutual support.

The suppressed sector: underground civil society. This sector of civil society is highly diverse, including a wide variety of political and social organiza-

39. For analyses of the relationship between intellectuals and the emergence of this new associational sphere, see David Kelly and He Baogang, "Emergent civil society and the intellectuals in China", in Miller (ed.), *The Development of Civil Society*, pp. 24–39, and the chapter by Michel Bonnin and Yves Chevrier in this volume.

40. In Beijing, for example, a number of new "villages" have appeared, housing part of the city's estimated 1.5 million "floating population". They have names such as "Xinjiang Village", "Zhejiang Village" and "Henan Village" according to the regional origins of the migrants living there (*New China News Agency*, Beijing, 14 July 1993).

41. For example, an official in the Judicial Department of the Zengcheng county government in Guangdong province, interviewed in March 1994, admitted that fights between single-clan villages posed a threat to public order in the county.

42. This practice was recently observed by the author during a field-visit to Zengcheng county in Guangdong province in March–April 1994.

tions as well as secret societies and other criminal organizations. The degree of official repression varies. In some cases, it involves monitoring with repression kept as an option in reserve. A document reportedly issued by the CCP in mid-1992, for example, drew attention to the rise of "spontaneous mass organizations which were neither officially reported to nor sanctioned by government organs" which required close surveillance. These included organizations such as the All-China Qigong Association, the National Alliance of Demobilized Servicemen of the Rural Areas, the Association of Urban Unemployed, and the Association of Individual Households. While these kinds of organization do not pose an explicit threat to the regime, they are regarded as worrisome because they have been organized independently and represent groups which could potentially cause trouble (notably demobilized soldiers, who have a long history of self-organization and "trouble-making", going back to the Hundred Flowers Movement).[43]

Other organizations are classified as hostile agencies and are rigorously suppressed. Some of these are explicitly political organizations, such as those suppressed after the Beijing Massacre of 4 June 1989, when governments in Beijing and other cities took steps to identify and disband organizations involved in the urban mass movement.[44] However, there was already an accumulation of political organizations banned before 1989 and others have appeared since. Some of these can be identified in an internal document issued by the Ministry of Public Security in 1993 and leaked in the Hong Kong press. This reported that, over the period from June 1986 to September 1992, the public security forces had banned 1,370 "illegal organizations of all kinds" and a further 69 had either voluntarily disbanded or surrendered to the police. In spite of these measures, however, the document reported that illegal organizations were still spreading "like a prairie fire". It directed particular attention to 62 "hostile forces opposing the socialist system", which included political and social organizations from the 1989 Democracy Movement (such as the National Autonomous Federation of Workers), and assorted "ultra-leftist reactionary" organizations, relics of the Maoist period, with names such as The Defend Mao Zedong Doctrine Alliance and The Jiangxi Red Uprising Column. The list also included regional/ethnic organizations such as the Xinjiang Justice Party and the Independent Party of Inner Mongolia and religious organizations such as the China Christian Association and China Catholic Association.[45]

Religious sentiment spread rapidly in the early to mid-1990s in both

43. Yang Po, "CCP takes strict precautions against 'rebellion' by non-governmental mass organizations", *Cheng Ming*, Hong Kong, 8 June 1992, in *SWB: FE*, No. 1409.
44. For a valuable survey of these organizations, see Andrew G. Walder, "Popular protest in the 1989 Democracy Movement: The pattern of grass-roots organization", published in the Seminar Series of the Universities Service Centre, Chinese University of Hong Kong (n.d.).
45. "On cases of underground illegal organizations cracked and banned or surrendering themselves to the police over recent years", reported in *Cheng Ming*, Hong Kong, 1 January 1993, in *SWB: FE*, No. 1581.

urban and rural areas and public opinion surveys reported an upsurge of interest in religion, particularly among young people. Religious organizations have proliferated in the early–mid-1990's—Christian, Islamic, Buddhist, and Daoist—and the authorities responded with a mixture of repression, toleration, and attempts to incorporate them into the officially recognized religious bodies. They have also tried to crack down on "spontaneous churches", with limited success.[46] Regional policies towards grassroots religious organizations have varied significantly, with authorities in Guangdong apparently showing more tolerance while other provinces such as Sichuan have been more repressive.[47] By mid-1994, however, the national picture was causing such alarm in official circles that the Minister of Justice, Xiao Yang, asserted that, in some rural areas, "people are using the power of religion to deceive and control the masses and to interfere with party and government work; they are struggling with us to seize grass-roots political power."[48]

There has apparently been a comparably rapid spread of secret societies and other criminal fraternities and gangs. A circular reportedly issued by the Ministry of Public Security in 1992 claimed that there were over 1,830 underworld organizations of various types, some of them having as many as 30,000 members and operating not only across regions but also internationally, particularly through co-operation with Triad organizations in Hong Kong.[49] These organizations are regarded as dangerous not merely because of their characteristic involvement in vice and crime, but also because of their overseas connections and their sporadic political involvements (for example, in smuggling Democracy Movement activists out of China after 4 June).

In general, illegal organizations have spread rapidly in the early to mid-1990s and have clearly outrun the capacity of the authorities to control them. While some of them, such as the criminal secret societies, would be illegal under any form of political system, and some, such as remnant "ultra-leftist" and Democracy Movement organizations, represent a clear political challenge, the vast majority represent the associational urges of a rapidly changing society which is increasingly restless and resentful of restrictions. The regime faces a Catch-22 situation: suppression is increasingly unfeasible and, even where effective, is often counter-productive; tolera-

46. For attempts to control national-level religious organizations, see Lu Yusha, "Tension in spring—utmost 'solicitude' is shown for national churches", *Tangtai*, Hong Kong, 15 June 1994, in *SWB: FE*, No. 2028.

47. For the Sichuan case, see *Zhongguo Xinwenshe* (China News Agency), Beijing, 25 March 1993 (in *SWB: FE*, 1964), which reports a change of policy in the direction of religious liberalization after a decade of conflict and repression.

48. This is from a speech by Xiao on 25 August at a "National Work Conference on exchanging experiences in legal system propaganda and education work in 100 counties and cities", reported in *Fazhi Ribao* (*Legal Daily*), Beijing, 26 August 1994, in *SWB: FE*, No. 2124.

49. "Circular on resolutely banning and cracking down on the organizations and activities of secret societies", reported in *Cheng Ming*, Hong Kong, 1 May 1992, in *SWB: FE*, No. 1385.

tion will allow a widening range of organizations to increase their influence and exert stronger pressures for official acceptance, thereby undermining the party/state's capacity to maintain its institutional monopoly over society. This Catch-22 provides a powerful political dynamic towards not only the formation of civil society in terms of new social organizations, but also towards pressuring the authorities to change the political framework to provide some form of institutionalized guarantees for their existence and operational autonomy. How this might come about is one subject of our concluding section.

Conclusions: The Nature of Chinese Civil Society and its Implications for Democratization

The utility of the concept of "civil society"

Using the sociological definition of "civil society" advanced at the beginning of this chapter, one can argue that there is a burgeoning sphere of intermediate social association in China which embodies, in different ways and to differing degrees, the basic characteristics of a "civil society"—voluntary participation, self-regulation, and separation from the state. It is equally true that this organizational realm is partial and incipient in the sense that very few of the organizations described embody these characteristics to the full, nor do they operate in a political context which guarantees them the right to do so. This emergent associational universe is very diverse, containing sectors which are "traditional" and "modern",[50] urban and rural, national and grass-roots, political and non-political, progressive and reactionary, liberal and ultra-leftist, open and underground. They also vary widely in the types of relationship they have with the party/state, ranging from the caged and incorporated sectors—the "mass organizations" and the new-style "social organization"—through the interstitial, tolerated and monitored, to the suppressed. There is a kind of "core–periphery" arrangement with a relatively well-integrated core of caged and incorporated associations at the centre and a large and rapidly growing periphery of associations which are relatively fragmented but increasingly disorderly.

---

50. The mention of "traditional" and "modern" raises the usual question about the extent to which currently emergent civil society is something new or a resurgence of pre-revolutionary social forms. Many of the organizations emerging in the countryside seem to be clear examples of resurgence, though some of them are being used for new purposes. Moreover, the incorporated sector of "social organizations", marking an interpenetration of the realms of state and society, is redolent of the "third realm" which Huang holds to be a perduring characteristic of Chinese social structure (Philip Huang, "'Public sphere'/'civil society' in China? The Third Realm between state and society", *Modern China*, Vol. 19, No. 2 (April 1993), pp. 216–40. This writer is sceptical of both the notion and the reality of the "third realm", but a proper discussion of this thesis is beyond the bounds of this paper. For a review

Yet this sociological conception of civil society has its limitations. As a structural analysis, it tends to provide static "snapshots" of an increasingly complex and dynamic social constellation and blinds us to important elements of the reality. It needs to be related more explicitly to the changing nature of its basic institutional building blocks, particularly the "unit" (*danwei*), the new enterprises of the private, collective, and joint-venture sectors, and the proliferating mass media.[51] It also tends to privilege formal association and needs to be set within the social texturing of informal connections and networks which provides the underlying weave of Chinese social relationships across both state and society.

But to gain a better understanding of the development of civil society in contemporary China, we need to go beyond a structural analysis to investigate the dynamics of the process, as suggested in our initial distinction between the political and the market dynamics of civil society. The shifting constellation of intermediate associational life described above reflects the operation of both. The market dynamic opens up socio-economic space, endows social actors with resources and power to use them, and makes state control over the socio-economic system more difficult. The political dynamic, operating in different ways according to the specific nature of the relationship between each sector or layer of social organization and the state, creates political organizations which can draw strength from the social changes wrought by the market, can operate more freely within the increasing space created thereby, and can take advantage of the diminishing capacities of the state to expand their influence. Each layer of emergent civil society has its own dynamic: the balance of power within the caged and incorporated layers is shifting gradually in favour of their social constituencies, the interstitial layer is relentlessly expanding, and the illegal layer is worrying away at and weakening the coercive capacities of the party/state. These movements suggest the image of tectonic plates shifting before an earth tremor.

In their different ways, these two dynamics are moving in a direction which presages major changes in the balance of power and the nature of the relationship between state and society in contemporary China. The party/

of different scholarly positions on the issue of historical continuity, see Gu Xin, "A civil society", pp. 42–7.

51. The *danwei* was an important matrix of social mobilization both for the April 5th Movement of 1976 and the Democracy Movement of 1989. For the changing nature of the *danwei*, see Jutta Hebel and Gunter Schucher, "From unit to enterprise? The Chinese *tan-wei* in the process of reform", *Issues and Studies*, Taibei (April 1991), pp. 24–43, and numerous pieces by Andrew Walder (for example, "Factory and manager in an era of reform", *China Quarterly*, No. 118 (June 1989), pp. 242–64). For a thought-provoking analysis of a collective enterprise as part of an emergent civil society, analogous to my analysis of the dual character of the incorporated "social organizations", see Mayfair Mei-hui Yang, "Between state and society: The construction of corporateness in a Chinese socialist factory", *The Australian Journal of Chinese Affairs*, No. 22 (July 1989), pp. 31–60. Moreover, private companies (notably the Stone Corporation), research institutions and other *danwei* played a crucial role of social and political *animateur* in the pre-Tiananmen mobilization.

state's coping strategy—a combination of incorporation and repression—has channelled and staunched the rise of organized society, but was increasingly problematic as the pace of socio-economic change accelerated in the mid-1990s. As pressures from below have mounted yet not found adequate channels for expression and the tension between state and society has increased in consequence, the force of incipient civil society has increasingly taken on the form of spontaneous and sporadic bursts of activity—demonstrations, riots, protests, sit-ins, beatings, and fights—in both urban and rural areas. This can itself be seen as an index of the lack of a fully institutionalized civil society in which organizations have the ability not merely to form and operate autonomously within an orderly regulatory framework, but also have the legally guaranteed right to represent the interests and concerns of their constituencies to the authorities. The image of a boiler building up a dangerous level of steam pressure is an apt one.

The dynamic of civil society in China is becoming an increasingly generalized contestation between state and society. Indeed, the intellectual paradigm of "civil society" owes much of its influence to the fact that it is an effective way to interpret this struggle. It is this very fact that "civil society" is an idea rooted in real political struggles which gives it its force but weakens its usefulness as a scientific concept. If we try to render the term serviceable as a social-scientific concept, we drain it of its meaning. If we try to define it purely in sociological terms, the term becomes otiose and the social phenomena it refers to can equally well be labelled by some anodyne phrase such as "intermediate associations".

The sociological and political conceptions of "civil society" are in fact inextricable. *Nolens volens*, the use of the term "civil society" involves us in an analytical exercise which may be both ethnocentric (*qua* rooted in expectations derived from the Western experience of civil society) and teleological (*qua* positing certain political consequences of a market economy and an intermediate associational sphere). As such, the idea has heuristic value. Rather than beating our breasts about ethnocentrism or teleology, it is worth embarking on an analysis of the politics of civil society, but with the awareness that our usual expectations about the political consequences of an intermediate associational sphere may be wrong or only partly right when applied to China.

Civil society and political change

With this methodological caveat in mind, let us move to a discussion of the question we raised at the outset—the relationship between the rise of civil society as a sociological entity and the constitution of civil society as a political framework which legitimizes the free operations of social associations through the rule of law and guaranteed civil and political rights (essentially some form of liberal democracy). Our analysis suggests that political change, when it comes, is likely to be an outcome of an increasingly intense and generalized struggle in an increasingly complex and conflictual society. This could lead in the direction of chaos and collapse rather than orderly transition to an alternative and more preferable form of political society. Common sense and comparative experience suggest that the latter transition—a process of political liberalization or democratization—can only be successfully achieved through political accommodation and agreement between key sets of political actors.[52] This partly depends on the availability of a reform leadership within the CCP which is willing to read the writing on the wall and come to terms with new socio-political forces through policy concessions and institutional changes. However, it also depends on the ability of influential social forces to come together and agree on the desirability of new political arrangements. This implies a capacity for social forces to play a *constitutive* role by redefining the rules of the political game and underpinning their consolidation. Przeworski emphasizes this point when he argues that "democracy is consolidated when compliance—acting within the institutional framework—constitutes the equilibrium of the decentralised strategies of all the relevant political forces."[53]

However, the current character of China's incipient civil society makes such a smooth transition problematic because it is so diverse, fragmented, and potentially anarchic. For example, while some of the underground political organizations may be in favour of liberal democracy, others advocate a return to Maoist politics or, in the case of ethnic separatist organizations, a break-up of the existing political community. Moreover, certain key potential counter-elites—most notably the new entrepreneurial class—have shown little interest in the prospect of radical political change, because their interests are bound up with the stability of the current process of market reform under the auspices of an authoritarian regime with which they are deeply intermeshed.[54] As Wang Shaoguang has pointed out, civil societies in general—and Chinese civil society in particular—are riven by conflicts and inequalities and carry the potential for a wide variety of different political outcomes, of which democracy is but one.[55] The tendency to idealize the politics of civil society, which pervades much of the intellectual and political discourse on the issue, must be resisted.

The ideological climate among political reformers in China has indeed moved in a more sober and conservative direction over recent years. After

52. For comparative experience on the political dynamics of democratic transitions, see Guillermo O'Donnell, Philippe C. Schmitter and Laurence Whitehead (eds.), *Transitions from Authoritarian Rule: Prospects for Democracy*, 4 vols. (Baltimore: Johns Hopkins University Press, 1991).

53. Adam Przeworski, *Democracy and the Market: Political and Economic Reforms in Eastern Europe and Latin America* (Cambridge: Cambridge University Press, 1991), p. 26.

54. This point is made cogently by Dorothy J. Solinger, "Urban entrepreneurs and the state: The merger of state and society", in Rosenbaum (ed.), *State and Society in China*, pp. 121–42.

55. Wang Shaoguang, "Some reflections of 'civil society'", *Ershiyi Shiji* (*Twenty-First Century*), Hong Kong, No. 8 (December 1991), pp. 102–14.

the radical political fervour of Tiananmen died away, there has been a gradually growing consensus that, if a process of political liberalization and democratization is to take place, it should be a gradual, managed process. This does not merely represent the desire of political elites either to cling to their power or go out gracefully (or at least comfortably). To a considerable extent it also represents the fears provoked by and the conflicts inherent in China's incipient civil society: the new entrepreneurial class worries that radical political change might lead to instability, mass rule, or a recalcitrant labour force; the industrial working class fears that it might lead to a rapid erosion of its privileged position in society and to greater economic insecurity and exploitation by capital; intellectuals fear that it could lead either to chaos or rule by an illiterate numerical majority. Paradoxically, considerations of this kind lead one to suspect that civil society in its current form may be an obstacle rather than an impetus to democratization and that, like the Soviet precedent, a successful political transition towards democracy, if indeed it can be achieved, will need to be sponsored and organized by reformist elements within the current political elite.

Index

DATE DUE

MAR 1 9 '00		
APR 2 7 '00		